The Utah State Constitution

The Oxford Commentaries on the State Constitutions of the United States
G. Alan Tarr, Series Editor

Professor G. Alan Tarr, Director of the Center on State Constitutional Studies at Rutgers University, serves as General Editor for this important new series which in its entirety will cover each of the 50 states. Each volume of The Oxford Commentaries on the State Constitutions of the United States contains a historical overview of the state's constitutional development, plus a section-by-section analysis of the state's current constitution. Other features included in the volumes are the text of the state's constitution, a bibliographic essay, table of cases, and index. This series provides essential reference tools for those investigating state constitutional development and constitutional law.

The Utah State Constitution

Jean Bickmore White

Foreword by Michael O. Leavitt

THE OXFORD COMMENTARIES ON THE STATE CONSTITUTIONS OF THE UNITED STATES
G. Alan Tarr, Series Editor

OXFORD
UNIVERSITY PRESS

OXFORD
UNIVERSITY PRESS

Oxford University Press, Inc., publishes works that further Oxford University's objective of excellence in research, scholarship, and education.

Oxford New York
Auckland Cape Town Dar es Salaam Hong Kong Karachi Kuala Lumpur Madrid Melbourne Mexico City Nairobi New Delhi Shanghai Taipei Toronto

With offices in
Argentina Austria Brazil Chile Czech Republic France Greece Guatemala Hungary Italy Japan Poland Portugal Singapore South Korea Switzerland Thailand Turkey Ukraine Vietnam

Previously published in 1998 by Greenwood Press

Published by Oxford University Press, Inc.
198 Madison Avenue, New York, New York 10016

Library of Congress Cataloging-in-Publication Data

White, Jean Bickmore.
The Utah State Constitution / Jean Bickmore White; foreword by Michael O. Leavitt.
p. cm. — (The Oxford commentaries on the state constitutions of the United States)
Includes bibliographical references and index.
ISBN 978-0-19-977928-4 (hardback)
1. Constitutions—Utah. 2. Constitutional law—Utah.
3. Constitutional history—Utah. I. Utah. Constitution. II. Title.
KFU4011895.A6 W478 2011
342.79202—dc22 2011002739

Note to Readers
This publication is designed to provide accurate and authoritative information in regard to the subject matter covered. It is based upon sources believed to be accurate and reliable and is intended to be current as of the time it was written. It is sold with the understanding that the publisher is not engaged in rendering legal, accounting, or other professional services. If legal advice or other expert assistance is required, the services of a competent professional person should be sought. Also, to confirm that the information has not been affected or changed by recent developments, traditional legal research techniques should be used, including checking primary sources where appropriate.

(Based on the Declaration of Principles jointly adopted by a Committee of the American Bar Association and a Committee of Publishers and Associations.)

To Barbara and John

CONTENTS

■ SERIES FOREWORD

In 1776, following the declaration of independence from England, the former colonies began to draft their own constitutions. Their handiwork attracted widespread interest, and draft constitutions circulated up and down the Atlantic seaboard, as constitution-makers sought to benefit from the insights of their counterparts in sister states. In Europe, the new constitutions found a ready audience seeking enlightenment from the American experiments in self-government. Even the delegates to the Constitutional Convention of 1787, despite their reservations about the course of political developments in the states during the decade after independence, found much that was useful in the newly adopted constitutions. And when James Madison, fulfilling a pledge given during the ratification debates, drafted the federal Bill of Rights, he found his model in the famous Declaration of Rights of the Virginia Constitution.

By the 1900s, however, few people would have looked to state constitutions for enlightenment. Instead, a familiar litany of complaints was heard whenever state constitutions were mentioned. State constitutions were too long and too detailed, combining basic principles with policy prescriptions and prohibitions that had no place in the fundamental law of a state. By including such provisions, it was argued, state constitutions deprived state governments of the flexibility they needed to respond effectively to changing circumstances. This—among other factors—encouraged political reformers to look to the federal government, which was not plagued by such constitutional constraints, thereby shifting the locus of political initiative away from the states. Meanwhile, civil libertarians concluded that state bills of rights, at least as interpreted by state courts, did not adequately protect rights and therefore looked to the federal courts and the federal Bill of Rights for redress. As power and responsibility shifted from the states to Washington, so too did the attention of scholars, the legal community, and the general public.

During the early 1970s, however, state constitutions were "rediscovered." The immediate impetus for this rediscovery was former President Richard Nixon's appointment of Warren Burger to succeed Earl Warren as Chief Justice of the United States Supreme Court. To civil libertarians, this appointment seemed to signal a decisive shift in the Supreme Court's jurisprudence, because Burger was expected to lead the Court away from the liberal activism that had characterized the Warren Court. They therefore sought ways to safeguard the gains they had achieved for defendants, racial minorities, and the poor during Warren's tenure from erosion by the Burger Court. In particular, they began to look to state bills of rights to secure the rights of defendants and to support other civil-liberties claims that they advanced in state courts.

The "new judicial federalism," as it came to be called, quite quickly advanced beyond its initial concern to evade the mandates of the Burger Court. Indeed, less than two decades after it originated, it has become a nationwide phenomenon. For when judges and scholars turned their attention to state constitutions, they discovered an unsuspected richness. They found not only provisions that paralleled the federal Bill of Rights but also constitutional guarantees of the right to privacy and of gender equality, for example, that had no analogue in the U.S. Constitution. Careful examination of the text and history of state guarantees revealed important differences between even those provisions that most resembled federal guarantees and their federal counterparts. Looking beyond state declarations of rights, jurists and scholars discovered affirmative constitutional mandates to state governments to address such important policy concerns as education and housing. Taken altogether, these discoveries underlined the importance for the legal community of developing a better understanding of state constitutions.

Yet the renewed interest in state constitutions has not been limited to judges and lawyers. State constitutional reformers have renewed their efforts with notable success: since 1960, ten states have adopted new constitutions and several others have undertaken major constitutional revisions. These changes have usually resulted in more streamlined constitutions and more effective state governments. Also, in recent years political activists on both the left and the right have pursued their goals through state constitutional amendments, often enacted through the initiative process, under which policy proposals can be placed directly on the ballot for voters to endorse or reject. Scholars too have begun to rediscover how state constitutional history can illuminate changes in political thought and practice, providing a basis for theories about the dynamics of political change in America.

Jean Bickmore White's excellent study of the Utah Constitution is the thirtieth volume in the series, The Oxford Commentaries on the State Constitutions of the United States, which reflects this renewed interest in state constitutions and will contribute to our knowledge about them. Because the constitutional tradition of each state is distinctive, the volume begins with the history and the development of the Utah Constitution. It then provides the complete text of Utah's current constitution, with each section accompanied by commentary that explains the provision and traces its origins and its interpretation by the courts and by other governmental bodies. Finally, the book concludes with a table of cases cited in the history and the constitutional commentary, as well as a subject index.

G. Alan Tarr

FOREWORD

A constitution is the fundamental document of government. Constitutions provide stability and continuity, which are essential to our quality of life. They also reflect the will of the people in agreeing to a set of guiding principles under which they are willing to live.

Utah's Constitution contains the two fundamental purposes of state constitutions—guaranteeing the basic civil rights of its citizens and establishing the framework and structure of state government. But Utah's Constitution also reflects the unique history of the founding of our state.

While Utah's Constitution is our fundamental document, it has by no means been static. The constitutional framers of this and every state provided for means whereby the constitution could be amended. This allows the state constitution to act as a living document, to reflect the changing needs of our citizens and the increasing complexities of modern life. The people of Utah have shown great wisdom in their willingness to approve amendments that make Utah's Constitution one of the most vibrant and highly respected documents of its kind in America.

This guide recounts the history of the making of our state constitution and provides an excellent section-by-section review of its development. As active citizens in our body politic, we should learn about the historical and societal importance of our state constitution and understand what it contains. This work provides an excellent source for all of us to do just that.

I congratulate Dr. White for her tireless efforts in producing this work and thank all those Utahns past and present who had a hand in making the Utah Constitution the living document that it is.

Governor Michael O. Leavitt

ACKNOWLEDGMENTS

To write about a topic on which so little has been published has been a challenge—one that could not have been met without the encouragement and assistance of many who shared their expertise and insights with me. My editor, G. Alan Tarr, provided much-needed critical perspective, advice, and encouragement during the writing process. For access to much of the recent background research on the Utah State Constitution, and for critiques of parts of the text, I am deeply indebted to Lisa Watts Baskin, former director of the Utah Constitutional Revision Commission.

Legislative General Counsel Gay Taylor and Jerry Howe, Tani Downing, John Fellows, William Asplund, Robert Rees, and other researchers and attorneys with the Office of Legislative Research and General Counsel shared their knowledge, assisted in locating sources, or read parts of the text.

I thank the attorneys and others who are experienced in dealing with state constitutional issues for providing valuable critiques—Dallin H. Jensen, Douglas F. Bates, Margaret Bird, Karl Kappe, Robin Riggs, Roger Tew, Michelle Bush, and Brian Farr. I also appreciate the expert research assistance of Happy Morgan and the patient support of my husband, John Stephen White.

I am grateful to all of these colleagues and friends who generously shared with me their time and insight in the preparation of this first reference guide to our constitution. Any errors or omissions are, of course, my responsibility.

PART ONE

The History of the Utah Constitution

UTAH TERRITORY

Utah's constitutional history can only be understood by recognizing the unique circumstances of the state's founding and its turbulent, divisive territorial history. In July of 1847, a small group of members of the Church of Jesus Christ of Latter-day Saints (commonly known as Mormons) arrived in Great Salt Lake valley under the leadership of Brigham Young. They were the first of thousands of Mormons who would settle in the Great Basin during the next half century. These settlers gave Utah a distinctive character among the other nineteenth-century western territories. Far from the popular stereotype of ruggedly individualistic western pioneers, the Mormons came as part of a new religious movement pursuing a millennial dream. The move west was, as one historian has noted, part of "a quest for cultural unity erected upon a religious base." Believing that their mission was to establish the kingdom of God on earth, they were "set upon separating themselves from American Society and awaiting the destruction of all governments that would precede their own rise to power."[1]

Since the founding of the church in New York State in 1830, the Mormons had followed the direction of their prophet-president, Joseph Smith, in political,

[1] Marvin S. Hill, *Quest for Refuge: The Mormon Flight from American Pluralism* (Salt Lake City: Signature Books, 1989), 30–31.

economic, and social matters. Wherever they lived, they had formed a distinct culture within the main political and social culture, causing sometimes violent reaction against their political solidarity and their claims to direct revelation from God through their prophet. As a consequence, they were driven from Ohio to Missouri, then forced by an official "extermination order" to leave Missouri for refuge in Illinois. In a few short years they built up a prosperous settlement they called Nauvoo on the banks of the Mississippi. But this was not to last. Granted a municipal charter that gave them a large amount of home rule, the Mormons in effect lived under the ecclesiastical rule of Joseph Smith and church apostles. Their political solidarity and suppression of dissenting voices—along with rumors that they were secretly practicing polygamy—again provoked hostility among their neighbors. Mormon homes in nearby settlements were burned, and it became clear that once again they would have to leave the area or be driven out by violence.

After an angry mob killed Joseph Smith in 1844, his followers agreed to move to a place far from established settlements where they could finally live in peace. In 1846 they set out for one of the most isolated places on the continent, the semiarid Great Basin between the Rocky Mountains and the Sierra Nevadas, a part of Mexican territory. Partially explored by Catholic missionaries in 1776 and later by trappers, it was home to several Native American tribes. Despite warnings that the desert climate would make farming difficult, it seemed like a good place to put down roots once again.

Under the leadership of Brigham Young, the Mormons moved west, to start again with nothing but their wagonloads of possessions and their dream of being left alone to build a religion-based community. When they arrived in the Great Basin, the Mormons already had a clearly defined church government to provide law and order, distribute land, and direct economic affairs. Church leaders at first felt no need for a separate civil government. With the end of the Mexican War in 1848, however, the United States acquired a vast domain under the Treaty of Guadalupe Hidalgo, including the area occupied by the Mormons. The discovery of gold in California increased the numbers of travelers heading west through the Great Basin, bringing the outside world to their doors. The Mormons' self-imposed isolation was coming to an end, and some kind of legal relationship to the country they had fled was inevitable.

The Constitution of the "State of Deseret"

Mormon leaders at first sought territorial status in 1849. They soon decided instead to seek statehood, so that they could elect their own officials and have a greater degree of self-government. A constitution for the "State of Deseret"—supposedly written by a hastily called constitutional convention, but actually drafted under the direction of the Council of Fifty (a political arm of the Mormon church)—was sent to Congress.[2] This constitution, the first of seven written before achievement of statehood in 1896, was a simple document of just eight articles, outlining the structure of government, setting qualifications for voting and holding public office (limited to white males), and enumerating rights of citizens. In view of later conflicts over religious beliefs and separation of church and state, it is noteworthy that it had a strong provision affirming the right to worship according to one's conscience, forbidding an establishment of religion, and prohibiting a religious test for public office.[3]

This basic, no-frills constitution served as the organic law for the provisional "State of Deseret" until 1851 and would serve as a model for two documents drafted later in an effort to attain statehood.

The Deseret Constitution was accompanied to Washington by a petition for statehood and a slate of state officers—all Mormon church leaders. Congress then was embroiled in the conflict over extension of slavery, and admission of a new state was out of the question. Instead, Utah gained territorial status for an area vastly larger than Utah today, including virtually all of Nevada and parts of present-day California, Wyoming, Colorado, Oregon, New Mexico, and Arizona.

The Organic Act of 1850 and Territorial Government

After Congress passed the Organic Act creating the Territory of Utah in September 1850, President Millard Fillmore appointed a new slate of territorial judges and officials, headed by Brigham Young.[4] The Act provided for popular election of the bicameral Legislative Assembly, and a nonvoting delegate to Congress, as well as local officials. Territorial officers and judges were political patronage appointees from outside the Territory, as they were in other western territories, a practice that led to complaints throughout the West about the character and abilities of the "carpetbaggers." Utah's territorial governors—all from outside the Territory after Brigham Young's term—probably were no better and no worse than those in surrounding territories, but they were seen from the start as "political adventurers of the lowest grade" who were "glad to accept the crumbs of government patronage."[5] In fact, even capable men found it difficult to govern

[2] Peter Crawley, "The Constitution of the State of Deseret," *BYU Studies* 29 (1989): 13–15. The name "Deseret" is a term from the *Book of Mormon,* meaning "honeybee" and denoting industry.

[3] Art. VIII, sec. 8, draft Constitution of the State of Deseret, 31st Cong., 1st Sess., House of Representatives Mis. Doc. No. 18 (1850).

[4] Organic Act of the Territory of Utah, Ch. 51, 9 Stat. 453, 9 September 1850.

[5] Hubert Howe Bancroft, *History of Utah: 1540–1886* (San Francisco: The History Company, 1889), 486.

people who openly resented them.[6] It was doubly difficult in Utah, where the predominant power of the Mormon church and its leaders led to confrontations that did not enhance the political careers of its governors. Appointed governors and judges became the focus of discontent with territorial status—as they did in other western territories.[7] Relationships between the Mormons and their territorial officials were not the only reasons to seek statehood, however. The Mormons soon found their religious beliefs and practices would doom their dream of a separate social culture within the union.

The 1856 Constitution

In 1852 the Mormon church formally acknowledged the practice of plural marriage, or polygamy, which had long been the subject of rumors. This generated a wave of moral indignation that was to wash over the Territory for the next four decades. The image of Mormons in the national press ranged from ridicule to threats of national action; they were universally censured for resurrecting this Old Testament practice. The reaction of the Mormon-dominated Legislative Assembly was to seek self-government through statehood, and it sent memorials to Congress in 1852, 1853, and 1854 asking for the creation of a convention to write a new constitution. Since Congress refused to do so, the Legislative Assembly of 1855 authorized an election of delegates to a constitutional convention the following year. Meeting early in 1856, the elected delegates used the State of Deseret Constitution as a model, with only minor changes.[8] Congress refused to accept it. National hostility to the Mormons was rising, shown clearly in the 1856 Republican platform condemning the "twin relics of barbarism," polygamy and slavery.

Responding to complaints in the popular press that the Utah Territory was a sinkhole of moral decay, ruled by an ecclesiastical dictator, President James Buchanan decided early in 1857 to appoint a new governor to replace Brigham Young. He dispatched an army to escort the new governor, an experienced Georgian, Alfred Cumming. This prompted Brigham Young to evacuate Salt Lake City and prepare to burn it rather than surrender. Fortunately, Cumming

[6] Jack Ericson Eblen, *The First and Second United States Empires: Governors and Territorial Government, 1874–1912* (Pittsburgh: University of Pittsburgh Press, 1968), 271. Also Earl S. Pomeroy, *The Territories and the United States: 1861–1890* (Philadelphia: University of Pennsylvania Press, 1947), 62–63.

[7] Donald Crowley and Florence Heffron, *The Idaho State Constitution: A Reference Guide* (Westport, Conn.: Greenwood Press, 1994), 4; Robert B. Keiter and Tim Newcomb, *The Wyoming State Constitution: A Reference Guide* (Westport, Conn.: Greenwood Press, 1993), 3.

[8] Draft Constitution of the State of Deseret, 35th Cong., 1st Sess., Senate Mis. Doc. No. 240 (19 April 1858).

proved to be an able and diplomatic executive, and a compromise was arranged for a peaceful transfer of governmental power.

Brigham Young still held de facto power in the Territory, however. He continued to build Mormon economic power by promoting boycotts of businesses owned by non-Mormons (commonly known as gentiles, whether Catholic, Jewish, or Protestant). He also promoted development of cooperative enterprises by his followers to weaken the economic power of the gentiles. He wielded political power over the non-Mormon minority by sheer power of numbers in elections, and defied national pressure to end polygamy—claiming it to be a commandment of God. He was backed by an intensely loyal following. A past marked by violent rejection and expulsion from mainstream America had made Utah's Mormons, according to sociologist Thomas F. O'Dea, "into a people apart, separated by the ever widening chasm of divergent values and history from their fellow Americans."[9] By the late 1850s the Mormon people had come to accept this status; still, they were part of the United States and they wanted the self-rule statehood would bring.

The 1862 Constitution

In its first decade, the population of the Territory had grown to more than 40,000, and the time seemed ripe in 1862 for another constitutional convention. The document that emerged from the convention was similar to the 1849 and the 1856 State of Deseret constitutions, except for changes in the judicial article to give constitutional status to circuit and probate courts.[10] Although it seemed that a Congress concerned with the Civil War would be happy to rid itself of the expenses of a distant territory, Utah failed again to gain statehood. The lawmakers apparently were more concerned with the morals of the Mormons than with money. They finally passed the Morrill Anti-Bigamy Act of 1862, a measure that had languished in Congress since 1856, bitterly opposed by the now-departed southerners in their concern for states' rights. It applied only to the Territory of Utah. It provided penalties against anyone married to more than one partner, disincorporated the Mormon church, and limited the value of property the church could acquire to $50,000. Although it was not vigorously enforced for another decade, the Morrill Act was the pattern for subsequent legislation designed to break the power of the church and stamp out Mormon marriage practices that offended mainstream Christianity.[11] As a reaction, the Territorial Legislative Assembly sent another memorial to Congress in 1867, accompanied by a constitution of the State of Deseret only slightly altered from the 1862 document. It had

---

[9] Thomas F. O'Dea, *The Mormons* (Chicago: University of Chicago Press, 1957), 115.

[10] Art. VI, sec. 1, draft Constitution of the State of Deseret, 37th Cong., 2d Sess., House of Representatives Mis. Doc. No. 78 (1862), Serial 1141.

[11] Morrill Anti-Bigamy Act, Ch. 126, 12 Stat. 501 (1862).

been changed by the Assembly to recognize new boundaries drawn after the creation of the state of Nevada in 1864, not by a constitutional convention. It was ignored by Congress.

The 1872 Constitution

A decade after the discouraging events of 1862, Utahns launched their next exercise in constitution writing. By 1870, despite losing the vast area of Nevada, the population had reached more than 86,000. More important, the demographic makeup had begun to change. Although thousands of new converts to the Mormon religion had poured into the Territory from other parts of the country and from Europe, the introduction of metal mining in the Wasatch Mountains in the early 1860s also fed the immigration stream. The Catholic Church and several Protestant churches had put down roots in the Territory, and by the end of the decade a number of Jewish businessmen were settled in Salt Lake City. The transcontinental railroad, completed in Utah in 1869, opened a new era of transportation and trade. These developments challenged Brigham Young. He had fostered the development of home industries to meet the needs of a self-sufficient economy, and now manufactured goods from the East threatened this goal. He had preached the virtues of a stable, family-oriented agrarian commonwealth, now challenged by the lure of instant riches in the mines. His early disapproval of Mormons' involvement in mining meant that this new industry would be dominated by "outsiders." Utah's partial isolation from the rest of the nation was ending.

Other important changes added to the religious polarization of the Territory. Non-Mormon citizens were tired of legislative and other elections entirely dominated by the Mormons and founded their own Liberal party in 1870. The Mormon leadership then established its own party, the People's party, to formally nominate candidates approved by church leaders. It seemed like a good time to call another constitutional convention and try again for statehood.

The 1872 convention was different from those before it, both in its makeup and the kind of document that emerged from it. This time, there was a conscious effort to draw non-Mormons into the effort. Several leading non-Mormons were elected (although at least one declined to serve), and one of them, Eli M. Barnum, was chosen president of the convention. To attempt to deal with the polygamy barrier to statehood, this constitution included a provision inviting Congress to add an amendment containing an unspecified qualification for admission to the union. This obviously was an invitation to Congress to add a prohibition against polygamy; the catch was that the people of the Territory would have to approve it in an election, and this had all the survival prospects of a glacier at the equator.

This draft constitution marked a departure from the simple documents that preceded it. Hoping to repeat Nevada's swift acceptance into the union with its

1864 Constitution, delegates used their neighboring state's document as a model. It marked the beginning of more detailed and specific documents drafted by Utah constitutional conventions. It included more detailed legislative and judicial articles and provided for a powerful Board of Examiners to "examine all claims against the state."[12] The 1872 draft died in the House Committee on Territories after a rancorous debate that showed deep distrust of Utah's Mormon majority and its religious, political, and economic practices. Two years later, Congress passed the Poland Act. It strengthened prosecution of polygamists under the Morrill Act and limited jurisdiction of the Mormon-dominated probate courts, which were perceived to be biased toward church members.[13] More anti-polygamy legislation was to follow.

In March of 1882, Congress passed the Edmunds Act, which strengthened enforcement of the Morrill Act and placed Utah's electoral machinery in the hands of a commission appointed by the president.[14] Known as the Utah Commission, this five-member body was established to curb the political power of the Mormon church by vigorously enforcing a main provision of the law prohibiting polygamists from voting or holding public office. This began to erode the Mormons' political power by eliminating many of them from the voting rolls. In response, another constitutional convention was called in April of 1882.

The 1882 Constitution

The 1882 convention drafted a constitution that varied little from the Nevada-inspired 1872 document, but it gave up the fight for the name "Deseret," and called the new draft the "Constitution of the State of Utah."[15] For the first time, women (who had been given the vote by the territorial Legislature in 1870) were among the delegates. The House Committee on Territories—predictably—rejected this appeal for statehood, and the federal government continued efforts to deal with the "Mormon problem" by vigorous enforcement of the anti-polygamy laws. This resulted in the imprisonment of large numbers of Mormon men (most Mormon men did not practice polygamy) and severe economic hardship for many families.[16] This was not the first time Mormons had suffered for their

[12] Art. V, sec. 18, draft Constitution of the State of Deseret, 42d Cong., 2d Sess., House of Representatives Mis. Doc. No. 165 (1972), Serial 1526.

[13] Poland Act, Ch. 469, 18 Stat. 253 (1874).

[14] Edmunds Act, Ch. 47, 22 Stat. 30 (1882).

[15] Draft Constitution of the State of Utah, 47th Cong., 1st Sess., House of Representatives Mis. Doc. No. 43 (1882), Serial 2046.

[16] Leonard J. Arrington, *Great Basin Kingdom: An Economic History of the Latter-day Saints, 1830–1900* (Cambridge, Mass.: Harvard University Press, 1958), 360.

beliefs and practices, however, and they followed their church leaders in clinging to polygamy—whatever the costs.

Pressure on the church and its members became even more intense with the passage of the Edmunds-Tucker Act in February of 1887. It attempted to extinguish the legal existence of the church and seize all of its property except that used strictly for religious purposes; appropriated its assets; abolished the vote for women; and eliminated from voting rolls not only polygamists, but those who would counsel or advise others to practice it.[17] Mormons responded—typically—by another try for statehood.

The 1887 Constitution

In June of 1887, the sixth major attempt at statehood began with a constitutional convention spurned by the non-Mormon Liberal party. The draft constitution supposedly met the polygamy problem head-on by declaring bigamy and polygamy a misdemeanor.[18] It also tried to meet the charge of church-state mingling by a provision in the Bill of Rights forbidding "union of church and State."[19] The anti-polygamy provision could hardly be considered seriously, since church leaders still clung to the plural marriage doctrine. Other provisions were typical of those found in other late-nineteenth-century state constitutions, and some of them were to be found in the next—and final—constitution drafted in 1895 on the eve of statehood. The 1887 draft included an item veto for appropriations bills, stringent debt limits for local governments, and tax exemptions for mines and irrigation facilities. The tax exemptions illustrate the strength of both mining and agriculture as players in the political arena—which would continue through the next decade. The 1887 draft constitution was buried in the Senate Committee on Territories with a terse statement condemning both polygamy and control of civil affairs of the Territory by "the Priesthood of the Mormon Church."[20]

Breaking Barriers to Statehood

The polarization of the Territory along religious, political, economic, and social lines had produced, by the late 1880s, a situation that no one liked. The stringent federal anti-polygamy laws had sent most of the Mormon leadership—and large numbers of other men—to prison and embittered the membership. The seizure of church property by the federal government, and the threatened seizure of even their sacred temples in the future, was an alarming prospect. Non-Mormons

---

[17] Edmunds-Tucker Act, Ch. 397, 24 Stat. 635 (1887).

[18] Art. XV, sec. 12, draft Constitution of the State of Utah, 50th Cong., 1st Sess., House of Representatives Mis. Doc. No. 104 (1887), Serial 2565.

[19] Ibid., Art. I, sec. 3.

[20] U.S., *Congressional Record,* 50th Cong., 1st Sess., 1888, XIX, Part 3, 2391.

were gaining political strength, and some were prospering in mining and other enterprises. Allied with the appointed territorial officials, prosecutors, and judges, they kept the pressure on the federal government in Washington to keep the pressure on the Mormons to change the economic and political climate of the Territory. A change in the atmosphere was sorely needed, and slowly it came. Territorial governor Caleb W. West, a patient, diplomatic advocate of change, noted in his 1888 annual report that "The Mormon people in some measure have relaxed the old rule of rigorous exclusiveness. . . . They have exhibited a spirit of liberality and enterprise in appropriating money for needed charitable and educational institutions. . . . Without having the control, they have united with non-Mormons in public organizations for the protection and increase of trade."[21] The latter probably was the most important observation, for it recognized such events as the formation of chambers of commerce that brought Mormon and non-Mormon business leaders together in a common effort to boost the economy of the Territory.

Like an immense iceberg, a massive mound of distrust had stood between Mormons and non-Mormons during most of their territorial history. Now it was being chipped away. A Mormon and non-Mormon Citizens' ticket for the Salt Lake City election in 1888 won handily. Other events hastened the process of accommodation between the two factions. In 1889 the non-Mormon Liberal party won the city election in Ogden, to the surprise and dismay of the usually triumphant Mormon People's party. In 1890 the Liberals again showed their growing strength by winning the city offices in the Salt Lake City election, showing that Mormon political power in Utah's larger cities was now seriously diminished. The major event that sliced open the iceberg was the Manifesto (a policy declaration) of Mormon President Wilford Woodruff in September of 1890 advising Mormons to refrain from violating the laws against plural marriages. This move deprived the national press of its main complaint against the Mormons.

Other events quickly followed. In 1891 the Mormon church disbanded its People's party, and both the Republican and Democratic parties, which had been entirely overshadowed by the two religion-based parties, reached out for both Mormon and non-Mormon members. The Liberal party virtually folded after the election of 1892, except for a lingering effort in Salt Lake City. Utah's political system was now following the national model. In the 1880s and early 1890s the Mormon church leadership was working closely with national Republican leaders to pave the way for statehood.[22] After Grover Cleveland and the Democrats proved victorious in 1892, Utah's Democratic delegate to Congress,

---

[21] Report of the Governor of Utah to the Secretary of the Interior, 1888, 19, Utah State Archives.

[22] Edward Leo Lyman, *Political Deliverance: The Mormon Quest for Utah Statehood* (Urbana and Chicago: University of Illinois Press, 1986), 69–92.

Joseph L. Rawlins, worked carefully with both parties to assure passage of the Enabling Act. This Act was passed and signed by President Cleveland on 16 July 1894. It contained several requirements, including a provision banning polygamy "forever," a mandate that shaped the deliberations of the constitutional convention that was established by the Act.[23]

Later in 1894, after lively campaigning, the Territory held its first election based on national rather than religious party lines, and elected 107 delegates to a constitutional convention to be held early in 1895. To reach this point, Mormons had to abandon the dream of a self-sufficient, religion-based commonwealth, to give up political power for a party system like those in the rest of the country, and to change the marriage practices that had drawn the wrath of the nation. Non-Mormon leaders had come to realize that without statehood, the area would never be able to attract eastern capital and develop its economy. The constitutional convention would test the commitment of both Mormons and non-Mormons to unite in a common cause—statehood for Utah.

THE CONSTITUTIONAL CONVENTION OF 1895

The men who met on 4 March 1895 to write a constitution, under the guidance of a long-sought enabling act of Congress, approached their jobs with high hopes, but also with some fears. After so many failures to gain statehood, debates in the convention were peppered with warnings that nothing should be done to jeopardize it now. They were determined to "play it safe," to avoid experimentation, and to copy provisions from the constitutions of other states to avoid uncertainty. Their unique territorial history, with its deep social, political, and economic divisions along religious lines, reminded them that it was crucial to bridge these divisions in the convention. A rebirth of the old animosities might defeat the document at the polls in November. Economic prosperity was a primary aim of all the delegates, and they knew it could only come after large investments of eastern capital. Another aim of the convention, though seldom articulated, was to improve the national image of Utah.

These hopes were part of a goal repeatedly expressed—to attract eastern capital and build industrial prosperity in the new state. The emphasis on economic development, a theme common to other western states, was heightened by the severe effects of the 1890s depression in Utah. Unemployment was dangerously high: some estimates placed it at nearly half of the labor force in Salt Lake City.[24]

---

[23] Sec. 3, "An Act to Enable the People of Utah to Form a Constitution and State Government . . .," Ch. 138, 28 Stat. 107, 16 July 1894.

[24] Leonard J. Arrington, "Utah and the Depression of the 1890s," *Utah Historical Quarterly* 29 (January 1961): 5–6.

Farm income had plummeted, and the mining boom of the 1880s had slowed nearly to a halt for lack of capital to exploit deeper, lower-grade ores.[25]

The Delegates

The 107 delegates from the Territory's twenty-seven counties represented diverse interests and geographic origins. More than a third were foreign-born, and only twenty-eight were born in the Territory. Farmers and ranchers formed the largest occupational group, followed by merchants and manufacturers. Lawyers and mining entrepreneurs had smaller but effective representation. Nearly all of the delegates had some previous governmental experience, as mayors, city council members, legislators, or judges. Sixteen had served in one or more of the previous constitutional conventions, so they were not new to the process of constitution writing.

There were twenty-nine non-Mormons, including several who were prominent in mining and others who were leading lawyers. One was a Methodist Episcopal minister from Sevier County. All but three of the non-Mormons were Republicans. Despite being in a minority, the non-Mormons dominated the floor debates, making speeches far out of proportion to their numbers.[26] The most influential, dominating figure of the convention was a Unitarian lawyer, Charles S. Varian, who had served in both the Nevada and Utah legislatures and had been a United States district attorney in Utah. Although he won fame for prosecuting polygamists during territorial days, he won respect in the convention for his encyclopedic knowledge of state constitutions and laws and his well-reasoned arguments.

Mormon church interests were represented by several of its highest ranking members, including apostles John Henry Smith (who was unanimously elected president of the convention) and Moses Thatcher; Presiding Bishop William B. Preston; and Brigham H. Roberts, one of the presidents of Quorum of the Seventy. Two dozen lower-ranking officials from Mormon congregations throughout the Territory assured a strong voice for church interests.

Most of the main issues at the convention did not divide the delegates along religious lines, and few brought out partisan differences. Republicans had a clear majority in convention delegates, fifty-nine to forty-eight, a notable shift in the political balance in the previously Democratic-leaning Territory. Economic and sectional issues proved to be the most divisive in the convention. Mining and agricultural interests clashed over rights of eminent domain, water policy, and taxation. Delegates from agricultural counties far from the population

[25] Dean L. May, "Towards a Dependent Commonwealth," in Richard D. Poll, ed., *Utah's History* (Provo, Utah: Brigham Young University Press, 1978), 223.

[26] Stanley S. Ivins, "A Constitution for Utah," *Utah Historical Quarterly* 25 (April 1957): 114. Also Stanley S. Ivins Papers, Utah State Historical Society.

centers of the Wasatch Front (the western slopes of the Wasatch Mountains) fought for greater representation in future legislatures and a fair share of state institutions and services. Two concerns helped to dull the sharp edges of contention: fear of reviving the bitterness of the Mormon–gentile conflicts of the past (seldom mentioned but an underlying current), and fear of losing the battle for statehood.

Polygamy and Church-State Issues

Since polygamy had been the main rallying cry against the Mormons, Congress settled this nettlesome issue by mandating in the Enabling Act that it would be banned "forever." To the relief of the delegates, it was put in the Ordinance (Art. III) without debate. The Enabling Act also required "perfect toleration of religious sentiment" and public schools "free from sectarian control."[27] Still, the issue of a Mormon church theocracy hung over the convention, stimulating other provisions aimed at settling the church–state issue.

Most sections of the Declaration of Rights were picked up with little argument, copied from the United States Bill of Rights or from other state constitutions. Stronger provisions regarding church and state were written, in view of the political strength of the Mormons: some 65 percent of the new state's population would be Mormon.[28] The Declaration of Rights forbade a religious test for voting or holding office; use of public money for any religious worship, exercise, or instruction; or support of any ecclesiastical establishment. It also forbade any "union of Church and State." It prohibited any church from dominating the state or interfering with its functions and forbade use of public money or property for "religious worship or instruction or support of any ecclesiastical establishment" (Art. I, sec. 4). Three provisions in the Education article guaranteed schools free from sectarian control, prohibited religious or partisan tests for students or teachers, and public aid to church schools (Art. X, secs. 1, 12, and 13). Mormon delegates, whose children primarily attended public schools, willingly accepted these conditions in the overriding interest of gaining statehood.

Private Property and Public Use

One of the most emotionally charged issues of the convention was a simple provision regarding eminent domain, because of the almost sacred right to private property, the keen interest of both farming and mining delegates in the issue, and the possible impact on future development of mining, agriculture, industry, and transportation. It provided that "Private property shall not be taken or damaged

[27] Enabling Act, Ch. 138, 28 Stat. 107, sec. 3.

[28] Dean L. May, "A Demographic Portrait of the Mormons, 1830–1980," in D. Michael Quinn, ed., *The New Mormon History* (Salt Lake City: Signature Books, 1992), 133.

for public use without just compensation" (Art. I, sec. 22). There was much agonizing over the meaning of public use: when could use of private property constitute a public use? Other western states had dealt with the same issue; while trying to protect private property rights, Colorado and Wyoming constitutions permitted use of private property for "private ways of necessity" such as reservoirs, drains, flumes, or ditches for agricultural, mining, milling, domestic, or sanitary purposes. In the Utah convention, mining men argued that blocking entry to their claims would strangle the industry. Farming delegates would not honor the miners' claims without specific protection of their right to build irrigation ditches and reservoirs where they were needed.

Although some delegates favored a specific statement in the constitution to protect their interests—and tried repeatedly to revive the issue—the lengthy debates ended with the simple provision for just compensation for taking or damaging private property taken for public use (Art. I, sec. 22). For once, the delegates decided not to legislate for the future but leave the "public use" definition to future legislatures and courts—perhaps because it had become so divisive.

The Lawyers and Right to Juries

In a time when other states were examining the right to jury trials and questioning the use of the grand jury, the lawyers in Utah's convention led out in debate on these questions. A leading Mormon attorney and future state supreme court justice, Samuel R. Thurman eloquently pleaded for reducing the twelve-person jury as an economy measure that would not jeopardize justice for the accused. Since few other delegates wanted to take on the lawyers, a small group of Mormon and non-Mormon lawyers shaped the section. Mormons David Evans and William Creer joined non-Mormons Charles Varian, William Van Horne, Dennis Eichnor, and others to simplify and save money in the state's justice system. They preserved the right of trial by jury in capital cases and the unanimous verdict in criminal cases, but cut the size of other juries (Art. I, sec. 10). They also provided for filing an "information" (a statement of sufficient evidence to hold a suspect for trial), rather than requiring grand juries (Art. I, sec. 13). This creation of an alternative to grand juries reflected a common concern of many states with the inquisitorial nature and abuses of some grand juries.[29]

The Woman Suffrage Issue

In sharp contrast to the ease with which consensus was reached on most issues of individual rights, the issue of woman suffrage occupied the convention floor

[29] Gordon Morris Bakken, *Rocky Mountain Constitution Making, 1850–1912* (Westport, Conn.: Greenwood Press, 1987), 25–26. Also Keiter and Newcomb, *The Wyoming State Constitution,* 12.

longer than any other issue. This was surprising, since both the Democratic and Republican parties had endorsed the vote for women in their 1894 platforms, and the *Salt Lake Tribune* noted that the delegates exhibited "a strong sentiment in favor of giving women the right to vote."[30]

Women had been given the right to vote (but not to hold office) by the territorial Legislative Assembly in 1870. They had exercised this right until 1887, when Congress took it away in the Edmunds-Tucker Act, in order to reduce the number of Mormons qualified to vote. Utah's Mormon and some non-Mormon women had been active in the national woman suffrage movement in the early 1890s, and by 1894 they had organized suffrage associations throughout the state. Their political pressure on both political parties—along with the tacit approval of Mormon church leaders—probably would have assured a quick victory in the convention, but the issue became tangled in the sensitive church-state issue. It also raised the fear of putting unpopular or "experimental" provisions in the constitution. Utah was trying to shed the image of being "different" from the rest of the nation, and only two states, Wyoming and Colorado, had given women the right to vote and hold office.

The fear of upsetting a delicate political balance between Mormons and non-Mormons in future elections was raised by Fred J. Kiesel, an influential non-Mormon merchant, and for a time the issue seemed to be polarizing the convention along religious lines. Then one of the Territory's leading orators and a high official of the Mormon church, Brigham H. Roberts, launched an oratorical blitzkrieg against the vote for women, arguing that good women should not get into the dirty business of politics, and Utah should not jeopardize statehood. Soon the state's leading newspapers joined the fray, the entire Territory was aroused, and petitions bearing thousands of signatures for and against a separate vote of the electorate on the issue flooded the convention.[31] To the dismay of many delegates, the issue took up most of the convention time from 15 March to 18 April, when a motion to reconsider the previous vote in favor of woman suffrage was defeated. In the end both Mormons and non-Mormons had voted for and against the provision (Art. IV, sec. 1), but most non-Mormons opposed it to the end. The issue had not proved as divisive as many had feared, but the long battle for the vote for women had shown clearly that the political wounds of the past were not completely forgotten.

Governmental Structure and Powers

Design of the three major branches of government generally followed the pattern of the ill-fated constitutions drafted during the later territorial period: an

---

[30] *Salt Lake Tribune,* 4 March 1895.

[31] Ibid., 19 April 1895.

executive branch fragmented into several different offices and boards, a legislative branch sharply limited in its fiscal functions, and an elected judiciary with detailed instructions for its operation.

The Executive Department article defined the Executive Department as "consisting of Governor, Secretary of State, State Auditor, State Treasurer, Attorney-General, and Superintendent of Public Instruction" (Art. VII, sec. 1). Each was independently elected, and some sat on boards that supervised state institutions such as the state prison and the reform school. The governor, attorney general, and secretary of state served as the Board of Examiners with power to examine all claims against the state except salaries or compensation of officers fixed by law (Art. VII, sec. 13). In practice it gave the board power to disapprove expenditures for which the Legislature had authorized funds and created endless controversy until it was abolished in 1993. The usual pardoning power of governors was limited to temporary pardons, good only until the Board of Pardons (consisting of the governor, supreme court justices, and attorney general) could meet. The governor was, however, given an item veto over appropriations bills. The fragmentation of the executive branch was typical of other state constitutions written at the time and was not essentially changed until the early 1990s.

Convention delegates, many of whom had served in territorial legislatures, vacillated between strict elaboration of the legislative branch powers and duties and a broad outline of its responsibilities. On any given issue, the substance of the controversy determined its treatment. Delegates who opposed curbs on legislative action fought to keep limitations out of the document; they usually lost the battle to those who felt detail was necessary to chart the path of the future state government. The distrust of future legislative bodies was typical of the times, and it took nearly three-quarters of a century to effect reforms that would enable the Legislature to meet twentieth-century needs. The constitution mandated that the Legislature not enact special laws where general laws could apply, but then it went on to list eighteen specific cases where there should be no private or special laws. It also instituted the "one subject" rule for bills, which made amendment of entire articles difficult until modified in 1971 (Art. XXIII, sec. 1).

A proposed section prohibiting the Legislature from granting state subsidies or lending its credit to private business provided one of the few occasions for division along party lines. The Democratic minority members of the Legislative Committee recommended that any grant or appropriation of public property or money by the state or any political subdivision, or any lending of credit to any individual, association, or corporation, be prohibited.[32] Republicans played on

[32] *Proceedings and Debates of the Convention*, 2 vols. (Salt Lake City: Star Printing Co., 1898), 1: 394. Hereinafter, cited as *Proceedings of the Convention*.

the need for development of Utah's resources by outside capital and pointed out that the struggling sugar industry had been subsidized from territorial coffers. Democrats pointed to examples of states that had incurred crippling debts by subsidizing failed enterprises and wanted to protect future legislatures from the temptation to do the same. A prominent Salt Lake attorney, Franklin S. Richards, argued that "the State ought not to be authorized to engage in any business enterprises, construction and operation of railroads, or the building of manufactories of any kind . . . or for any purpose except strictly governmental purposes."[33] The combative editor of the *Salt Lake Tribune*, Charles C. Goodwin, joined his fellow Republican delegates in urging that future legislatures have the power to help private enterprises when "they can benefit themselves."[34]

When the influential Charles Varian broke ranks with his fellow Republicans, he took a dozen party members with him to join the Democrats in a provision to prohibit the state or its local governments from lending credit or subscribing to stock or bonds "in aid of any railroad, telegraph or other private individual or corporate enterprise or undertaking" (Art. VI, sec. 31). This ignored the subsidy issue, but it lessened fears of future legislative corruption by railroad or other corporate interests looking for credit from the state.

Rural interests fought hard to keep the large Wasatch Front counties from dominating future legislatures. The apportionment issue was argued from every possible angle. There was the high-ground federal analogy of equal representation in the United States Senate. There was also the low-ground argument that everyone should have a chance at the benefits to be parceled out by future legislatures. The smaller counties won the battle for at least one representative from each county in the House and hung onto their victory until reapportionment was forced by United States Supreme Court decisions (*Baker v. Carr,* 1962; *Reynolds v. Sims,* 1964) in the early 1960s.[35]

The Judicial Department article (Art. VIII) was crafted almost entirely by the lawyers from both political parties. They provided for a supreme court and seven district courts. Since each district contained several counties, rural counties fought for their share of court services; each court was required to meet at least four times each year in each county (Art. VIII, sec. 5).

The probate courts were a bone of contention between Mormons and non-Mormons in territorial days. They were local courts whose jurisdiction could be determined by the Mormon-dominated Legislature. Their reach soon was expanded far beyond the traditional role of probate courts into competition with the federally controlled district courts, until it was curbed by the United States Supreme Court in 1874 in *Ferris v. Higley* and in the Poland Act. The probate

---

[33] Ibid., 1: 889.

[34] Ibid., 1: 902.

[35] Frank H. Jonas and Brad E. Hainsworth, "Utah," in Eleanore Bushnell, ed., *Impact of Reapportionment on the Thirteen Western States* (Salt Lake City: University of Utah Press, 1970), 263–64.

courts remained a symbol of Mormon domination to non-Mormons, and the idea that they might be enshrined in the new constitution was anathema to the non-Mormon lawyers. Charles C. Goodwin, chairman of the Judiciary Article Committee, said county officials felt their probate judges were "not fit to be blown up" and "they begged us to remove them so that they could get competent men."[36] This probably was an exaggeration, but in the late stages of the convention no one wanted to linger on sensitive and divisive issues, and the probate courts were written out of the judiciary in Article XXIV, section 9.

Education and Sectional Interests

Since early territorial days, development of an adequate school system had been a struggle. In most rural areas the grammar schools had lived a hand-to-mouth existence until passage of a territorial school act in 1890. Even then, this support was not generous enough to guarantee a full school year, and only Utah's two largest cities had high schools. There appeared to be a consensus that a guarantee of free schools (but not free colleges or universities) should be in the constitution; the issue was whether the state school fund should support free high schools while many districts could not adequately support their grammar schools. Eventually, a compromise was reached. The schools would be free, but high schools would be supported by local taxes if state school funds were not sufficient. This debate centered on some deep concerns of the delegates—their desire to create an inviting atmosphere for outside investment, but at the same time to keep governmental expenditures low.

Sectional antagonisms reached an even more contentious level when a proposal to combine the University of Utah, located in Salt Lake City, and the Utah State Agricultural College (now Utah State University), located 100 miles north in Logan. William J. Kerr, president of Brigham Young College, persuasively argued that Utah was too poor to support two higher education institutions, and many delegates agreed with him. The battle for location, however, doomed the proposal. After a long and divisive debate, the institutions remained separate, and in their original locations.

Corporations and Labor

Although many issues in the convention grew out of Utah's unique territorial experience, delegates also faced many of the same problems their western neighbors—Idaho, Wyoming, Montana, Washington, and the Dakotas—had struggled with during their conventions. Although Utah delegates were desperate to attract new capital and industry, they shared the national concern with the

[36] *Proceedings of the Convention*, 2: 1397.

rising power of corporations and trusts in the 1880s and 1890s. Some infant industries in the Territory, notably the sugar industry, could be hurt by regulation designed to curb rapacious trusts. Provisions were artfully drawn to avoid this problem, and a long, detailed article (Art. XII), replete with limitations and directions for future legislatures, was the result. Most of it was eliminated in the 1990s. But in the 1890s the debate over the Corporations article and the Labor article (Art. XVI) showed a deep concern with shaping the economic future of the new state. Delegates tried to promote the welfare of workers by outlawing blacklisting and importation of "Pinkertons" or any private army to break up strikes. After much controversy, they provided for a Board of Labor, Conciliation and Arbitration to "fairly represent the interests of both capital and labor" (Art. XVI, sec. 2), a mandate largely ignored by future legislatures. They also showed the influence of the progressive movement by prohibiting employment of women and children in mines, limiting the use of prison labor, and setting an eight-hour day for public employment, as well as banning railroad consolidation and combinations resulting in restraint of trade. Taken together, the corporations and labor articles were a patchwork of compromises designed to promote a more prosperous economy in the future state, and amendments were needed later to meet twentieth-century conditions.

The taxation and debt provisions (Arts. XIII and XIV) were strongly influenced by the depressed economic environment of the mid-1890s. The lack of capital to boost mining and other industries out of the depression, along with dangerously high unemployment in the Territory fed fears that unless the power to tax and incur debt was stringently limited, the people of the Territory would refuse to ratify the new constitution in November. Since the Territory already had a debt of about $767,000, future debt (after paying off the territorial debt) was limited to $200,000, and property tax ceilings were placed on state government.

Taxation of mines and mining claims became a hot issue, with mining magnate Thomas F. Kearns (a future United States senator) pleading for taxation only on machinery and improvements until mines began to produce income. His pleas did not prevail. Taxation and Revenue Committee chairman George M. Cannon argued successfully for adoption of the Montana Constitution's provision for taxation of mines at the amount paid for the claims and on net proceeds of production, insisting that "mining should bear its just proportion of taxation and of the burdens of the state."[37]

Since farmers and stock raisers formed the largest single bloc in the convention, the needs of agriculture were given special consideration in the Taxation article. "Ditches, canals, and flumes" used for irrigating lands were not to be taxed while "owned and used exclusively for such purpose" (Art. XIII, sec. 3).

[37] Ibid., 1: 1078.

Property of the United States and other governmental units, as well as public libraries and property used exclusively for religious worship or charitable purposes were also exempted from taxation. This short list of exemptions was to be lengthened considerably during the next century.

Development of water resources made life in the semiarid Great Basin possible. Control of those resources sparked a spirited debate in the convention, as in other western conventions.[38] By 1895, legal rights to specific stream flows were incorporated in Utah territorial law, and water was distributed by local water districts throughout the Territory. The Wyoming constitutional assignment of water as property of the state was soundly rejected by the Utah convention, which passed a simple provision affirming water rights in existence at the time of statehood (Art. XVII).

At the end of sixty-six official days (fifty-five actual working days), the delegates had worked together with amazingly little personal conflict and rancor. Few issues threatened division on religious lines, and most issues were decided without marked political partisanship. Sectional and economic interests proved to be the most important. The constitution they produced was a product of extensive borrowing, which is not necessarily a bad thing—or due to a lack of creativity.[39] It was excessively long by model state constitution standards, and it needed many changes by the mid-twentieth century.

■ CHANGES IN THE FIRST CENTURY

At the end of its first century, Utah was one of nineteen states that had not rewritten their original constitutions.[40] At the end of Utah's centennial year, 1996, voters had approved ninety-one amendments out of 140 proposed. This figure is somewhat misleading in terms of the magnitude of change, since early amendments generally were limited to single sections, while amendments since 1970 frequently have made changes in several sections with one amendment (Art. XXIII, sec. 1).

Utah's Constitution provides for two methods of change (Art. XXIII). Both require action by the Legislature and approval by the voters. If a substantial change seems to be needed, the Legislature by a two-thirds vote may call for a convention, which must be approved by a majority of the voters who vote at the election. A new constitution produced by the convention must be ratified by the same majority. In 1966 Utah voters overwhelmingly opposed a proposal to call

---

38 Bakken, *Rocky Mountain Constitution Making*, 65–73.

39 Christian G. Fritz, "The American Constitutional Tradition Revisited: Preliminary Observations on State Constitution-Making in the Nineteenth-Century West," *Rutgers Law Journal* 25 (No. 4, 1994): 980–81.

40 *The Book of the States*, 1996–97 ed. (Lexington, Ky.: The Council of State Governments, 1996), 3, Table 1.1.

a new convention to completely revise the constitution, and no one has pushed for a convention since then.

The only other method of change is by amendment. The constitution requires passage of a proposed amendment by two-thirds of the members in both houses of the Legislature and subsequent approval by a majority of the voters who vote on the amendment in a general election. The initiative petition route is not available for constitutional amendment, although it is for proposal of statutes. Since Utah's Constitution contained the "single subject" provision that required amendments to be split into small pieces, the process of change was slow. Then in the mid-1960s, studies of the executive and legislative branches showed a need for significant constitutional revision. In 1969 the Legislature created a Constitutional Revision Commission to conduct comprehensive studies and recommend changes to the Legislature. The Commission recommended, and the voters approved in 1970, a "Gateway Amendment" to Article XXIII to permit amendment of an entire article as a single proposition. This accelerated the process of change. The Commission was made a permanent body in 1977, and since then it has made thorough studies of several articles, including the Executive Department (Art. VII), the Judicial Department (Art. VIII), the Education article (Art. X), and the Corporations article (Art. XII). These studies have resulted in amendment proposals that have been approved by the Legislature and the voters—along with many amendments to other articles.

Early Changes

The first proposals for change came early in Utah's statehood. The first five proposed amendments appeared on the ballot just two years after statehood, in 1898, and were soundly defeated by the minority of voters who took the trouble to vote on them. Just two years later, voters were in a more receptive mood. They approved three amendments, one on tax abatement for the poor, one on maintenance of public schools, and another providing for legislation by the initiative and referendum.

These amendments provided a foretaste of what was to come—frequent amendment of the Education article (Art. X) and the Taxation and Revenue article (Art. XIII). Since education generally is the most expensive activity of state government, and most of the amendments have involved state school funds, organized interests such as the Utah Education Association (teachers) and the Parent-Teacher Association have provided a powerful force behind change. Amendments have earmarked several revenue streams for support of education. The Revenue and Taxation article (Art. XIII) has had twelve amendments that provided or permitted full or partial exemptions to property taxation, including mortgages, armed forces veterans and their widows, poor and indigent homeowners, business inventories, homes, agricultural lands, farm equipment, and household furnishings. Another twenty-one amendments have dealt with taxation of mines, earmarking of taxes for roads, creation of an income tax, and other matters. No other article has had such a large number of amendments proposed and passed.

Protection of Rights

Only five sections of the Declaration of Rights (Art. I) have been amended: bail restriction, specifications for grand juries, the right to bear arms (to clarify its purpose and the Legislature's right to "define the lawful use of arms"), use of hearsay evidence in preliminary hearings for criminal suspects, and number of jurors required for trials in criminal cases. In 1994 a new section on victims' rights was approved by voters, part of a national backlash against perceived over-protection of criminals' rights. It permits victims to "be informed of, be present at, and be heard at important criminal justice hearings related to the victim." The strong "separation of church and state" provisions in Article I and in other articles have remained essentially the same. Although much of the tension over church-state relations during territorial days has attenuated, some still remains, and most voters are aware that it is risky to tamper with church-state barriers in a state where more than two-thirds of the population in the 1990s is (at least nominally) affiliated with the Mormon church.[41] In 1994 voters rejected an amendment that attempted to define the kind of school instruction relating to religion that would not be considered "religious instruction or a sectarian practice forbidden by the constitution." Church-state relations continue to be a sensitive area in Utah.

The Elections and Suffrage article (Art. IV) has remained stable, with only residency and age of voters changed to conform to federal changes in the 1970s.

The Structure of Government

The Legislative Department article (Art. VI) has had only a dozen amendment proposals accepted, but these have been significant. Over the years, the Utah Legislature has evolved from a body whose rights to have interim study committee meetings, research and legal assistance, and emergency powers were legally questionable. Beginning in 1972, the article has been extensively revised to

---

[41] Estimates of the Mormon population of Utah range between 69 percent and 75 percent. Lawrence A. Young uses the lower figure in "The Religious Landscape," in Tim B. Heaton, Thomas A. Hirschl, and Bruce A. Chadwick, eds., *Utah in the 1990s: A Demographic Perspective* (Salt Lake City: Signature Books, 1996), 158, Table 2. Another view is in Karl Cates, "'Changing' Utah Stays 75% LDS, Analyst Says," *Deseret News* (Salt Lake City), 29 January 1996. Also see Lowell C. Bennion, "The Geographic Dynamics of Mormondom, 1965–95," *Sunstone* 18 (December 1995): 30, for the distribution of the Mormon population of Utah.

permit the establishment of fiscal analysis, research, legal, and auditing staffs, and it has changed from biennial to forty-five-day annual sessions. The Legislature's most frustrating constitutional battles have been over its own pay. Voters refused until 1944 to raise the $4-a-day limit set in 1896, and after that rejected several attempts to keep legislators' pay current with inflation. Finally, in 1982 voters approved a salary commission to recommend salaries, which legislators must approve.

Over the years, the executive branch has been strengthened by the elimination of constitutionally decreed boards, by providing for tandem election of the governor and lieutenant governor (essentially letting the governor choose a compatible lieutenant governor), and by eliminating the Board of Examiners, which was often a hotbed of political controversy. The Executive Department article (Art. VII) has had few actual amendments, but the revisions approved in 1980 and 1992 substantially changed the institution by permitting the governor to make more appointments and to have legal counsel. An amendment also vested the "executive power of the State" in the governor, a change not conveying any specific powers but lending credence to the tendency of recent governors to vigorously promote an "activist" agenda.

The Judicial Department article (Art. VIII) has also had few—but sweeping—changes by amendment. The selection of judges has changed from partisan elections to selection by the governor after nomination by a commission. The revised article also provides for unopposed judicial retention elections, flexibility in establishing courts, a judicial compensation commission, a judicial conduct commission, and establishment of a unified court system with a judicial council to make rules for administering the system.

Corporations, Labor, and Money

The Corporations article (Art. XII) has had drastic surgery to prune away all but four of its original twenty sections. Voters in 1992 approved the Constitutional Revision Commission's recommendation to eliminate provisions written to deal with 1890s economic problems, some preempted by federal action and others that had survived through sheer inertia. The Labor article (Art. XVI) was amended to permit prison industries and to permit women to work in mines, the latter in response to federal requirements for equal employment opportunities.

The unrealistic debt limits set in the original Public Debt article (Art. XIV) in terms of dollars were changed in 1920 to 1.5 percent for the state and 2 percent for local governments. In the same year, voters rejected a "home rule" provision for cities, but approved it in 1932. In 1972 counties were given the option to change their forms of government, and some have done so (Art. XI, Counties, Cities, and Towns).

Voter Moods and Change

A study of constitutional change by amendment shows that Utah voters are willing to make changes that are carefully sold to them—or if the changes match the mood of the times. The prohibition issue is an illustration. In 1895 the constitution's framers refused to put a prohibition article in the document, or even to submit it as a separate proposition; they were reluctant to destroy a thriving industry during a depression. But by 1916 the national prohibition movement, the support of the Mormon church (whose health code prohibits use of alcoholic beverages), and the prohibition platform of Utah's first non-Mormon governor, Simon Bamberger (a popular German-born Jew), all converged, and in 1919 prohibition became part of the constitution. By the late 1920s the nation was having another look at the consequences of prohibition—crime, speakeasies, and bootlegging. In 1933 Utah not only ratified repeal of the U.S. Constitution's Eighteenth Amendment, but it eliminated its own prohibition amendment. The cycle was complete.

The conventional wisdom once proclaimed that Utah voters would not vote for more than a few propositions on each ballot and that they would just vote "no" on any proposition they did not easily understand. A study of Utah amendment patterns suggests that Utah voters will accept fairly large packages of change in a single amendment if they think they understand the changes. A Voter Information Pamphlet with pro and con arguments, introduced in 1976, has increased understanding of amendments. Careful study by the now permanent Constitutional Revision Commission of major amendments has produced information that has built support among both the legislators and the voters. Since 1970, proposed amendments have had a success rate of 84 percent—even though some are much more complex than earlier amendments—and the percentage of voters in elections who take the trouble to vote on amendments has increased. Of course, amendments that can be widely publicized by well-financed interest groups have always had an advantage over "good government" amendments with no specific constituency. Still, the track record of the latter has been remarkable in the 1980s and 1990s.

Some Utahns still view their constitution with a kind of reverence and wonder why it is amended so often. The answer is that too much legislation was written into it in the 1890s, and too much detail has been added since then—sometimes to achieve short-term purposes. It has been substantially changed, during its first 100 years, but generally not through judicial fiat. It has proved not to be carved in granite, but it is not just wet cement, either. Like the conservative citizens it serves, it changes slowly. But it does change as times change, which is the reason why it survives.

PART TWO

The Utah Constitution and Commentary

Part II contains a section-by-section analysis of the Utah State Constitution. Historical background of the various articles is presented, and the changes in the original sections which have been made by amendment are explained. Significant decisions by the Utah Supreme Court and Utah Court of Appeals are noted, as well as statutes in the Utah Code Annotated that are pertinent for sections implemented by legislative action. Although not all repealed sections are discussed, some are mentioned briefly to illustrate the patterns of change in the constitution. Citations of cases discussed are in the Table of Cases.

PREAMBLE

> Grateful to Almighty God for life and liberty, we, the people of Utah, in order to secure and perpetuate the principles of free government, do ordain and establish this CONSTITUTION.

This statement expresses the philosophy of the writers of the constitution. It is similar to preambles in the constitutions of the other western states in declaring gratitude to God and emphasizing the creation of the constitution as an act of the people of Utah. Although the Preamble is sometimes quoted in court cases to emphasize that political power is vested in the people of the state, it carries no legal authority on its own. The sovereign power of the people to establish or alter their government is also expressed in Article I, section 2 (Declaration of Rights).

Article I

Declaration of Rights

SECTION 1

Inherent and inalienable rights. All men have the inherent and inalienable right to enjoy and defend their lives and liberties; to acquire, possess and protect property; to worship according to the dictates of their consciences; to assemble peaceably, protest against wrongs, and petition for redress of grievances; to communicate freely their thoughts and opinions, being responsible for the abuse of that right.

This section was in the original constitution and has not been changed. It expresses in general terms the rights described in the First and Fifth amendments of the U.S. Constitution pertaining to individual liberties. It includes the right to acquire, possess, and protect property and contains a final clause making individuals responsible for libelous or slanderous use of the freedom to communicate. Freedom of worship does not include the right to practice polygamy, the Utah Supreme Court held (*In re State ex rel. Black,* 1955). The court distinguished between freedom to worship and the right to engage in a practice punishable in criminal law, citing *Reynolds v. United States* (1878). It also stated that Utah's Constitution forbids the practice, a provision that could not be voided by provisions in sections 1, 4, and 15 of Article I. (See commentary on Article III.) In *State v. International Amusements* (1977), upholding a conviction for distributing pornographic material, the supreme court observed that in this section the "fundamental and most important right of freedom of expression is stated in clear and comprehensive language." Noting that the U.S. Supreme Court in *Miller v. California* (1973) had denied constitutional protection to material deemed obscene by contemporary community standards, the court upheld in this case the use of a local community standard rather than a statewide standard for determining whether material met the *Miller* tests for obscenity.

This section is frequently cited in litigation along with other sections of this article. See commentary on section 4 (freedom of worship), section 7 (due process of law), section 15 (freedom of speech and of the press), and section 22 (taking private property for public use).

SECTION 2

All political power inherent in the people. All political power is inherent in the people; and all free governments are founded on their authority for their equal protection and benefit, and they have the right to alter or reform their government as the public welfare may require.

This section was in the original constitution and has not been changed. It emphasizes the source of political power, the purpose of government to provide equal protection and benefit, and the right of the people to change their government. The "equal protection and benefit" provision is occasionally cited along with section 24 of this article to challenge statutes that treat certain classes of citizens differently. The Utah Supreme Court, in a note in *Malan v. Lewis* (1984) stated: "Occasionally, we have referred to either Article I, Sec. 24 or Article I, Sec. 2, or both, as the constitutional source of state equal protection principles. Article I, Sec. 2 uses the language 'equal protection,' but, although it is relevant to the construction of Article I, Sec. 24, it is more a statement of a purpose of government than a legal standard that can be used to measure the legality of governmental action." (See commentary on section 24 of this article, uniform operation of laws.) The right to reform government has not been the subject of litigation.

SECTION 3

Utah inseparable from the Union. The State of Utah is an inseparable part of the Federal Union and the Constitution of the United States is the supreme law of the land.

This section was in the original constitution, as required by section 3 of the Enabling Act of 16 July 1894 (Ch. 138, 28 Stat. 107), and it has not been changed. There has been no significant litigation on this section.

SECTION 4

> **Religious liberty—No property qualification to vote or hold office.** The rights of conscience shall never be infringed. The State shall make no law respecting an establishment of religion or prohibiting the free exercise thereof; no religious test shall be required as a qualification for any office of public trust or for any vote at any election; nor shall any person be incompetent as a witness or juror on account of religious belief or the absence thereof. There shall be no union of Church and State, nor shall any church dominate the State or interfere with its functions. No public money or property shall be appropriated for or applied to any religious worship, exercise or instruction, or for the support of any ecclesiastical establishment. No property qualification shall be required of any person to vote, or hold office, except as provided in this Constitution.

This section was in the original constitution and has not been changed. It is the cornerstone of the commitment by the constitution's framers to guarantee religious freedom and separation of church and state in Utah, and to overcome the perception in the rest of the nation that Utah was a de facto Mormon theocracy. It elaborates on the mandates in the Enabling Act "That perfect toleration of religious sentiment shall be secured, and that no inhabitant of said State shall ever be molested in person or property on account of his or her mode of religious worship," and that a system of public schools be established "open to all the children of said State and free from sectarian control." These requirements were common to the requirements of statehood for other western territories in the late nineteenth century, but they had a special resonance for Utah's Constitution writers, who wanted to leave no doubts about their determination to build a secular, pluralist society.

Section 4 is one of six sections of the Utah Constitution containing specific references to freedom of religious worship or separation of church and state. Other references include Article I, section 1 ("to worship according to the dictates of their consciences") and Article III (perfect toleration of religious sentiment and unmolested religious worship); Article X, Education, has three provisions: section 1 (schools free from sectarian control), section 8 (no religious or partisan tests in schools), and section 9 (no "direct support of any school or educational institution controlled by any religious organization"). Section 4 repeats, expands, or makes more specific these guarantees of free exercise of religion and separation of church and state found in the other sections. It received little discussion in the constitutional convention, probably because both Mormon and non-Mormon delegates agreed that a strong emphasis on church-state separation was necessary to change perceptions of Utah by citizens of other states and to foster a favorable vote for the constitution by Utah's non-Mormon voters.

Section 4 includes one statement on property qualifications for voting, which is not operative now. (See commentary on Article XIV, section 3.) It contains six provisions regarding religion, which prohibit: (1) infringement on rights of conscience, (2) laws passed respecting an establishment of religion or prohibiting the free exercise thereof, (3) religious tests for voting or holding office, (4) religious belief (or the absence thereof) as a measure of competence for serving as a witness or juror, (5) union of church and state or domination or interference with state functions by a church, (6) appropriation of public money or property for "any religious worship, exercise or instruction, or for the support of any ecclesiastical establishment." Several of these prohibitions were in constitutions drafted earlier in the quest for statehood; the public appropriations wording is almost identical to that in the much-copied Washington State Constitution (Art. I, sec. 11).

In view of the Territory's contentious past, the framers obviously wanted to leave nothing to chance, and voters have never been asked to change this section. They did, however, defeat a proposal in 1994 to create a new section in Article X defining certain studies of religion (such as comparative study of religions) as *not* constituting either "religious instruction or a sectarian practice forbidden by the Utah Constitution." Passage of this amendment could have influenced the interpretation of the "religious worship, exercise or instruction" phrase in this section. Sponsors of the amendment maintained that it was needed to assure the right to discuss the influence of religious beliefs and movements on historical events. Opponents of the proposed amendment argued that the speech it was designed to protect was adequately protected by the U.S. Constitution's First Amendment and warned that it could be a dangerous opening for religious indoctrination in the schools.[1] Defeat of the amendment left inoperative a "Maintaining Constitutional Freedom in the Public Schools" statute passed in 1993 to accomplish the same objective as the defeated amendment (U.C.A. 53A-13101.1).[2]

In 1948 the Utah Supreme Court approved the leasing of a portion of the state capitol grounds to the Daughters of Utah Pioneers for erection of the Pioneer Memorial building, and appropriated funds to pay part of the building's cost. Although membership in the organization was predominantly Mormon, and the main purpose of the group was to honor and perpetuate the memory of the Mormon founders of Utah, the court noted that there were non-Mormon members of the organization and there was no evidence that it was a proselytizing agency of the Mormon church. State support of the building, therefore, was held not to be support of an "ecclesiastical establishment" (*Thomas v. Daughters of Utah Pioneers,* 1948). The Utah Supreme Court held in 1973, however, in *Manning v. Sevier County* (1973) that an agreement providing for a gift of a

[1] Utah Voter Information Pamphlet, General Election, November 8, 1994, "For and against Proposition No. 3," 18 and 19.

[2] Citations to the Utah Code refer to Utah Code Annotated, 1953, as amended, current volumes or supplements. They will be cited hereinafter as U.C.A.

hospital partially funded by municipal and county bonds to a church-owned nonprofit corporation violated this section.

Prayers in public meetings and school-related activities in Utah have been the subject of litigation in both state and federal courts. Although required prayers during regular school sessions have been banned under the U.S. Constitution since 1962 (*Engel v. Vitale*), questions were raised regarding the constitutionality of prayers at school graduation, and at meetings of state, city, and county governmental bodies. Since several Utah school districts faced lawsuits either challenging or supporting such prayers, Utah's state school superintendent contributed $10,000 to the Providence [Rhode Island] School Committee to assist in the cost of their appeal to the U.S. Supreme Court, to settle the graduation ceremony prayer issue. The high Court ruled in the Rhode Island appeal that graduation prayers were unconstitutional under the U.S. Constitution (*Lee v. Weisman,* 1992). The Society of Separationists challenged the use of state funds to provide financial support for the Rhode Island appeal under section 4, and the Utah Supreme Court upheld the grant in *Society of Separationists, Inc. v. Taggart* (1993). The court held that the money given to Rhode Island was not for "religious worship, exercise or instruction or for the support of any ecclesiastical establishment," and therefore this section was not violated.

The most significant case defining the use of public money or property under this section was decided by the Utah Supreme Court in *Society of Separationists, Inc. v. Whitehead* in 1993. The court made it clear that its decision upholding prayer in Salt Lake City Council meetings was not based on a similar case, in which the U.S. Supreme Court had upheld the practice of praying in open legislative sessions (*Marsh v. Chambers,* 1983). In *Marsh* the right to prayer in the legislative session was upheld primarily because it was part of a long-standing tradition. The Salt Lake City Council, on the other hand, had not had an opening prayer or reading from 1911 until 1979. In *Whitehead,* the court reversed a district court holding that the Council's prayers violated the section 4 ban on use of public money or property for "any religious worship, exercise or instruction or for the support of any ecclesiastical establishment." After a lengthy review of Utah's territorial history and constitution-writing, the court noted that the City Council had made an effort to include all organizations interested in providing an opening thought, reading, or invocation (not all included a prayer). The court concluded that an indirect benefit was provided. It survived constitutional scrutiny, however, because it met two requirements: First, money or property must be provided on a nondiscriminatory basis; second, public money or property must be equally accessible to all. In this case, the court also concluded that the Council's policy of permitting prayer during the part of the meeting set aside for opening remarks did not violate the section 4 prohibitions against union of church and state or domination of government by any church.

In 1992 this section and several other sections of Article I were cited in *Jane L. et al. v. Bangerter* in an effort to invalidate Utah's abortion law. Claims that the law (U.C.A. 76-7-301 et seq.) violated the state constitution's establishment and free exercise clauses (among other constitutional provisions) were all dismissed with prejudice (barring the right to maintain an action on the same claim or cause) by the federal district court for Utah. Several limits on abortion were, however, struck down by the Tenth Circuit Court of Appeals for violation of the federal Constitution in 1995, and the remaining part was held not to be severable. This interpretation was overruled by the U.S. Supreme Court in 1996 (*Leavitt v. Jane L.*), leaving standing the severable provision in the statute (which regulated abortions after twenty weeks' gestational age).

SECTION 5

Habeas corpus. The privilege of the writ of habeas corpus shall not be suspended, unless, in case of rebellion or invasion, the public safety requires it.

This section protects the privilege of the writ of habeas corpus, a writ requiring a person to be brought before a court to determine whether the person has been detained or imprisoned legally. The section was in the original constitution and has not been changed. During the constitutional convention debates, some delegates wanted the Legislature to provide by law for suspension of the writ; others noted that this traditionally was a function of the executive that required timely action in times of peril.[3] The importance of this writ to prisoners challenging their incarceration was affirmed in 1993 by the Utah Court of Appeals in *Currier v. Holden*. The court struck down a statute which gave prisoners only three months after the occurrence of specific events (such as denial of a new trial) to file for the writ. The purpose of the statute, according to legislative records, was to deter serial filing of habeas corpus petitions by prisoners in order to prevent undue delay in the execution of sentences. The court held that the statute adversely impacted habeas corpus actions unrelated to the problems described by the Legislature. It held that the constitutional right to petition for habeas corpus relief is a basic individual right that is particularly important to a group needing protection, and this statute unreasonably limited prisoners' access to the courts under the constitution's open courts provision. (See commentary on Article I, section 11.)

Use of the writ of habeas corpus is covered in the Utah Rules of Civil Procedure, Rule 65B et seq. and Utah Rules of Appellate Procedure, Rules 18 and 20.

---

[3] *Proceedings and Debates of the Convention,* 2 vols. (Salt Lake City: Star Printing Co., 1898), 1: 252–57. Hereinafter cited as *Proceedings of the Convention.*

SECTION 6

Right to bear arms. The individual right of the people to keep and bear arms for security and defense of self, family, others, property, or the state, as well as for other lawful purposes shall not be infringed; but nothing herein shall prevent the Legislature from defining the lawful use of arms.

In the original constitution, this provision read simply: "The people have the right to bear arms for their security and defense, but the Legislature may regulate the exercise of this right by law." In 1974 the Utah Supreme Court held in *State v. Beorchia* that the Legislature was authorized by this section to forbid the possession of dangerous weapons by noncitizens, convicted criminals, or persons addicted to drugs. Utah has a strong anti-gun-control movement that opposes most restrictions on the right to own firearms, and an amendment reflecting this concern was approved by voters in 1984. The amendment changed this section to emphasize the right of *individuals* to own and use arms. It limited the Legislature to the right to define the lawful use of arms. Subsequently, the Utah Supreme Court held in *State v. Wacek* (1985) that this amendment was to be prospective only, leaving in place statutes passed prior to its enactment.

The current statute regulating firearms (U.C.A. 76-10-501 et seq.) reserves to the state all authority to regulate firearms, except as the Legislature might specifically delegate responsibility to local authorities, and it forbids municipalities or other political subdivisions to enact or enforce any ordinance, regulation, or rule pertaining to firearms.

The statute defines the right of a citizen or lawful alien to own or keep a firearm. It prohibits any person who is addicted to drugs, has been convicted of any crime of violence, is on parole or probation for a felony, or is declared mentally incompetent from possessing a "dangerous weapon." Dealers in firearms must obtain a criminal history background check through the state Department of Public Safety or a local law enforcement agency before selling a handgun.

Under the state's law enforcement statute, individuals may obtain a permit to carry a concealed firearm "for lawful self defense" after a determination of good character and a background check. The permit is valid throughout the state, "without restriction" for two years (U.C.A. 53-5-704 (1). The concealed-weapons provision has met strong opposition from some school and church officials and business owners who want to exclude individuals carrying concealed weapons from their premises.

SECTION 7

Due process of law. No person shall be deprived of life, liberty, or property, without due process of law.

This section was in the original constitution and has not been changed. Since this provision is identical to the clause in the U.S. Constitution's Fifth Amendment, now applied to the states, it has had a substantial amount of judicial interpretation on the federal and state levels. The concept of due process of law requires access to legal proceedings conducted in accordance with rules and principles established within a system of jurisprudence for the enforcement and protection of private rights. Under the U.S. Constitution's Fifth Amendment, a law should not be unreasonable, arbitrary, or capricious, and the means used shall have a reasonable and substantial relation to the objective of the law.

In 1938 the Utah Supreme Court, in *McGrew v. Industrial Commission,* upheld a wage and hours statute as a proper use of the state's police power but held that the Industrial Commission's failure to hold the required hearing before issuing its order deprived the plaintiffs of due process of law. In a challenge by employers to a 1933 minimum wage law providing for minimum pay and maximum hours for women and minors, the court in *McGrew* examined the meaning of liberty and property and the right to due process of law. The court found that the challengers to the statute had no property interest in the labor of their employees and that right to regulate hours of labor was a lawful exercise of the state's power to protect the public safety, health, and morals of women and minors—not an unconstitutional infringement on their "liberty of contract." Since the statute required a hearing of interested parties before setting the wage and hour requirements, the court stated that "due process" under this section required that a hearing be provided "before some officer, tribunal, board, or court" so that those persons whose property is affected may present evidence, objections, and arguments. In *Christiansen v. Harris* (1945), the court noted that rules of procedure may be found in statutes for criminal and civil cases, as well as in rules of the courts, but all have the same basic requirements. They include the provision that no party's legal rights can be affected until these legal rights have been the subject of an inquiry by a person or body authorized by law to determine such rights. Additionally, the party must have due notice of such inquiry (including the time and purpose of the inquiry) and there must be an opportunity to be heard and to give evidence.

"Due process" is not necessarily limited to judicial action; the order of an administrative body issued without notice to affected individuals violates due process (*Morris v. Public Service Commission,* 1958). In a prosecution for contempt, not committed in the presence of the court, due process requires that the person charged be advised of the nature of the action against him, have assistance of counsel (if requested), have the right to confront witnesses, and have the right to offer testimony on his behalf (*Burgers v. Maiben,* 1982). In a criminal case, the due process clause requires that a sentencing judge act on reasonably reliable and relevant information in exercising discretion in fixing a sentence; relevant documents, such as the presentence investigation report, should be made available to the defendant prior to the sentencing hearing (*State v. Howell,* 1985).

Since 1913, Utah has used an indeterminate sentencing system; with few exceptions, judges sentence offenders within a given time range, such as five-years-to-life imprisonment. After an offender arrives at the state prison, the Board of Pardons and Parole holds an original parole grant hearing to determine (subject to future review) the minimum amount of time the inmate will serve and the time of the next hearing. In 1993 the Utah Supreme Court noted that (except for certain mandatory minimum sentences and for the Utah Sentence and Release Guidelines the Board has adopted) this decision usually is the "real" sentence. Accordingly, the inmate's "liberty" interest is involved in the Board's procedures, and the due process requirement of section 7 applies at this point. The Supreme Court in 1992 held that the inmate is entitled at the original parole grant hearing to know what information the Board will be considering at the hearing and have a reasonable opportunity to prepare responses and rebut inaccuracies (*Labrum v. State Board of Pardons,* 1993). The following year, the court held that due process requirements of this section should also apply to post-revocation parole grant hearings and stated that an inmate is entitled to see psychological reports which will be considered in hearings at which an inmate's release date may be fixed or extended (*Neel v. Holden,* 1994). The *Labrum* and the *Neel* holdings were not made retroactive by the court.

In 1955 the Utah Supreme Court held that there was no violation of due process of law in depriving parents of custody of their children, where all the procedural steps were followed in the determination of whether the children were neglected children, and where the parents were duly served in all respects and represented by counsel (*In re State ex rel. Black*).

SECTION 8

Offenses bailable.

(1) All persons charged with a crime shall be bailable except:

(a) persons charged with a capital offense where there is substantial evidence to support the charge; or

(b) persons charged with a felony while on probation or parole, or while free on bail awaiting trial on a previous felony charge, when there is substantial evidence to support the new felony charge; or

(c) persons charged with any other crime, designated by statute as one for which bail may be denied, if there is substantial evidence to support the charge and the court finds by clear and convincing evidence that the person would constitute a substantial danger to any other person or to the community or is likely to flee the jurisdiction of the court if released on bail.

(2) Persons convicted of a crime are bailable pending appeal only as prescribed by law.

This section explains limits on the right to bail of persons charged with a crime. The section in the original constitution originally read: "All prisoners shall be bailable by sufficient sureties, except for capital offenses when the proof is evident or the presumption strong." By the early 1970s, public clamor to do something about crime resulted in passage of an amendment in 1972 adding to the list of those who could be denied bail. The 1972 amendment provided that bail could be denied to a person who was accused of the commission of a felony while on probation or parole, or while free on bail awaiting trial on a previous felony charge, and where the proof was evident or the presumption strong.

In 1988 voters approved by a 77 percent majority another amendment to this section, which changed part of subsections (1)(a) and (b) from the previous wording, "when the proof is evident or the presumption strong," to read "when there is substantial evidence" to support the charge. This amendment also added subsection (c), which gave the Legislature the power to designate crimes for which bail could be denied, under certain conditions: if there is substantial evidence to support the charge *and* the court finds by clear and convincing evidence that the person would constitute a substantial danger to other persons or to the community *or* is likely to flee the jurisdiction of the court if released on bail. Proponents of the change in 1988 argued that Utah judges needed more discretion to deny bail to persons who present a clear and present danger to the community, and bail for most offenses still would be granted. Opponents claimed that the change in evidentiary standard from "proof is evident or the presumption is strong" to "substantial evidence" left a vague standard of proof.[4]

In *State v. Kastanis* (1993), the Utah Supreme Court found that the history of the amendment showed no intention to make a substantive change in the standard of proof, but the wording was changed to "substantial evidence" because the term was more commonly used and understood by the courts and attorneys. A new subsection to section 8 in 1988 provided that persons convicted of a crime are bailable pending appeal only as prescribed by law. The court held in *Kastanis* that a defendant must be allowed to attend the bail hearing and may present evidence and witnesses and cross-examine the state's witnesses. The defendant must be given adequate notice to prepare for the hearing, and at the hearing the trial court may not revoke bail unless the facts furnish a reasonable basis for a jury finding of a verdict of guilty of a capital crime. The current bail statute is U.C.A. 77-20-1 et seq.

---

[4] Utah Voter Information Pamphlet, General Election, November 8, 1988, "For and against Proposition No. 2," 12 and 13.

SECTION 9

Excessive bail and fines—Cruel punishments. Excessive bail shall not be required; excessive fines shall not be imposed; nor shall cruel and unusual punishments be inflicted. Persons arrested or imprisoned shall not be treated with unnecessary rigor.

This section, unchanged from the original constitution, is a counterpart to the U.S. Constitution's Eighth Amendment. It prohibits excessive bail or fines and the administration of cruel and unusual punishments, and it also prohibits "unnecessary rigor" in the treatment of prisoners. The need for this addition was questioned by some delegates during the convention as novel and unnecessary, but it was approved.

The death penalty and the manner in which it sometimes is carried out in Utah (by firing squad, if chosen by the offender, rather than by lethal injection) has attracted national attention and raised questions under both the "cruel and unusual punishment" and the "unnecessary rigor" provisions. The length of sentences and the minimum mandatory sentence for some crimes have been challenged under this section.

In 1986 the Utah Supreme Court ruled in *State v. Bishop* that the minimum mandatory sentence for sodomy on a child did not violate this section or the Eighth Amendment to the U.S. Constitution (although one justice dissented on the grounds that the court did not clarify the principles governing the state and federal provisions). The court used a proportionality standard, quoting the U.S. Supreme Court in *Solem v. Helm* (1983); in *Solem* the Court held that the Eighth Amendment prohibited not only barbaric punishments but also sentences disproportionate to the crime committed and the sentences meted out to others convicted of a similar offense. In *State v. Gardner* in 1989, the Utah Supreme Court held that the death penalty under Utah law meets the requirements of the state and federal constitutions. A sentence with a five-year minimum and life maximum for those convicted of sodomy on a child was not disproportionate to the nature of the crime and thus did not constitute cruel and unusual punishment, since the penalty was proportionate to the seriousness of the offense, and an automatic review was provided to determine proportionality and recognize differences in rehabilitation possibilities among individual offenders. In *State v. Russell* (1990) the Utah Supreme Court held that two minimum mandatory sentences of fifteen years each for aggravated sexual assault and aggravated kidnapping, plus a five-years-to-life sentence for robbery did not constitute cruel and unusual punishment and did not constitute "unnecessary rigor" in treatment. The standard for determining whether a punishment is cruel and unusual, the court stated, was "whether the sentence imposed in proportion to the offense committed is such as to shock the moral sense of all reasonable men as to what is right and proper under the circumstances." Acknowledging that this section is somewhat broader than the federal provision because of the "unnecessary rigor" provision, the court found that in this case the sentence was not unnecessarily rigorous because the manner of committing the crimes was "severe and shocking"; it concluded that unnecessary rigor should be decided on a case-by-case basis.

The Utah Supreme Court held in *State v. Andrews* (1992) that execution after the lapse of nearly eighteen years following conviction was not cruel and unusual punishment under this section or the Eighth Amendment, because the defendant had waived the issue and his numerous appeals had created the time lapse. The court in *Andrews* found that the standard of proportionality met both the federal and state constitutional requirements, using the same standard enunciated in *Russell*.

In *State v. Deli* (1993), the defendant argued that he was treated with unnecessary rigor because all of his sentences were ordered to run consecutively and because the trial court had recommended to the Board of Pardons and Parole that he not be entitled to parole at any time. The Utah Supreme Court noted that it had previously observed that the section 9 content and limitations were best explicated on a case-by-case basis (citing *Russell*). The court found that the trial court had considered "the gravity and circumstances of the offenses and the history, character, and rehabilitative needs of the defendant in determining whether to impose consecutive sentences." In affirming the sentences imposed, the supreme court noted that the trial court had found the offenses were "characterized by extreme cruelty or depravity" and that society would be at risk if the defendant should ever be released from prison—facts that do not show treatment with unnecessary rigor.

Utah's prisoners have filed numerous lawsuits in federal courts, using the U.S. Constitution's Eighth Amendment and the Civil Rights Act of 1871 (42 U.S.C. 1983) to challenge the constitutionality of conditions in Utah's correctional institutions.

SECTION 10

Trial by jury. In capital cases the right of trial by jury shall remain inviolate. In capital cases the jury shall consist of twelve persons, and in all other felony cases, the jury shall consist of no fewer than eight persons. In other cases, the Legislature shall establish the number of jurors by statute, but in no event shall a jury consist of fewer than four persons. In criminal cases the verdict shall be unanimous. In civil cases three-fourths of the jurors may find a verdict. A jury in civil cases shall be waived unless demanded.

This section specifies the size of juries in criminal cases, maintaining the traditional twelve-person jury in capital cases, mandating an eight-person jury for other felony cases, and permitting a lesser number of jurors (but not fewer than four) in other criminal and civil cases. The size of juries was debated vigorously during the constitutional convention, as delegates weighed the traditional twelve-person juries against substantial savings that could be realized with fewer jurors in most cases. They wanted, as Delegate C.C. Goodwin put it, to "do exact justice by the people, if we can, and do it at the least possible expense."[5] In the original article, the right of trial by jury in capital cases was assured. Eight jurors were mandated in courts of general jurisdiction, four jurors in courts of inferior jurisdiction. A unanimous verdict was required in criminal cases; in civil cases three-fourths of the jurors could find a verdict. A jury in civil cases would be waived unless demanded.

After a reorganization of the court system in 1985, and further changes abolishing the circuit courts in the mid-1990s, this section was amended to relate the jury size to the type of crime rather than to a specific court system. In 1996 voters approved the present version, which preserves the twelve-person jury for capital cases, and a jury of at least eight members for other felony cases. In all other cases, both criminal and civil, the number of jurors will be determined by statute, but shall consist of at least four persons. The number of jurors needed to reach a verdict in criminal and civil cases remains the same—unanimous in criminal cases, a three-fourths majority in civil cases. The waiver provision for civil cases remains the same as in the original constitution. The provision for fewer than twelve jurors in the original section was upheld by the U.S. Tenth Circuit Court of Appeals in 1970 in *Johnson v. Turner*. The court held that the Sixth and Fourteenth amendments to the U.S. Constitution did not bar the use of a jury of eight as provided in the Utah Constitution.

Utah follows the practice of death qualification for jurors, which excludes from a jury in a capital case not only those jurors who would never vote to impose the death penalty, but also those who would always vote to impose the death penalty upon a finding of first-degree murder. The Utah Supreme Court held in *State v. Young* (1993) that the trial court should have excluded for cause a juror who said that he would not be able to consider any information about a murderer to persuade him that something other than death was appropriate, because such a juror could not follow his oath and apply the law as instructed by the court. The defendant in *Young* also challenged the impartiality of the jury selected for his trial under the federal Sixth and Fourteenth amendments and the Utah Jury Selection and Service Act (U.C.A. 78-46-1 et seq.), since the random drawing for the jury panel did not produce a panel with Hispanic representation. The court rejected the challenge for lack of evidence of systematic exclusion of Hispanics during the jury selection process. The court noted that the constitution does not require that each trial jury chosen contain the requisite percentage of minority members in order to meet the "fair cross section" standard. A defendant who challenges a jury selection must show that the excluded group represented

---

[5] *Proceedings of the Convention,* 1: 261.

a distinctive group in the community, that the group was not fairly and reasonably represented in jury venires, and that underrepresentation is due to systematic exclusion of the group during the jury selection process.

SECTION 11

Courts open—Redress of injuries. All courts shall be open, and every person, for an injury done to him in his person, property or reputation, shall have remedy by due course of law, which shall be administered without denial or unnecessary delay; and no person shall be barred from prosecuting or defending before any tribunal in this State, by himself or counsel, any civil cause to which he is a party.

This section, which is unchanged from the original constitution, has been described by the Utah Supreme Court as a guarantee of access to the courts and a judicial procedure that is based on fairness and equity, assurance that an individual may not be arbitrarily deprived of effective remedies designed to protect basic individual rights, and entitlement to a remedy by law for injuries to person, property, or reputation (*Berry v. Beech Aircraft Corporation,* 1985).

This section has been held not to create new rights or give new remedies where none previously existed, but to prevent the judicial system from closing the doors of the courts against any person who has a legal right which is enforceable in accordance with some known remedy (*Brown v. Wightman,* 1915).

The Utah Supreme Court established in *Berry* a two-part test to determine whether a statute abrogating a remedy violates the open courts provision: (1) an effective and reasonable alternative remedy by due course of law must be provided, and (2) if the law does not provide such an alternative remedy, the abrogation may be justified only if there is a clear social or economic evil to be eliminated and the elimination of an existing legal remedy is not an arbitrary or unreasonable means for achieving the objective. In *Condemarin v. University Hospital* (1989), the Utah Supreme Court struck down a legislative limitation on medical malpractice recoveries because it failed both parts of the test established in *Berry*. It disallowed recovery from government employees (the hospital staff) and capped the damages recoverable from the hospital; the statute was also held to be an unreasonable, arbitrary limitation on the right of seriously injured plaintiffs to recover adequate damages.

This section has been used to challenge statutes of limitation and statutes of repose (the latter cuts off right of action after a specified time measured from delivery of product or completion of work). In *Berry,* the Utah Supreme Court held that Utah's Product Liability Act (a statute of repose that barred all personal injury, property damage, and death claims six years after the initial purchase) violated the open courts provision. A statute specifying a three-month limitation for prisoners' petitions for a writ of habeas corpus, to challenge the legality of their incarceration, was held to be an unreasonable limitation on a constitutional right in *Currier v. Holden* (1994). (See commentary on section 5.) A statutory classification that discriminates against a person's constitutionally protected right to a remedy for personal injury under this section is constitutional only if it is reasonable, substantially furthers a valid legislative purpose, and is reasonably necessary to further a legitimate legislative goal (*Lee ex rel. Lee v. Gaufin,* 1993).

The sovereign immunity of the state has been challenged under this section. The Utah Court of Appeals found in *Wright v. University of Utah* (1994) that the state has immunity from tort actions arising out of an assault or battery under the state's governmental immunity act (U.C.A. 63-30-10(2)) while performing governmental functions, but not when the state performs a nongovernmental function. The eight-year time limitation on temporary total disability benefits in the Workers' Compensation Act was held not to be an unconstitutional statute of repose within this section (*Stoker v. Workers' Compensation Fund,* 1994).

The provision that "no person shall be barred from prosecuting or defending before any tribunal in this State, by himself or counsel, any cause to which he is a party" does not render unconstitutional a statute making the practice of law without a license a crime. The right to prosecute or defend a cause to which one is a party is, however, protected from abrogation either by the Legislature or the courts under this section (*Nelson v. Smith,* 1944).

SECTION 12

Rights of accused persons. In criminal prosecutions the accused shall have the right to appear and defend in person and by counsel, to demand the nature and cause of the accusation against him, to have a copy thereof, to testify in his own behalf, to be confronted by the witnesses against him, to have compulsory process to compel the attendance of witnesses in his own behalf, to have a speedy public trial by an impartial jury of the county or district in which the offense is alleged to have been committed, and the right to appeal in all cases. In no instance shall any accused person, before final judgment, be compelled to advance money or fees to secure the rights herein guaranteed. The accused shall not be compelled to give evidence against himself; a wife shall not be compelled to testify against her husband, nor a husband against his wife, nor shall any person be twice put in jeopardy for the same offense.

Where the defendant is otherwise entitled to a preliminary examination, the function of that examination is limited to determining whether probable cause exists unless otherwise provided by statute. Nothing in this constitution shall preclude the use of reliable hearsay evidence as defined by statute or rule in whole or in part at any preliminary examination to determine probable cause or at any pretrial proceeding with respect to release of the defendant if appropriate discovery is allowed as defined by statute or rule.

This section defines the rights of an individual accused of committing a crime; it limits compulsory testimony, prohibits double jeopardy for the same offense, and permits use of "reliable hearsay" evidence in pretrial proceedings. The first paragraph of this section was in the original constitution and has not been changed. The second paragraph was approved in 1994 as part of an amendment creating specific rights for crime victims; the other part of this amendment created a declaration of the rights of victims as the new section 28 in this article. The addition to this section and the new section 28 were drafted by the Utah Council on Victims, which concluded that crime victims needed constitutional protection for their right to fair and considerate treatment in the criminal justice system; the proposal passed both houses of the Legislature unopposed in 1994. It relieves crime victims of the need to testify and be cross-examined at virtually all preliminary hearings, a provision designed to avoid further traumatizing abused children and victims of sex crimes. Under the "reliable hearsay" provision, the investigating police officer could testify in lieu of the victim. Opponents of this part of the amendment argued that this provision would hamper discovery of the truth at preliminary hearings and discourage the dismissal of groundless prosecutions.[6] Proponents argued that eliminating hearsay at preliminary hearings often forced victims to testify in order to establish probable cause—and causing them unnecessary further anguish.[7]

The first paragraph of this section, which was modeled on the Washington State Constitution of 1889 (Art. I, sec. 22), includes procedural rights of accused persons that are protected in the U.S. Constitution and in most state constitutions. The provision that no costs would be incurred prior to final judgment was inserted by the framers of the constitution to make certain that poor defendants would not be denied access to the courts by having to pay court fees or the costs of their prosecution.[8] The right to be confronted by witnesses and have a chance to cross-examine them was emphasized by delegate-attorney John Foy Chidester as "the only way to have a fair trial."[9]

In criminal trials to determine guilt (as opposed to pretrial proceedings, which determine whether the accused person will be bound over for trial) the traditional rights of the accused in the first paragraph of this section are given the same protection as is required by the federal Constitution, and the extent of these rights under the two constitutions has been determined on a case-by-case basis over the years.

---

[6] Utah Association of Criminal Defense Lawyers, in Utah Voter Information Pamphlet, General Election, November 8, 1994, "For and Against Proposition 1," 9.

[7] Paul G. Cassell, " Balancing the Scales of Justice: The Case for and the Effects of Utah's Victims' Rights Amendment," *Utah Law Review* 1994 (No. 4): 1434–36.

[8] *Proceedings of the Convention,* 1: 308–11.

[9] Ibid., 1: 307.

There is no separate constitutional standard (different from federal constitutional standards) governing admissibility of confessions under the Utah Constitution, the Utah Court of Appeals stated in *State v. James* (1993). Upholding use of a confession given after the reading of the Miranda warning against self-incrimination, the appeals court in *James* held that the federal Fifth Amendment protects only coerced confessions. The court declined to make a separate determination under section 12 out of concern that "a separate state standard might generate general confusion in this area."

The Utah constitutional guarantee of notice requires that the prosecutor state the charge with sufficient specificity to protect the defendant from multiple prosecutions for the same crime, and to supply information sufficient for the person charged to prepare a defense, the Utah Supreme Court held in *State v. Wilcox* (1991). The court stated that a defendant whose crimes took place over a significant period of time need not be given the exact time, date, and place of each offense, since the lack of specificity did not (1) impair his defense or (2) expose him to multiple prosecutions for the same crime. A defendant must be apprised of enough of the state's evidence so that he or she can prepare to meet that case.

A defendant is not entitled to have African Americans on the jury panel as long as the jury is selected from a fair cross-section of the community (*State v. Price,* 1995). On the right to effective counsel, the Utah Supreme Court held in *State v. Hay* (1993) that the failure to recognize self-defense evidence may have shown a deficient performance by counsel, but the defendant was not deprived of effective assistance of counsel and would not receive a new trial. To gain a new trial the defendant must show (1) a deficient performance by counsel, and (2) that this deficiency prejudiced the trial result.

The Utah Court of Appeals held that a trial court did not err in allowing a defendant to represent himself, where the court properly inquired into the defendant's wish to represent himself and took defendant's questionable mental health into account (including psychological evaluations) in considering the request (*State v. Drobel,* 1991). The test is whether a person desiring to represent himself or herself has chosen this course "knowingly and intelligently," and to determine this, the court must consider the total circumstances of the case.

This section recognizes the marital privilege of a husband or wife not to be compelled to testify against a spouse during a trial. The supreme court held in *State v. Carter* (1995), however, that the state is free to interrogate and receive information from a witness spouse on any matter—including confidential communications—so long as the witness spouse's statement is not introduced into evidence at trial over the objections of the accused spouse. The state is also free to act upon any information received from a spouse in a criminal investigation and to use evidence obtained based on this information, subject to statutory or evidentiary rules of exclusion.

SECTION 13

Prosecution by information or indictment—Grand jury. Offenses heretofore required to be prosecuted by indictment, shall be prosecuted by information after examination and commitment by a magistrate, unless the examination be waived by the accused with the consent of the State, or by indictment, with or without such examination and commitment. The formation of the grand jury and the powers and duties thereof shall be as prescribed by the Legislature.

This section provides for the use of an information or for a grand jury to determine whether someone accused of a crime should be tried for that offense. The grand jury (a body convened to determine whether a person should be tried for the commission of a crime) could return an indictment charging a public offense on which the accused person would then be tried by a petit (trial) jury. Perceived abuses by grand juries during the nineteenth century led to diminished use of these bodies by the time Utah's Constitution was written in 1895.[10] As an alternative method of bringing an accused person to trial, delegates provided for use of an "information," an accusation alleging a criminal offense which is presented, with some supporting evidence, by a public prosecutor before a magistrate (in Utah any justice of the supreme court or the judge of any court created by law). When the accused person appears before the magistrate, if the charge is a misdemeanor the person enters a plea. Persons charged with a felony are entitled to a preliminary hearing (which may be waived) to determine probable cause that they have committed a crime. At this hearing, the defendant has the right to testify under oath, call witnesses, present evidence, and cross-examine the accusing witnesses; the burden of proof is on the state. If the magistrate finds probable cause, the defendant can be bound over for trial in a district court. (See commentary on section 12 on use of hearsay evidence at preliminary hearings.)

The first sentence of this section was in the original constitution, followed by a sentence providing for grand juries of seven members to be summoned only when "in the opinion of the judge of the district, public interest demands it." In 1948 an amendment was approved which deleted the last sentence and left the grand jury's formation, powers, and duties to be prescribed by the Legislature. This is done in the current statute (U.C.A. 77-10a-1 et seq.), which provides for a meeting of a committee of five district court judges at least every three years to determine whether or not to call a grand jury. Such calls are rare; use of the information and preliminary hearing is routine. A defendant may not, however, lawfully be tried and convicted on a charge upon which he was not given, or on which he did not waive, any preliminary hearing (*State v. Jensen*, 1943).

---

[10] Gordon Morris Bakken, *Rocky Mountain Constitution Making, 1850–1912* (New York, Westport, Conn., and London, 1987), 25–27.

SECTION 14

Unreasonable searches forbidden—Issuance of warrant. The right of the people to be secure in their persons, houses, papers and effects against unreasonable searches and seizures shall not be violated; and no warrant shall issue but upon probable cause supported by oath or affirmation, particularly describing the place to be searched, and the person or thing to be seized.

This section was in the original constitution, a virtual copy of the Fourth Amendment to the U.S. Constitution, and the text has not been changed. The meaning of this section has been changed by interpretations of the Fourth Amendment and the extension of the exclusionary rule to the states. This rule, which excludes from the courts evidence produced by an illegal search and seizure, was applied to federal cases in *Weeks v. United States* in 1914, but it was not held to apply to the states until the Supreme Court extended it to state searches in *Mapp v. Ohio* (1961). There is speculation that Utah's provision springs from the state's territorial past, when unannounced raids on the homes of Mormon polygamous families created both fear and resentment toward federal law enforcement officers. It is true that many delegates to the constitutional convention of 1895 were polygamists and some had been the targets of searches by U.S. marshals. If delegates wanted a more strictly interpreted law on searches and seizures, it is not shown in the *Proceedings of the Convention*; this section was adopted without debate.[11] Attorney Kenneth R. Wallentine believes that this section has roots in Utah's past, and that Utah's search laws were intended to be strict in protection of persons and property because of the hardships caused by the anti-polygamy raids during the territorial period.[12] On the other hand, law professor Paul G. Cassell asserts that section 14 was simply designed to track prevailing law; he argues that there is no evidence to show that the anti-polygamy raids of the 1880s caused the constitution's framers to adopt an expansive protection against unreasonable searches and seizures.[13]

There is continuing disagreement in the courts over the use of this section. Prior to 1990, this section was interpreted in the same manner as the federal Fourth Amendment, with no distinctions drawn between the protections offered in the two provisions—but without ruling out the possibility of an independent construction of section 14 in the future (*State v. Watts*, 1988). Two years later, in *State v. Larocco* (1990), the Utah Supreme Court stated in a plurality opinion that it intended to interpret the exclusionary rule (exclusion of illegally obtained evidence from trials) based on the state rather than the federal Constitution, in

---

[11] *Proceedings of the Convention*, 1: 319.

[12] Kenneth R. Wallentine, "Heeding the Call: Search and Seizure Jurisprudence under the Utah Constitution, Article I, Section 14," *Journal of Contemporary Law* 17 (No. 2, 1991): 278–91.

[13] Paul G. Cassell, "Search and Seizure and the Utah Constitution: The Irrelevance of the Antipolygamy Raids," *Brigham Young University Law Review* 1995 (No. 1): 16.

order to adequately protect the rights of Utah citizens. The precedential value of this case is not clear; in several cases since *Larocco*, courts have either questioned or relied on distinctions from *Larocco*. In *State v. Bean* in 1994, the Utah Court of Appeals stated that a defendant or appellant who is seeking to take advantage of additional protection suggested in *Larocco* must offer a specific analysis regarding how the state provision should be read more broadly under either the circumstances of the matter or because of the legal issues raised. If this is not done, the court will not engage in an independent state constitutional analysis. In *State v. Anderson* (1996) the Utah Supreme Court said there was a need to support with analysis and legal authority reasons why the court's analysis of this issue should diverge from federal analysis. Noting that the court had endeavored to establish uniformity in the application of the search and seizure requirements of the state and federal constitutions, the majority opinion observed that imposing different and possibly conflicting constitutional standards on law enforcement officers could have the effect of diminishing, not increasing, protection of rights of privacy. The court held that the arrest of Anderson and two subsequent searches of his vehicle conformed to requirements of both the Utah and U.S. constitutions—probable cause and exigent circumstances. The court in *Anderson* also stated that Utah courts should "construe Article I, section 14 in a manner similar to constructions of the Fourth Amendment except in compelling circumstances."

The Court of Appeals has dealt with numerous cases challenging stops of motorists. It has held that suspicionless, investigatory motor vehicle roadblocks that are conducted without legislative authorization are per se unconstitutional (*State v. Sims*, 1991). When a reliable source with reasonable suspicion based on articulable facts reports the commission of a crime, the dispatcher communicates the information to police, and the responding officer's own observations corroborate the dispatch, reasonable suspicion exists for a stop (*State v. Roth*, 1992). The appeals court held in *State v. Hewitt* (1992), however, that the defendant's nervous behavior was insufficient to give the investigating officer a reasonable articulable suspicion to detain him once the initial purposes of the traffic stop were completed. This section continues to be interpreted on a case-by-case basis.

SECTION 15

Freedom of speech and of the press—Libel. No law shall be passed to abridge or restrain the freedom of speech or of the press. In all criminal prosecutions for libel the truth may be given in evidence to the jury; and if it shall appear to the jury that the matter charged as libelous is true, and was published with good motives, and for justifiable ends, the party shall be acquitted; and the jury shall have the right to determine the law and the fact.

This section, unchanged from the original constitution, is similar to the First Amendment of the federal Constitution in protecting freedom of speech and of the press. It also gives specific protection in criminal libel prosecutions for material printed if it is found to be truthful and published with good motives for justifiable ends. It is usually invoked along with the provision in section 1 of this article that there is an inherent and inalienable right to "communicate freely" thoughts and opinions while "being responsible for the abuse of that right." It is more specific than section 1, however, in forbidding governmental interference with freedom of the press and providing a specific defense in criminal libel actions. The section was adopted after a discussion of then-current libel law and a rejection of an amendment to include civil actions (libel suits brought by individuals) as well as criminal defamation actions (cases where persons accused of defamation, libel, or slander, are prosecuted by the state).[14]

Utah has statutes in the criminal code covering criminal defamation, injunctive relief against privacy offenses, and libel and slander. Libel statutes also are included among the statutes covering newspapers and broadcasting.

Criminal defamation is defined in U.C.A. 76-9-404 as knowing communication to any person orally or in writing any information which a person knows to be false and knows will "tend to expose any other living person to public hatred, contempt, or ridicule." It is a class B misdemeanor. A person injured by defamation as defined in this section may seek an injunction against the person who perpetrated the injury and may seek damages (U.C.A. 76-9-406). Libel is defined in the criminal code as follows: "For the purpose of this part: 'Libel' means a malicious defamation, expressed either by printing or by signs or pictures or the like, tending to defame or darken the memory of one who is dead, or to impeach the honesty, integrity, virtue, or reputation, or publish the natural defects of one who is alive and thereby expose him to public hatred, contempt, or ridicule" (U.C.A. 76-9-501). A person is guilty of libel, a class B misdemeanor, "if he intentionally and with a malicious intent to injure another publishes or procures to be published any libel" (U.C.A. 76-9-501).

The criminal code defines a "fair reporting privilege" that protects newspapers and broadcasting stations from prosecution for "a fair and true report or broadcast of any judicial, legislative, or other public official proceedings, or of any statement, speech, argument, or debate in course of the same except upon proof of malice in making the report, which shall not be implied from the mere fact of publication." It does not protect libelous remarks connected with matter privileged by this section (U.C.A. 76-9-504 and 505). This section of the code, which was revised in 1973, has not been the subject of litigation since statehood.

---

[14] *Proceedings of the Convention,* 1: 320–23.

Civil actions for libel and slander are covered by statutes covering newspapers and broadcasting (U.C.A. 45-2-1 through 10). The definition of libel is virtually the same as the libel definition in the criminal code noted above (it uses the word "blacken" rather than "defame or darken" the memory of an individual). Both the criminal libel statutes and the newspapers and broadcasting statutes establish standards for privileged publication or broadcasting of judicial, legislative, or other public official proceedings, except on proof of malice (U.C.A. 76-9-504 and 45-2-3). Because there have been no criminal libel suits since statehood and because the civil statutes cover most of the same ground, the criminal libel statutes are felt by some critics to be redundant.[15]

The First Amendment to the U.S. Constitution protects free speech and also provides minimum standards for state defamation and libel laws, including interpretations of the U.S. Supreme Court in *New York Times Co. v. Sullivan* (1964) and *Gertz v. Robert Welch, Inc.* (1974). In *New York Times* the Court prohibited a public official from recovering damages for a defamatory falsehood relating to his official conduct unless the official proves that the statement was made with actual malice, knowing that it was false, or with reckless disregard of whether it was false or not. In *Gertz* the Court held that public persons (not just public officials) may recover for defamation only upon a clear and convincing showing of the defendant's knowledge or reckless disregard of the falsity of the defamatory publication, and that states may define their own standards of liability in civil defamation actions against the news media—so long as they do not impose liability without fault.

The Utah Supreme Court stated in *Russell v. Thomson Newspapers* in 1992 that the malice standard in the Utah statute defining privileged publication of official proceedings is not the same as the malice defined in *New York Times.* Utah's standard is derived from the common law standard, and the plaintiff in this case needed only to prove negligence. In this case the newspaper had gone beyond the information disclosed in a malpractice proceeding.

In *West v. Thomson Newspapers* (1994) the Utah Supreme Court held in a defamation suit against a newspaper that an editorial column critical of the mayor of a Utah town was protected by this section and section 1 of Article I. The court addressed the protection guaranteed by this section and the proper analysis to be used when a court confronts an issue involving a question of both state and federal constitutional law. After reviewing four possible standards of review in cases where state constitutional provisions are similar to federal constitutional provisions, the court concluded that the "primacy" model (analyzing the state's law, including its constitutional law, before reaching a federal constitutional

[15] Thomas N. Thompson, "Defamation—Constitutional Standards and Utah Law," *Utah Law Review* 1974 (Winter): 817–18.

claim) was the best method to address this case.[16] The material published in this case had minimum protection from the federal First Amendment, the court noted, but the Utah Constitution provided an independent source of protection for expressions of opinion in Article I, sections 1 and 15. In *Thomson* the court reviewed the history of section 15 and concluded that its framers were particularly concerned with protecting a robust exchange of thoughts and opinions. Section 15, the court found, limits the reach of defamation actions for *opinion,* which differs from verifiable facts, and the statements in this case were protected by sections 1 and 15 as expressions of opinion.

Court cases invoking this section involve a broad range of interests in addition to libel actions. They include, among others, suits seeking access to criminal proceedings and government documents. The Utah Supreme Court has held that the public has a right of access to criminal trials and preliminary hearings, but this right is subject to restrictions where necessary to assure that a defendant receives a fair trial (*Kearns-Tribune Corp. v. Lewis,* 1984). The public does not, however, have a constitutional right of access to juvenile court proceedings (*In re N.H.B.,* 1989). Pretrial documents associated with a preliminary hearing for a criminal case warrant a presumptive right of access under this section, but when disclosure of documents was likely to prejudice defendants' fair trial rights, barring access may be upheld (*State v. Archuleta,* 1993).

The Utah Supreme Court held in 1980 that the right of the public to have access to and publish the salaries paid to state college employees outweighs considerations as to the privacy right of the employees, or the right of the institution to conduct its operations in secret (*Redding v. Brady*).

SECTION 16

No imprisonment for debt—Exception. There shall be no imprisonment for debt, except in cases of absconding debtors.

This section was in the original constitution and has not been changed. There has been little significant case law. In 1977 the Utah Supreme Court held that one who disobeys a court order or judgment requiring payment of a debt and who is in willful defiance of the court may be found in contempt of court and punished by imprisonment (*Thomas v. Thomas,* 1977).

---

[16] Other possible models for state constitutional analysis are discussed by Utah Supreme Court Justice Christine M. Durham in "Employing the Utah Constitution in the Utah Courts," *Utah Bar Journal* 2 (November 1989): 25–27.

SECTION 17

Elections to be free—Soldiers voting. All elections shall be free, and no power, civil or military, shall at any time interfere to prevent the free exercise of the right of suffrage. Soldiers, in time of war, may vote at their post of duty, in or out of the State, under regulations to be prescribed by law.

This section guarantees free exercise of the right of suffrage and the right of soldiers in time of war to vote as provided by law; it is unchanged from the original constitution.

The power of the Legislature to regulate the electoral process was upheld in *Anderson v. Cook* in 1942 when the Utah Supreme Court held that this provision does not guarantee any person the unqualified right to appear as a candidate on the ticket of any political party. Nor can this section be construed to deny the Legislature the power to provide regulations, machinery, and organization for elections and prescribing reasonable methods for selecting the persons who may be voted for at an election. The Utah election code is U.C.A. Title 20A.

SECTION 18

Attainder—Ex post facto laws—Impairing contracts. No bill of attainder, ex post facto law, or law impairing the obligation of contracts shall be passed.

This section, which is unchanged since the original constitution, forbids three types of laws that are also forbidden to states in Article I, section 10 of the U.S. Constitution.

A bill of attainder is one that imposes guilt and inflicts punishment upon an identifiable individual or group without judicial process. A county ordinance prohibiting massages by members of the opposite sex (with certain exceptions) was held not to be a bill of attainder by the Utah Supreme Court because no identifiable individual or group was the subject of legislative punishment without due process (*Redwood Gym v. Salt Lake County Commission,* 1981).

The court has held that nothing in the U.S. or the Utah constitutions prohibits retroactive legislation except for ex post facto laws—and this exception pertains only to criminal matters (*Garrett Freight Lines v. State Tax Commission,* 1943). Statutes that alter the degree or lessen the amount or measure of the proof that was necessary to conviction when a crime is committed are ex post facto when applied in prosecuting crimes committed prior to the statute's passage. A conviction cannot be based on uncorroborated testimony if the statute that permitted this was passed after the alleged murder was committed, but before the trial, the Utah Supreme Court held in *State v. Schreuder* (1986).

The impairment of contract provision has been held not to apply to regulation of rates for public utilities. Regulation of utility rates is a governmental function and a valid exercise of the state's police power to promote the welfare of the citizenry, the Utah Supreme Court held, in *United States Smelting, Refining & Milling Co. v. Utah Power & Light Co.* (1921). When the Public Service Commission revoked a certificate of convenience and necessity (the authority to operate in a given area) held by a trucking company, this was held to be an administrative act and did not constitute impairment of a contract between the company and the state (*Fuller-Toponce Truck Co. v. Public Service Commission,* 1939).

SECTION 19

Treason defined—Proof. Treason against the State shall consist only in levying war against it, or in adhering to its enemies or in giving them aid and comfort. No person shall be convicted of treason unless on the testimony of two witnesses to the same overt act.

This section was in the original constitution and has not been changed or interpreted by case law. It is similar to the first paragraph of Article III, section 3 in the U.S. Constitution. The federal provision gives Congress the power to provide for punishment for treason within limits. There is no case law on this section.

SECTION 20

Military subordinate to the civil power. The military shall be in strict subordination to the civil power, and no soldier in time of peace shall be quartered in any house without the consent of the owner; nor in time of war except in a manner to be prescribed by law.

This section was in the original constitution and has not been changed or interpreted by case law.

SECTION 21

Slavery forbidden. Neither slavery nor involuntary servitude, except as a punishment for crime, whereof the party shall have been duly convicted, shall exist within this State.

This section was in the original constitution and has not been changed. There is little case law. In 1961 the Utah Supreme Court held that a provision requiring a city to withhold state income taxes due from city employees does not constitute involuntary servitude (*Salt Lake City v. State Tax Commission*).

SECTION 22

Private property for public use. Private property shall not be taken or damaged for public use without just compensation.

This section, which is unchanged from the original constitution, is similar to the federal Constitution's Fifth Amendment provision for compensation when property is taken for public use; it adds a provision for compensation for property damaged. The section was passed by the constitutional convention after a series of debates on related issues, including private property rights, time of payment of damages, past abuses by railroads, and potential harm to economic development of the new state.[17] The delegates rejected a Washington State Constitution provision authorizing use of eminent domain for "private ways of necessity" (use of private property for private purposes that had a public benefit) and for agricultural or mining benefits. This was one of the most contentious issues at the convention and passed only after a number of compromises had been made.

Just compensation for property taken for a public use means compensation in money, and other property cannot be substituted for money, no matter how valuable, against the wishes of the condemnee (*Shurtleff v. Salt Lake City,* 1938). A standard of just compensation usually is the market value of the property taken; however, where this is not readily ascertainable, opinion evidence of what the property would probably sell for, if there were others who could use it, would be a proper basis for determining such value (*Southern Pacific Co. v. Arthur,* 1960).

In *Colman v. Utah State Land Board* in 1990 the Utah Supreme Court held that this section is self-executing, and property owners who suffer a taking or damaging of property have a constitutional right to sue the state for just compensation; they did not need a waiver of the state's sovereign immunity to sue. The court also established standards for determining inverse condemnation claims. These claims seek compensation for property taken for a public use without being condemned through eminent domain, such as property that has been diminished in value by the presence of a nearby public property that was taken for a public purpose. In *Colman,* a lessee of state land used for a canal to aid in mineral extraction from Great Salt Lake sought compensation for destruction of the canal as a result of measures employed to prevent flooding of the lake. The court found that there were alleged sufficient facts to constitute a "taking" or "damage" under this section. While acknowledging that the precise limits of

[17] *Proceedings of the Convention,* eminent domain debates during the convention: 1: 328–44; 1: 345–51; 2: 1414–31.

taking or damaging had not been spelled out, the court found three elements necessary for an inverse condemnation: (1) the nature of the property, (2) the existence of a taking or damage, and (3) the damage be effected for a legitimate public use. These elements require a protectable interest in property, not limited to land and improvements; a substantial interference with private property which permanently destroys, materially lessens its value, or impairs its use; and damages due to a direct and necessary consequence of the public use, not damages due to careless or negligent acts by a state agency.

Although the operators of a garbage collection service were put at a severe competitive disadvantage by a city ordinance forcing residents to use the city's collection services, the ordinance did not result in a taking of the private business property (*Bagford v. Ephraim City*, 1995). The court observed that the company had only a terminable oral agreement with the city—which did not constitute a protectable property interest and establish the elements of a "taking," and it was not prevented from competing for garbage collection business. In 1996 the court held in *Strawberry Electric Service District v. Spanish Fork City* that under the analysis provided in *Colman*, the District could claim compensation from Spanish Fork City for "taking" the District's facilities which had been used to provide services to an area later annexed by the city. In this case there was a statute (U.C.A. 10-2-424) which provided that a municipality annexing a territory and providing services formerly provided by another entity must pay the fair market value of a utility's affected facilities.

The eminent domain statute is U.C.A. 78-34-1 et seq. Its provisions describe the uses for which eminent domain may be exercised and the way in which the process of condemnation shall be conducted. The Legislature in 1993 enacted the Private Property Protection Act, which defines "constitutional taking" or "taking" as meaning governmental action that requires compensation to the owner of property under the Fifth or Fourteenth Amendment to the U.S. Constitution or Article I, section 22 of the state constitution. This statute, U.C.A. 63-90-1 et seq., requires state agencies to identify "taking" issues, develop guidelines in dealing with such issues, and minimize the impact of necessary actions on the property owner. In 1994 the Legislature added a statute on constitutional taking issues that apply to political subdivisions of the state (U.C.A. 63-90a-2). Both statutes reflect legislators' awareness of the implications of the Utah Supreme Court's decision in *Colman*.

Development of the meaning of this section has been similar to the development of "takings" law under the federal Fifth Amendment.[18]

[18] David W. Tufts, Comment: "Taking a Look at the Modern Takings Clause Jurisprudence: Finding Private Property Protection under the Federal and Utah Constitutions," *Brigham Young University Law Review* 1994 (No. 4): 7–10.

SECTION 23

Irrevocable franchises forbidden. No law shall be passed granting irrevocably any franchise, privilege or immunity.

This section was in the original constitution and has not been changed. It was proposed by lawyer-delegate David Evans to prevent irrevocable grants to railroads or to individuals for rights to timber or other natural resources. Unless the Legislature had the right to revoke such franchises or privileges, he argued, it would be powerless to withdraw them without violating the obligation of contract.[19] There is has been no judicial elaboration of the meaning of this section in case law.

SECTION 24

Uniform operation of laws. All laws of a general nature shall have uniform operation.

This section reflects the concern with treating citizens alike that was also expressed in Article 6, section 26, which forbids private laws where a general law can be applicable. It relates to, and is frequently cited with, section 2 of this article, which states that equal protection of the people is a purpose of free governments. The Utah Supreme Court, in *Malan v. Lewis* (1984) noted, however, that section 2 is more a statement of a purpose of government than a legal standard that can be used to measure the legality of governmental action, and stated that section 24 was generally considered the equivalent of the equal protection clause of the Fourteenth Amendment of the U.S. Constitution. But in *Malan* the court also noted that while Fourteenth Amendment case law may be persuasive in applying Utah's section 24, federal law is not binding in interpretation of section 24, so long as the court does not reach a result that violates the federal equal protection clause. In the same case, the court held that section 24 requires a law to meet two tests: (1) a law must apply equally to all persons within a class, and (2) statutory classifications and the different treatment given the classes must be based on differences that have a reasonable tendency to further the objectives of the statute.

Since many general laws create classifications that apply to different groups, the constitutionality of such classifications has been challenged under sections 2 and 24 of this article. The Utah Supreme Court held in 1941 that the inability of the Legislature to make perfect classification does not render a statute unconstitutional (*State v. J.B. & R.E. Walker, Inc.*). The court, in rejecting a challenge to a Sunday closing law, held, in *Gronlund v. Salt Lake City* in 1948, that discrimination

---

[19] *Proceedings of the Convention*, 1: 366.

is the very essence of classification and is not objectionable unless it is founded upon unreasonable distinctions. There must, however, be some reasonable basis for differentiation between classes which is related to the purposes to be accomplished by the act, and it must apply uniformly to all persons within the class (*Hansen v. Public Employees' Retirement System Board of Administration,* 1952).

A Utah child support statute (now changed to a gender-neutral provision) which established a lower age of majority for females than for males was discriminatory because it mandated support for male minors until age twenty-one and for female minors only until age eighteen. The statute denied equal protection of the laws in the context of child support, the U.S. Supreme Court held in *Stanton v. Stanton* (1975). A statute giving prosecutors undirected discretion to choose where to file first degree or capital felony charges against juvenile offenders aged sixteen years or older was held unconstitutional under this section in *State v. Mohi* (1995). The Utah Supreme Court found in *Mohi* that the selection process for juveniles who would be tried in the adult justice system (while others had the benefit of treatment in the juvenile system) was arbitrary and without standards and did not meet the requirements of this section. The court stated that the most important difference between the Fourteenth Amendment equal protection clause of the federal Constitution and Utah's "uniform operation of laws" provision is that a law must not only be uniform on its face, but the uniform operation of the law is critical. A law does not operate uniformly if persons similarly situated are not treated similarly, the court stated.

SECTION 25

Rights retained by people. This enumeration of rights shall not be construed to impair or deny others retained by the people.

This section was in the original constitution and has not been changed. It has been used to assert rights not specified in the constitution, similar to rights claimed under the Ninth Amendment to the U.S. Constitution, which states that "The enumeration in the Constitution, of certain rights, shall not be construed to impair or deny others retained by the people." This section has been held by the Utah Supreme Court to secure the right of parents to raise their children, except on a showing of (1) parental unfitness, (2) abandonment, or (3) substantial neglect of their children (*In re J.P.,* 1988). The court held that this section protects the rights inherent in family relationships—husband-wife, parent-child, and sibling—as "the most obvious examples or rights retained by the people." The court cited numerous decisions of the U.S. Supreme Court involving marital and parental rights, in which the federal court held marital and family relationships to be among the most basic of civil rights. The Utah Court of Appeals, in *T.R.F. v. Felan* (1988), held that parental rights cannot be terminated by applying the "best interest of the child" standard but must show the parent's unfitness, abandonment, or substantial neglect. In 1996 the appeals court, *In re Adoption of B.O.*, upheld a provision of the Termination of Parental Rights Act (U.C.A. 78-3a-401 et seq.) which permitted termination of parental rights for abandonment, based on a showing of a parent's failure to make more than token efforts to support or communicate with a child. The court held that this provision did not violate federal due process, Ninth Amendment retained rights, or this section of the Utah Constitution.

SECTION 26

Provisions mandatory and prohibitory. The provisions of this Constitution are mandatory and prohibitory, unless by express words they are declared to be otherwise.

This section was in the original constitution and has not been changed. It has been interpreted by the courts to be more than a philosophical statement and to prohibit the Legislature from limiting or creating exceptions to constitutional guarantees. Utah's Fair Trade Act, which had allowed agreements fixing minimum prices for products, was held to be unconstitutional under this section because it violated Article XII, section 20 (since repealed), which prohibited price controlling. In *Berry v. Beech Aircraft* (1985), plaintiffs contended that the Product Liability Act that prohibited claims for personal injury more than six years after the injury denied them access to the courts guaranteed in Article I, section 11. The defense argued that this section was merely a philosophical statement that did not impose any limitations on legislative power, but the Utah Supreme Court disagreed, finding that section 26 "riveted" all the other rights in the Declaration of Rights into the fundamental law of the state, enforceable in a court of law.

SECTION 27

Fundamental rights. Frequent recurrence to fundamental principles is essential to the security of individual rights and the perpetuity of free government.

This section, copied from the Washington State Constitution of 1889, was in the original constitution and has not been changed. Although some delegates questioned the importance of the provision, it was defended by delegate Heber M. Wells (who became Utah's first governor) as "a patriotic utterance that did no harm."[20] The section has not been the subject of any case law.

[20] Ibid., 1: 362.

SECTION 28

Declaration of the rights of crime victims.

(1) To preserve and protect victims' rights to justice and due process, victims of crimes have these rights, as defined by law:

(a) To be treated with fairness, respect, and dignity, and to be free from harassment and abuse throughout the criminal justice process;

(b) Upon request, to be informed of, be present at, and to be heard at important criminal justice hearings related to the victim, either in person or through a lawful representative, once a criminal information or indictment charging a crime has been publicly filed in court; and

(c) To have a sentencing judge, for the purpose of imposing an appropriate sentence, receive and consider, without evidentiary limitation, reliable information concerning the background, character, and conduct of a person convicted of an offense except that this subsection does not apply to capital cases or situations involving privileges.

(2) Nothing in this section shall be construed as creating a cause of action for money damages, costs, or attorney's fees, or for dismissing any criminal charge, or relief from any criminal judgment.

(3) The provisions of this section shall extend to all felony crimes and such other crimes or acts, including juvenile offenses, as the Legislature may provide.

(4) The Legislature shall have the power to enforce and define this section by statute.

This section provides protection for the right of crime victims to be treated with respect and dignity during the criminal justice process, to be present at important criminal justice hearings related to the victim, and to have a sentencing judge consider, without evidentiary limitation, reliable information on the background and character of a person convicted of an offense. Provisions of the section extend to all felony crimes and such other crimes, including juvenile offenses, as the Legislature may provide. This section was enacted as part of the Rights of Crime Victims amendment approved by voters in 1994. (The other part is in section 12 of this article, which limits the scope of preliminary hearings and permits use of reliable hearsay in such hearings. See commentary on section 12 for background of the amendment.)

This section is implemented in the Code of Criminal Procedure by the Rights of Crime Victims Act (U.C.A. 77-38-2 et seq.). As amended in 1995, the act defines rights of victims not only to attend "important criminal justice hearings" but also "important juvenile justice hearings," which are defined as cases involving a minor's conduct which would be a felony if committed by an adult. The victim does not have a right to be heard at any criminal trial or preliminary hearing, or at any delinquency trial or preliminary hearing in a minor's case, unless called as a witness. The right to attend the hearing may be limited by the Utah Rules of Evidence. The victim's address, telephone number, and victim impact statement maintained by state agencies are to be protected information. The court may exclude any oral statement from a victim on the grounds of the victim's incompetency as provided in Rule 601(a) of Utah Rules of Evidence.

To monitor implementation of this section, the Legislature created a victims' rights committee in each judicial district. Membership is to be designated by the presiding district court judge, and is to include local law enforcement representatives, county and city attorneys, a victim advocate, and other representation as appropriate (U.C.A. 77-37-5). Each committee is to meet at least semiannually to review progress and problems related to the Victims' Rights Act and section 28. If a person fails to perform duties so that rights under the act are not provided, an action for injunctive relief may be brought against the individual and the government entity that employs the individual (U.C.A. 77-37-5(4)).

Section 28 was challenged in *State v. Beltran-Felix* in 1996; the defendant claimed that the presence of the victim in the courtroom denied him the right to a fair trial. The Utah Supreme Court disagreed and upheld the right of the victim to be present at the trial.

Article II

State Boundaries

SECTION 1

State boundaries. The boundaries of the State of Utah shall be as follows: Beginning at a point formed by the intersection of the thirty-second degree of longitude west from Washington, with the thirty-seventh degree of north latitude; thence due west along said thirty-seventh degree of north latitude to the intersection of the same with the thirty-seventh degree of longitude west from Washington; thence due north along said thirty-seventh degree of west longitude to the intersection of the same with the forty-second degree of north latitude; thence due east along said forty-second degree of north latitude to the intersection of the same with the thirty-fourth degree of longitude west from Washington; thence due south along said thirty-fourth degree of west longitude to the intersection of the same with the forty-first degree of north latitude; thence due east along said forty-first degree of north latitude to the intersection of the same with the thirty-second degree of longitude west from Washington; thence due south along said thirty-second degree of west longitude to the place of beginning.

When Mormon colonizer Brigham Young first sought statehood for a "State of Deseret" in 1849, the area claimed for Deseret included the lower third of what is now California, a major part of Arizona, part of New Mexico, parts of Oregon, Idaho, and Wyoming, the western third of Colorado, and all of Nevada. Gradually, this massive land claim was whittled away, as other western territories were established by national lawmakers who were notably unsympathetic to Young's dreams of a western empire.

California quickly claimed its present boundaries when it gained statehood in 1850. When Utah gained territorial status in the Organic Act of 1850, the area recognized in this act reflected the loss of Brigham Young's claim to most of Arizona, a slice of New Mexico, a piece of Oregon, and parts of Nevada and Wyoming.[21] Subsequently, the Territory of Nevada was created from the western part of Utah Territory in 1861, and in the same year Colorado was enlarged to its present borders at Utah's expense. Nevada gained two strips from western Utah, in 1862 and 1866. In 1868 the "slimming down" process was completed by granting Utah's northeastern corner to Wyoming. The Enabling Act passed by Congress in 1894 recognized the 1868 boundaries as the area that "may become the State of Utah" as provided in the act.[22] These boundaries were incorporated in the 1896 Constitution and have remained the same since statehood.

[21] Organic Act of the Territory of Utah, Ch. 51, 9 Stat. 453 (1850).

[22] Enabling Act, Ch. 138, 28 Stat. 107 (1894).

Article III

Ordinance

This article was placed in the original constitution in response to specific requirements in the Enabling Act passed by Congress and signed by President Grover Cleveland on 16 July 1894.[23] In addition to the provisions for religious tolerance, nonsectarian public schools, land grants to the new state, and assumption of territorial debts commonly found in the enabling acts of other western states, Utah's Enabling Act prohibited polygamous marriages forever. This was to provide assurance that polygamy—the most visible stumbling block to statehood—would not be legal in the new state. Although the "irrevocable" provision in the Ordinance is considered by some to be an unnecessary—and perhaps humiliating—part of Utah's Constitution, the article has survived with only one amendment and without serious efforts to remove the "irrevocable" language. It is at least questionable whether this provision could be enforced, since the U.S. Supreme Court in *Coyle v. Smith* (1911) upheld the moving of Oklahoma's state capital, despite a federal mandate to keep it in Guthrie, as a condition of statehood. The Ordinance is divided into four parts.

[23] Ibid.

The following ordinance shall be irrevocable without the consent of the United States and the people of this State:

> **Religious toleration—Polygamy forbidden.** First:—Perfect toleration of religious sentiment is guaranteed. No inhabitant of this State shall ever be molested in person or property on account of his or her mode of religious worship; but polygamous or plural marriages are forever prohibited.

Although "perfect toleration of religious sentiment" was required of other western territories in their state constitutions, the unusual religious background of Utah's history gives this provision more significance in Utah's Constitution. This mandate is augmented in other articles of the constitution: Article I, section 4 (Declaration of Rights), prohibits religious discrimination and union of church and state; Article X, section 8 prohibits religious or partisan tests in state schools.

Although the Church of Jesus Christ of Latter-day Saints (Mormon) has officially abandoned the practice of polygamy and excommunicates members who practice it, and it is banned under Utah law (U.C.A. 76-7-101), Utah still has a number of so-called "fundamentalist" groups which cling to the practice. Many polygamists live quietly in Utah communities, where they are virtually ignored by law enforcement agencies. Two major efforts to break up polygamous fundamentalist groups in 1944 and 1953 did not prove successful, although they allegedly were carried out with the cooperation of Mormon church officials and law enforcement agencies.[24]

The Utah Supreme Court held in a case arising out of the 1944 raid that Utah's statute prohibiting unlawful cohabitation did not violate the constitutional right of religious freedom. In *State v. Barlow* (1944), the Utah court reiterated an argument made earlier by the U.S. Supreme Court in *Reynolds v. United States* (1878) that religious beliefs, not religious practices, were protected. The Utah court rejected the idea that the Ordinance was invalid because of its alleged adoption under duress and held that it was within the power of the state to determine whether polygamy should be proscribed.

Other issues, involving the right of polygamists to adopt children and the right of a polygamist to be a police officer, have been addressed by Utah courts. In *Johanson v. Fischer* (1991), the Utah Supreme Court ruled against dismissal by a trial court of a petition for adoption of six children on the ground that the petitioners were living according to their religious belief in plural marriage. The lower court had held that the state's "interest of the child" standard could not be met by adoption into a home where polygamy was taught and practiced.

---

[24] Martha Sonntag Bradley, *Kidnapped from that Land: The Government Raids on the Short Creek Polygamists* (Salt Lake City: University of Utah Press, 1993), 148–53. Also B. Carmon Hardy, *Solemn Covenant: The Mormon Polygamous Passage* (Urbana and Chicago: University of Illinois Press, 1992), 343.

The supreme court held that the petition could not be denied on this ground alone and should be reviewed on its merits: "The fact that our constitution requires the state to prohibit polygamy does not necessarily mean that the state must deny any or all civil rights and privileges to polygamists."

In 1984, in *Potter v. Murray City*, a police officer who was terminated from his job for openly living with more than one wife unsuccessfully sought summary judgment against the city and the state under the First and Fourteenth amendments and a federal civil rights statute (42 U.S.C. 1983). Among other arguments, Potter claimed that he had a constitutional right to practice polygamy in accordance with his religious beliefs and that the state had not shown a compelling interest that would justify his termination. The federal District Court denied that any constitutional right had been violated. On appeal, the Tenth Circuit Court of Appeals affirmed the lack of a constitutional right—using the rationale in *Reynolds*—and rejected Potter's argument that the Enabling Act's prohibition of polygamy "forever" was voided by the "equal footing" of the state holding in *Coyle v. Smith* (1911). The U.S. Supreme Court refused to review the case. Some critics of the *Reynolds* dichotomy of religious belief and practice believe that this is an outmoded interpretation of the free exercise clause.[25] And as the court in *Barlow* noted, the fact that polygamy was forbidden in the Enabling Act would not prohibit the state from forbidding it in the light of social customs—as it does adultery and fornication.

As long as Utah's practitioners of polygamy keep a low profile, there seems to be little interest in prosecuting them. Given current liberal attitudes toward sex outside of marriage and the high rates of divorce in conventional marriages, it is not surprising that prosecution of polygamy (like adultery) has become a "nonissue." The brief in *Potter* stated that there were between 5,000 and 10,000 individuals living in polygamous families in 1983 and that there had been "not more than twenty-five" criminal prosecutions between 1952 and 1983 in Utah. Because of the difficulties over polygamy in Utah's past, periodic national interest in the topic produces brief flurries of national and local media attention. Otherwise, this part of the "irrevocable" section gets little attention from the public or from public officials.

Right to public domain disclaimed—Taxation of lands—Exemptions. Second:—The people inhabiting this State do affirm and declare that they forever disclaim all right and title to the unappropriated public lands lying within the boundaries hereof, and to all lands lying within said limits owned or held by any Indian or Indian tribes, and that until the title thereto shall have been extinguished by the United States, the same shall be and remain subject to the disposition of the United States, and said Indian lands shall remain under the absolute jurisdiction and control of the Congress of the United States. The lands belonging to citizens of the United

[25] Penelope W. Saltzman, "Polygamy," *Utah Law Review* 1986 (No. 2): 345–71.

> States, residing without this State shall never be taxed at a higher rate than the lands belonging to residents of this State; but nothing in this ordinance shall preclude this state from taxing, as other lands are taxed, any lands owned or held by any Indian who has severed his tribal relations, and has obtained from the United States or from any person, by patent or other grant, a title thereto, save and except such lands as have been or may be granted to any Indian or Indians under any act of Congress, containing a provision exempting the lands thus granted from taxation, which last mentioned lands shall be exempt from taxation so long, and to such extent, as is or may be provided in the act of Congress granting the same.

This section clarifies the right of the federal government to the public lands not appropriated in the Enabling Act to schools and other institutions and to lands owned or held by Indian tribes. It also provides for equal taxation of lands owned by residents and nonresidents. Lands owned by Indians who have severed their tribal relations, except those lands granted to them by the United States with a tax exemption included in this grant, are taxable by the state.

The Enabling Act, in sections 6, 7, 8, and 12, appropriated lands for the common schools, public buildings, the state university and agricultural college, permanent water reservoirs, an insane asylum, a school of mines, a deaf and dumb asylum, a reform school, state normal schools, an institution for the blind, and a hospital for disabled miners. It also gave the U.S. Territorial Penitentiary to the State of Utah. The acceptance of these lands as a trust is provided in Article XX of the constitution. More specifically, the proceeds from the sales of all lands granted to the state for the support of public elementary and secondary schools is provided in Article X, section 5, and proceeds from the sale of lands reserved for the benefit of the state's universities and colleges is provided in Article X, section 7.

Utah originally was granted seven million acres of public lands, and the state currently manages approximately 3,700,000 acres for the support of the common schools.[26] The disposition and uses of these lands have produced some heated debates in recent years. Amid criticism that sales, leases, and mineral royalties on trust lands had not produced revenues comparable to trust lands in other western states, the Legislature in 1994 passed the School and Institutional Trust Lands Management Act (U.C.A. 53C-1-101 et seq.). The act took management of trust lands from the state Division of State Lands and Forestry, and placed it in a new agency, the School and Institutional Trust Lands Administration, headed by a director selected by a board of trustees. The Board of Trustees is a seven-person board appointed by the governor, subject to confirmation by the Senate. Six of the governor's appointees are chosen from a list of candidates provided by a nominating committee of education and land users' representatives.

[26] 1995 Report, Western States Land Commissioners Association, reported in Salt Lake City *Deseret News*, 18 December 1996.

The Board's task is not easy, considering the desires of environmental activists to protect the adjacent federal land and the desires of public school officials to enforce the terms of the trust and enhance revenues for the perennially cash-starved schools. The act creating the administration, however, clearly states its purpose: to administer the trust for the exclusive benefit of the trust beneficiaries, not for the benefit of other agencies or the general welfare of the state (U.C.A. 53C-1-102).

Within the past two decades, some Utahns have joined with officials of other western states to protest the federal government's control of vast amounts of land within their borders designated as public domain, including national parks, forests, monuments, or recreational areas—in Utah approximately two-thirds of its land area. Since there are limits on activities within such areas, the 1996 proclamation by President Bill Clinton, without public comment, of a new Grand Staircase-Escalante National Monument—with 176,000 acres of trust lands within its boundaries—sparked outrage from rural Utah counties near the monument because of the potential for coal mining and other economic activities in the area. Potential losses to the public schools from coal royalties alone are estimated to exceed $1.8 billion.[27] But because the monument contained public lands retained by the federal government in the Enabling Act, and disclaimed in the Ordinance, there appeared to be little they could do but hope that President Clinton's promise to trade other lands for the school lands within the monument would be fulfilled.

The Utah Supreme Court in 1992 held that the term "Indian lands" refers to lands established as such by federal law, as opposed to land traditionally inhabited by specific Indian tribes (*State v. Gardner,* 1992).

There has been only one amendment to the Ordinance. In 1946 voters approved an amendment that removed the proviso that taxes would not be imposed by the state on U.S. government lands. The amendment's supporters pointed out that some activities on federal properties (such as the naval depot) established in Utah during World War II might be taxable; in any event, Congress had the power to exempt its own property without a state constitutional provision.

Territorial debts assumed. Third:—All debts and liabilities of the Territory of Utah, incurred by authority of the Legislative Assembly thereof, are hereby assumed and shall be paid by this State.

The amount of debt accumulated by the Territory of Utah at the time of statehood was a major concern and the subject of considerable debate by delegates in the 1895 constitutional convention. By 1895 the territorial debt had reached

[27] Douglas F. Bates, general counsel for the State Board of Education, note to author, 25 March 1997.

$767,000—an obligation that influenced the debate on the public debt article (Art. XIV) and persuaded delegates to set a low ceiling on future indebtedness.[28]

Free nonsectarian schools. Fourth:—The Legislature shall make laws for the establishment and maintenance of a system of public schools, which shall be open to all the children of the State and be free from sectarian control.

Despite years of efforts to force the Territory of Utah to establish a system of free public schools, this was not accomplished until 1890. Until then, there were meagerly financed local public schools that many non-Mormons felt were dominated by the Mormons. Catholics, as well as Methodists, Presbyterians, and other Protestant denominations, soon entered the Territory, and some established schools that generally were better than the public schools and sometimes attracted Mormon students. When the constitutional convention met in 1895, the issue was settled; there would be a public school system. The financing of such a system, and how much education should be free, were the main issues. The provisions for a school system are elaborated in the Education article (Art. X, sec. 1).

In 1995 parents of Navajo Indian school children and the Navajo Nation sued the San Juan School District to compel the district to provide secondary school facilities in a remote area of the Navajo reservation. In *Meyers v. Board of Education of the San Juan School District* (1995), the federal district court for Utah held that the Enabling Act requirement to make no distinction in civil or political rights on account of race or color, except as to Indians not taxed, did not exclude Native American children from the constitutional mandate in Article III to maintain a system of public schools "open to all children of the State."

[28] *Proceedings of the Convention,* 2: 1116–42.

Article IV

Elections and Right of Suffrage

SECTION 1

Equal political rights. The rights of citizens of the State of Utah to vote and hold office shall not be denied or abridged on account of sex. Both male and female citizens of this State shall enjoy equally all civil, political and religious rights and privileges.

This provision took up more time at the constitutional convention in 1895 than any other section of the constitution, because of its restoration of women's right to vote and hold office. At that time, only two states, Wyoming and Colorado, extended these rights to women, although Idaho was soon to grant them also. Only two territories, Utah and Wyoming, had granted the vote to women prior to statehood, Wyoming in 1869 and Utah in 1870. Congress took this right from Utah women in the Edmunds-Tucker Act of 1887 to reduce the number of Mormons on the voting rolls.[29] By 1894, when elections to Utah's constitutional convention were held, there was a strong network of woman suffrage groups affiliated with the National American Woman Suffrage Association throughout the Territory. They had lobbied vigorously for support in restoring their political rights, and they obtained promises in both the Democratic and Republican party platforms that this would be done in the new constitution.

[29] Ch. 397, 24 Stat. 635 (1887).

This achievement was threatened when a minority report of the Committee on Elections and Suffrage asserted that giving the vote to women would add some 40,000 new voters to the rolls and might upset the newly achieved political balance that had replaced the old Mormon-gentile political parties. Equal political rights for women was also opposed on the grounds that it was a "radical" move that might threaten statehood, and with the usual anti-suffrage arguments that women were too pure and good to be dragged into the filthy pool of politics. None prevailed, however, and with the votes of both Mormon and non-Mormon delegates, Utah joined its western neighbors in giving women the vote more than a decade before it was assured in the U.S. Constitution.[30]

SECTION 2

Qualifications to vote. Every citizen of the United States, eighteen years of age or over, who makes proper proof of residence in this state for thirty days next preceding any election, or for such other period as required by law, shall be entitled to vote in the election.

In the original constitution, the qualifications for voting were similar to those in other states at the time. United States citizenship for ninety days and attainment of the age of twenty-one were the basic personal requirements; in addition, voters were required to have resided in the state or territory one year, in the county four months, and in the precinct sixty days prior to any election. The Declaration of Rights (Art. I, sec. 4) provided that there be no property qualification for any person to vote or hold office, "except as provided in the constitution," and a permissible exception (elections levying a special tax or creating indebtedness) was placed in the original section 7 of this article.

In the constitutional convention, proposals to require the ability to read or the ability to read the constitution were discussed in a lively debate. This was a somewhat sensitive subject, since there were many foreign-born settlers who had not yet mastered English well enough to pass such tests. In the end it was decided not to have a literacy requirement, since literacy was no guarantee of intelligence, and in time the schools were expected to solve the problem.[31] No poll tax as a requirement for voting was imposed, although men generally were required to perform labor on the public streets or pay $2 to be exempt from this duty. This sometimes was called a poll tax, but it had no connection to the right to vote.

---

[30] *Proceedings of the Convention,* 1: 804.

[31] Ibid., 1: 601–17.

Over the years, the age and residency requirements have been changed in response to adoption of the Twenty-sixth Amendment to the U.S. Constitution, subsequent changes in the Voting Rights Act of 1965, and federal court decisions regarding voting requirements. In 1970 Utah voters approved an amendment to section 2 reducing the legal residency requirement to six months in the state and sixty days in the county. It also provided that in presidential elections, persons who could prove residence in the state for thirty days prior to the election might vote for a president and a vice-president of the United States, but not for other offices. This change, which became effective on 1 January 1971, proved to be too little, too late in conforming to national trends in the minimum voting age when the Twenty-sixth Amendment lowering the national voting age to eighteen was ratified in 1971. A year later, in *Dunn v. Blumstein* (1972), the U.S. Supreme Court used a "strict scrutiny" test to strike down Tennessee's requirement of one year's residence in the state and three months in the county. This time period was considered longer than necessary to meet the state's interest in honest elections and burdened not only the right to vote but the right of citizens to travel from state to state.

This left Utah lawmakers again behind the curve and wondering what minimal residency requirements would meet constitutional standards. In 1976 voters again approved changes in this section to provide a minimum residence period of thirty days "or for such other period as required by law," in an effort to keep Utah's rules flexible enough to deal with federal court interpretations on residency. The current minimum residency requirement is thirty days (U.C.A. 20A-2-101).

Although the constitution provides the basic rights of citizens to vote, the Legislature may prescribe reasonable rules and regulations, such as registration and voting procedures (*Evans v. Reiser*, 1931). The term "resident" is defined in Utah law (U.C.A. 20A-2-105 (1) et seq.) as an individual's principal place of residence within the state, one in which he or she intends to continue residency—even though temporarily living out of the state as a member of the armed forces, or for other reasons. Generally, a citizen's oath or affirmation is evidence of residency in a particular place, but this does not apply to persons incarcerated in a correctional facility. Convicted felons are not denied the vote in Utah, except for offenses listed in section 6 of this article. Prisoners are required, however, to register to vote at their place of residence prior to incarceration—even though they may no longer have ties to that location, the Utah Supreme Court decided in *Dodge v. Evans* (1985). The court concluded that even though the right to vote is a fundamental right, demanding a compelling state interest and strict scrutiny of laws regulating it, the Legislature has some latitude in enacting laws governing residency requirements, as long as the fundamental right to vote is not impaired and a law is not intended to favor one group of voters over another. An amendment denying felons the vote while incarcerated will be voted on in November 1998.

SECTION 3

Voters—Immunity from arrest. In all cases except those of treason, felony or breach of the peace, voters shall be privileged from arrest on the days of election, during their attendance at elections, and going to and returning therefrom.

This section was intended to enhance the right to vote, free of governmental interference, and was found in the original constitution. In the elections article revision approved in 1976, the word "electors" used in the original constitution was changed to "voters" to provide consistency in style. There is no essential difference in the meaning of the words.

SECTION 4

Voters—Immunity from militia duty. No voter shall be obliged to perform militia duty on the day of election except in time of war or public danger.

In this section, the word "elector" in the original constitution was changed to "voter" in the elections article revision approved in 1976 to provide consistency in style. Otherwise it is the same as it appeared in the original constitution.

SECTION 5

Voters to be citizens of United States. No person shall be deemed a qualified voter of this State unless such person be a citizen of the United States.

In this section the only change from the original constitution was from "elector" to "voter" in the revision approved in 1976.

SECTION 6

Mentally incompetent persons and certain criminals ineligible to vote. No mentally incompetent person or person convicted of treason, or crime against the elective franchise, unless restored to civil rights, shall be permitted to vote at any election, or be eligible to hold office in this State.

This provision was in the original constitution, but with the words "idiot" and "insane" instead of "mentally incompetent." This was the terminology of the time (the Territory then had an insane asylum), but by 1976 these terms were considered both insensitive and clinically inaccurate, and the change was approved in 1976.

Crimes against the elective franchise are crimes involving voter registration, false impersonation of a voter in order to vote more than once (U.C.A. 20A-2-401 and 20A-3-505). There are also a number of crimes against the franchise involving election returns, such as altering or assisting in altering the vote count (U.C.A. 20A-4-502 and 503), or interfering with the vote count (U.C.A. 20A-4-504).

SECTION 7

Property qualification forbidden. No property qualification shall be required for any person to vote or hold office.

Property qualifications were required in the original constitution for voters in elections to increase property taxes beyond a basic limit in the Revenue and Taxation article (Art. XIII, sec. 7) and also in the Public Debt article (Art. XIV, sec. 3) for elections to incur public debt. By 1976 the U.S. Supreme Court had applied strict standards of review in cases limiting the right of states to restrict voting in local bond elections. In *Cipriano v. City of Houma* (1969), a law limiting voting in revenue bond elections to property owners, and in *Phoenix v. Kolodziejski* (1970), a law requiring property ownership for voters in a general obligation bond election, the U.S. Supreme Court rejected arguments that property tax owners had a special interest in the outcome of these particular elections not shared by citizens who did not own property. In 1976 Utah voters approved a revision of this section that removed the property ownership requirement for approval of local property tax increases and replaced it in section 7 with the current language banning property qualifications.

Oddly enough, although court decisions in bond elections triggered concern with property ownership as a voting requirement, this requirement remains as "deadwood" in Utah's Public Debt article. The provision in the Declaration of Rights (Art. I, sec. 4) permitting a property qualification for voting in elections if "provided in this Constitution" also remains. In practice, the property ownership requirement is ignored in local bond elections.

SECTION 8

Ballot to be secret. All elections shall be by secret ballot. Nothing in this section shall be construed to prevent the use of any machine or mechanical contrivance for the purpose of receiving and registering the votes cast at any election: Provided, That secrecy in voting be preserved.

The matter of ballot secrecy was important at the time of Utah's constitutional convention because of the lack of secrecy in territorial elections until the 1880s. In 1896, the first year of statehood, a statute providing for identification of ballots by numbering in order to detect possible fraud was struck down in *Ritchie v. Richards*. This view was reemphasized in *Evans v. Reiser* (1931).

SECTION 9

General and special elections—Terms.

(1) All general elections, except for municipal and school officers, shall be held on the Tuesday next following the first Monday in November of the year in which the election is held.
(2) Special elections may be held as provided by law.
(3) The terms of all officers elected at any general election, except legislators, shall commence on the first Monday in January next following the date of their election.
(4) Municipal and School officers shall be elected at such time as may be provided by law.

This provision sets the day for general elections and leaves the timing of special elections, as well as municipal and school officer elections, to be provided by law. It is the same as it was in the original constitution, except for an amendment approved by voters in 1992. This section was divided into four subsections, and the terms of legislators were exempted in subsection (3) from starting on the first Monday in January. In the Legislative Department article (Art. VI, sec. 3), legislators' term of office was changed to begin from the first day of January after their election.

General elections for state officials, legislators, and county officials now are held every two years, in even-numbered years, the same years as federal elections. Municipal elections are held in the intervening odd-numbered years. Constitutional amendments and other statewide referenda are on the ballot only in general elections.

SECTION 10

Oath of office. All officers made elective or appointive by this Constitution or by the laws made in pursuance thereof, before entering upon the duties of their respective offices, shall take and subscribe the following oath or affirmation: "I do solemnly swear (or affirm) that I will support, obey and defend the Constitution of the United States and the Constitution of this State, and that I will discharge the duties of my office with fidelity.["]

This provision has remained unchanged from the original constitution. It has been construed to permit, in addition to the oath, a requirement of a bond for the state treasurer (*State ex rel. Stain v. Christensen,* 1934). Signing of an oath form, rather than going through a formal ritual, was held in 1962 to satisfy the requirements of this section (*State v. Mathews,* 1962).

Article V

Distribution of Powers

SECTION 1

Three departments of government. The powers of the government of the State of Utah shall be divided into three distinct departments, the Legislative, the Executive, and the Judicial; and no person charged with the exercise of powers properly belonging to one of these departments, shall exercise any functions appertaining to either of the others, except in the cases herein expressly directed or permitted.

This article was in the original constitution, and it has not been amended. It has, however, been interpreted by the courts to accommodate the growth of regulatory agencies and to monitor the boundaries of Legislative, Judicial, and Executive Department powers. Early in the state's history, the Utah Supreme Court held that the power of the courts to declare void any act of any department of government that violates the constitution did not invade the domain of the Legislative Department (*Ritchie v. Richards,* 1896). Utah's courts have, however, tended to give wide latitude to the Legislature within the scope of the police power. The Utah Supreme Court stated in *Utah Manufacturers' Association v. Stewart* in 1933 that every presumption will be indulged in favor of constitutionality and every reasonable doubt resolved in favor of validity of a legislative act. This philosophy has been emphasized many times since then. The constitutional powers of the district court given in Article VIII cannot be enlarged or abridged by the Legislature, the court held in *State ex rel. Robinson v. Durand* (1908).

In 1963 the court held in *In re Woodward* that establishment of a juvenile court system in the public welfare department of the executive branch violated this section; this court was later made part of the Judicial Department.

In 1984 the court held that a statute empowering district courts to appoint the board of directors of water conservancy districts violated this article by conferring a power not within the primary function of the judiciary (*Timpanogos Planning and Water Management Agency v. Central Utah Water Conservancy District,* 1984). A statutory provision for appointment of six members of the Utah State Board of Higher Education by the president of the Senate and the speaker of the House of Representatives was held to violate this section in *Rampton v. Barlow* (1970).

Challenges to the delegation of judicial power under this section generally have not been successful. The Workmen's Compensation Act, which delegated to the state Industrial Commission the power to hear controversies arising under the act, was upheld so long as the commission did not act arbitrarily or in excess of the express powers conferred by the statute (*Utah Fuel Co. v. Industrial Commission,* 1920). The authority of the Public Service Commission to deny a certificate of public convenience and necessity (permitting a company to operate a business regulated by the commission) was not considered a judicial function that would violate this section in *Mulcahy v. Public Service Commission* (1941).

The rulemaking powers of state agencies have survived many challenges as an unconstitutional delegation of legislative powers. An exception was a provision of a barbers' price and hour act, where the State Barber Board was authorized to establish minimum prices and hours for barbers if they were agreed on by at least 70 percent of the licensed barbers in any city or county; this was held to be unconstitutional as an improper delegation of legislative authority in *Revne v. Trade Commission* in 1948. The court held in *State v. Goss* (1932) that where a policy was prescribed by statute, the power to make rules may be delegated to an administrative agent. In *White River Shale Oil v. Public Service Commission* (1985) the court held that the delegation of legislative power is not unconstitutional if the Legislature sets general standards to provide direction to an administrative body possessing the expertise to adapt the legislative goals to varying circumstances; the guidelines should be sufficient to ensure that the agency's decisions will not be arbitrary or unreasoned. (See also commentary on Article VI, section 6.)

Article VI

Legislative Department

Utah's Legislative Department article was written in an era when attitudes toward legislatures were marked by memories of the corruption and excesses of early and mid-nineteenth-century legislatures and fear of unchecked legislative power. Framers of state constitutions at that time typically created lawmaking bodies hedged in by numerous limitations on their powers, and Utah's framers in 1895 followed this pattern.

The original Legislative Department article consisted of thirty-one sections. They established the basic pattern of bicameralism, limited the length of time the Legislature is in sessions, outlined legislative procedures, and established limits on action. In the first half century of statehood, only four amendments to the article were approved by voters, although there were numerous court cases interpreting the article. Then in the mid-1960s governmental reform efforts in Utah turned to an examination of the state's constitutional framework and the basic structures of state government. The Legislative article was the first to be studied in 1970 by the Constitutional Revision Commission that had been created after a constitutional convention proposal was rejected by the voters in 1966. The Commission soon concluded that the Utah Legislature was poorly equipped to deal with the problems of a growing population.

The Commission then proposed, and voters in 1972 approved, a package of constitutional changes that provided authority for the Legislature to hire legal, auditing, and other staff assistance, and pay for members to work on interim study committees; it also clarified several other sections. These changes profoundly affected the operation of the Legislature by enabling it to develop research, legal, fiscal, and auditing offices, to continue policy studies between sessions, to play a larger role in state budget development, and to significantly enhance its oversight of state agencies.

SECTION 1

Power vested in Senate, House, and People. The Legislative power of the State shall be vested:

1. In a Senate and House of Representatives which shall be designated the Legislature of the State of Utah.
2. In the people of the State of Utah, as hereinafter stated: The legal voters or such fractional part thereof, of the state of Utah as may be provided by law, under such conditions and in such manner and within such time as may be provided by law, may initiate any desired legislation and cause the same to be submitted to a vote of the people for approval or rejection, or may require any law passed by the Legislature (except those laws passed by a two-thirds vote of the members elected to each house of the Legislature) to be submitted to the voters of the State before such law shall take effect.

The legal voters or such fractional part thereof as may be provided by law, of any legal subdivision of the State, under such conditions and in such manner and within such time as may be provided by law, may initiate any desired legislation and cause the same to be submitted to a vote of the people of said legal subdivision for approval or rejection, or may require any law or ordinance passed by the law making body of said legal subdivision to be submitted to the voters thereof before such law or ordinance shall take effect.

This section vests the legislative power of the state in the two houses of the Legislature and in the people of the state through the initiative and referendum processes. The Legislature held the legislative power of the state exclusively until voters approved an amendment providing for the initiative and referendum in 1900. These Progressive Era procedures may be used by citizens of counties, cities, or towns to initiate or nullify local ordinances, as well as to enact statutes or nullify legislative acts. Over the years, there have been sixteen statewide initiative acts on the ballot in Utah, dealing with such diverse topics as liquor by the drink, fluoridation of water, term limits for office holders, tax and spending limits, pari-mutuel betting, and criminal penalties for "indecent" material on cable television. Most have failed to gain voter approval.

Determination of what types of legislation are subject to the initiative or referendum has fallen largely to the courts. The Legislature did, however, provide by statute that citizens of local governments may not initiate budgets or changes in budgets, and they may not require any budget adopted by the local legislative body to be subject to a referendum (U.C.A. 20A-7-201 through 213). The Utah Supreme Court has attempted to define what is meant by "legislation" subject to the referendum, and "administrative" actions, which are not (*Keigley v. Bench,* 1939). It has held that the original enactment of a zoning ordinance would generally be subject to referendum, while ordinances implementing the basic zoning law, such as by zoning variances, generally would not (*Wilson v. Manning,* 1982). In *Citizens' Awareness Now v. Marakis* (1994) the Utah Supreme Court further developed its distinction between legislative and administrative actions in the zoning context by asking lower courts to determine whether the community had received adequate notice of the ordinance, whether the zoning ordinance fell within the general purpose and policy of the original ordinance, whether it constituted a material variance from the original law, and whether the subject covered was appropriate for voter decision.

Delegation of rulemaking power to administrative bodies has been held to be constitutional when a policy has been prescribed by statute and when there are clear standards to guide the agency (*State v. Goss,* 1932; *Fry v. Utah Air Conservation Commission,* 1975).

SECTION 2

Time of general sessions. Annual general sessions of the Legislature shall be held at the seat of government and shall begin on the third Monday in January.

The original constitution provided for biennial sessions to begin on the second Monday in January for a period not to exceed sixty days. By 1968 it was evident that more frequent meetings were needed, at least for budgetary purposes. In that year voters approved an amendment providing for a regular sixty-day session in odd years and a twenty-day session limited to budget matters in even years. Nonbudget items could be added to the budget-session agenda if both houses agreed by a two-thirds vote. This soon became a frequent occurrence, and in 1984 voters approved a switch to annual forty-five-day sessions. The difficulty with this schedule was that it was difficult to make budget decisions until accurate revenue information was available for the previous calendar year. In 1992 an amendment changing the starting date to the third Monday in January was approved, to provide more time for obtaining revenue information.

SECTION 3

Election of House members—Terms.

(1) The members of the House of Representatives shall be chosen biennially on even-numbered years by the qualified voters of the respective representative districts, on the first Tuesday after the first Monday in November.

(2) Their term of office shall be two years from the first day of January next after their election.

Amendments approved in 1972 and 1992 made minor changes to eliminate reference to the first election in 1896 and to designate subsections.

SECTION 4

Election of senators—Terms.
(1) The senators shall be chosen by the qualified voters of the respective senatorial districts, at the same times and places as members of the House of Representatives.
(2) Their term of office shall be four years from the first day of January next after their election.
(3) As nearly one-half as may be practicable shall be elected in each biennium as the Legislature shall determine by law with each apportionment.

This section prescribes four-year terms for senators and for half of the Senate to be elected each two years. Style changes, including division into sections, were approved by amendment in 1972 and 1992. Otherwise this section is the same as the one in the original constitution.

SECTION 5

Who eligible as legislator. No person shall be eligible to the office of senator or representative who as of the last date provided by law for filing for the office is not a citizen of the United States, twenty-five years of age, a qualified voter in the district from which he is chosen, a resident for three years of the State, and for six months of the district from which he is elected. No person elected to the office of senator or representative shall continue to serve in that office after ceasing to be a resident of the district from which elected.

This provision contains the residency requirements for candidates for the Senate and the House of Representatives. The original constitutional provision required a year's residence in the district; a 1972 amendment changed this to six months. After a senator refused to resign his seat following his move to another district, an amendment approved in 1982 added the sentence requiring continued residence in the district.

SECTION 6

Who ineligible as legislator. No person holding any public office of profit or trust under authority of the United States, or of this State, shall be a member of the

Legislature: Provided, That appointments in the State militia, and the offices of notary public, justice of the peace, United States commissioner, and postmaster of the fourth class, shall not, within the meaning of this section, be considered offices of profit or trust.

This section prohibits any person holding a "public office of profit or trust" from serving in the Legislature, but it permits members of the state militia, justices of the peace, and holders of certain minor offices in the federal government to serve. The language has not been changed since it was placed in the original constitution. The definition of an office of "profit or trust" is unclear, but the Utah Supreme Court held in 1970 that members of the Legislative Council (a legislative study group) could not be legislators because counsel members were paid a per diem fee. This created an odd situation because only members of the Legislature could serve on the council (*Romney v. Barlow,* 1970).

The issues in interpreting this provision are closely related to those in Article V, which specifies that "no person charged with the exercise of powers properly belonging to one of these departments shall exercise any functions appertaining to either of the others, except in the cases herein expressly directed or permitted." They also relate to the provision in section 10 of this article providing that "each house shall be the judge of the election and qualifications of its members." The question of ineligibility has been raised when public school teachers or other state employees have been elected to the Legislature. In a 1978 per curiam opinion in *Jenkins v. Bishop,* the Utah Supreme Court ruled that school administrators and teachers were not disqualified from membership in the Legislature. The court did not decide, however, whether the defendants may maintain their position in their school districts during their service in the Legislature. In 1987 the attorney general sued to remove three state employees from membership in the House of Representatives after their election. The Utah Supreme Court declined in *State v. Evans* (1987) to review the decision of the House of Representatives regarding the election and qualifications of its members. The Constitutional Revision Commission submitted to the Legislature an amendment to clarify the separation of powers standard in Article V and also the ineligibility standard in Article VI in 1989, but it was not approved. The issue of eligibility seems to be one that both the Legislature and the courts find difficult to clarify.

SECTION 7

Ineligibility of member to office created at term for which elected. No member of the Legislature, during the term for which he was elected, shall be appointed or elected to any civil office of profit under this State, which shall have been created, or the emoluments of which shall have been increased, during the term for which he was elected.

This section, which was part of the original constitution, prohibits legislators from leaving the Legislature for a paid office which was created, or for which the pay was increased, during their term. The Utah Supreme Court has indicated that the purpose of the section was to avoid conflicts of interest on the part of legislators and to assure that they are not improperly influenced by a desire for personal gain (*State ex rel. Jugler v. Grover,* 1942; *Romney v. Barlow,* 1970). This provision did not prevent a state senator from running for the office of lieutenant governor/secretary of state, even though the salary of the office had been increased during the senator's term of office. The Utah Supreme Court ruled in *Jenkins v. Jensen* (1981) that the salary increase was an adjustment for inflation and had been given to other officers of the Executive Department; there was no indication that the office had been singled out for special treatment to favor the senator.

SECTION 8

Privilege from arrest. Members of the Legislature, in all cases except treason, felony or breach of the peace, shall be privileged from arrest during each session of the Legislature, for fifteen days next preceding each session, and in returning therefrom; and for words used in any speech or debate in either house, they shall not be questioned in any other place.

This section protects legislators from arrest during, before, and after each legislative session and frees them from lawsuits for speech on the floor of the house in which they are serving. This section is unchanged from the original constitution, and there has been no significant case law on it.

SECTION 9

Compensation of legislators—Citizens' salary commission. The Legislature shall not increase the salaries of its members on its own initiative, but shall provide by law for the appointment by the Governor of a citizens' salary commission to make recommendations concerning the salaries of members of the Legislature. Upon submission of the commission's recommendations, the Legislature shall by law accept, reject or lower the salary but may not, in any event, increase the recommendation. The Legislature shall provide by law for the expenses of its members. Until salaries and expenses enacted as authorized by this section become effective, members of the Legislature shall receive compensation of $25 per diem while actually in session, expenses of $15 per diem while actually in session, and mileage as provided by law.

This section provides for a citizens' salary commission to recommend salaries for members of the Legislature, which they may accept, reject, or lower—but not raise. It resolves a problem dating back to the beginning of statehood.

Delegates to Utah's constitutional convention, after a spirited debate, provided for a salary of $4 per day while in session and ten cents a mile for travel to and from the meeting place. The prevailing sentiment was to keep the figure low enough to avoid undue alarm to citizens who were financially pinched by the 1890s depression, but to keep it high enough to avoid bribery of legislators. Writing the amounts into the constitution created an uncomfortable situation for legislators, who had to seek a constitutional amendment for every raise in pay. Four amendments raising legislative pay were turned down by voters between 1896 and 1944, when a raise to $300 a year was passed. In 1950 the amount was boosted to $500 a year, but not until 1968 (after three more proposed amendments to raise salaries or expenses failed to get voter approval) did they receive a $25 salary and $15 expense allowance per day. A 1980 proposal to jump to $40 a day was turned down by voters, which prompted the legislators to propose a salary commission to take this politically difficult matter out of their hands. An amendment to establish a commission to review salaries was approved by the voters in 1982, and changes in the salary and expense structure since then have rendered the last sentence of the section obsolete. The Legslative Compensation Commission (U.C.A.36-2-3) has attempted to keep salaries in line with inflation, and further amendments on this topic do not appear to be needed.

SECTION 10

Each house to be judge of election, and qualifications of its members—Expulsion. Each house shall be the judge of the election and qualifications of its members, and may punish them for disorderly conduct, and with the concurrence of two-thirds of all the members elected, expel a member for cause.

This section allows each house of the Legislature to determine whether a member is legally elected and to discipline and expel members for cause. It is unchanged from the original constitution. Recently, a member of the House of Representatives resigned after she was convicted of shoplifting. No expulsions have occurred.

SECTION 11

Majority is quorum—Attendance compelled. A majority of the members of each house shall constitute a quorum to transact business, but a smaller number may adjourn from day to day, and may compel the attendance of absent members in such manner and under such penalties as each house may prescribe.

This section specifies the number of members needed to form a quorum and confers the right to compel attendance at sessions. It is unchanged from the original constitution. Attendance has not been a significant problem in the Utah Legislature, and there is no case law on this section.

SECTION 12

Rules—Choosing officers and employees. Each house shall determine the rules of its proceedings and choose its own officers and employees.

The Senate elects a president as presiding officer after his or her selection by the majority party caucus. The House of Representatives elects a speaker after his or her selection by the majority party caucus. The majority and minority parties in each house select their respective leaders and whips. Each house has its own rules, as well as joint rules governing legislative procedures, standing committees and interim committees, and floor actions. These rules change from time to time.

SECTION 13

Vacancies to be filled. Vacancies that may occur in either house of the Legislature shall be filled in such manner as may be provided by law.

The original constitution provided for the governor to issue writs of election to fill vacancies in the Legislature. In 1930 voters approved a change to the current language, which was implemented by statute to permit vacancies to be filled without a special election. Under current law, when a vacancy occurs in the Legislature, the governor appoints someone to fill the position until the next general election (U.C.A. 20A-1-503). This appointment must be made from a list of three persons nominated by the county central committee of the political party to which the former legislator belonged. The person chosen must be a resident of the district in which the vacancy occurs.

SECTION 14

Journals—Yeas and nays. Each house shall keep a journal of its proceedings, which, except in case of executive sessions, shall be published, and the yeas and nays on any question, at the request of five members of such house, shall be entered upon the journal.

This section, unchanged from the original constitution, requires each house to keep and publish a journal of its proceedings and to publish in its journal the vote on any question at the request of five members of that house. See, however, section 22, which also deals with constitutional procedures to be followed; as amended in 1972, section 22 calls for recording of yeas and nays on final passage of all bills and entry on the journal of the house in which the vote occurs.

In an early case, *Ritchie v. Richards* (1896), the Utah Supreme Court held that legislative journals are public records for courts to consider in determining the constitutionality of an enactment. They are not necessarily more reliable than other sources as proof that constitutional procedures were followed, however, since it is possible that mistakes could be made in making journal entries, and statutory enactments should not stand upon such a "sandy and uncertain foundation." Laws evidenced by the signatures of the presiding officers, and the approval and signature of the governor, and the filing in the public archives ought not to be overthrown by memoranda on the journals, the court ruled. Where the records are silent on the subject under investigation, the courts presume that the Legislature acted in accordance with its delegated power.

SECTION 15

Sessions to be public—Adjournments. All sessions of the Legislature, except those of the Senate while sitting in executive session, shall be public; and neither house, without the consent of the other, shall adjourn for more than three days, nor to any other place than that in which it may be holding session.

This section, which is unchanged from the original constitution, provides that all sessions of the Legislature shall be public except those of the Senate while in executive session (usually to discuss confirmation of the governor's appointees). It also prohibits one house from adjourning for more than three days or moving to another location.

SECTION 16

Duration of sessions. No annual general session of the Legislature shall exceed 45 calendar days, except in cases of impeachment. No special session shall exceed 30 calendar days, except in cases of impeachment. When any session of the Legislature trying cases of impeachment exceeds the number of days it may remain in session as provided in this section, the members shall receive compensation only for expenses and mileage for those days in excess of 30.

This section provides limits for both general and special sessions, and it limits pay and expenses for impeachment sessions longer than thirty days. The original section limited the Legislature to biennial sixty-day regular sessions, except in cases of impeachment, and special sessions to thirty days. It contained the same limits on pay for sessions involving impeachment. In 1968 voters approved a twenty-day budget session to be held during even-numbered years, while retaining the regular sixty-day session in odd-numbered years. The need for more time in regular session became apparent during the next decade, and in 1984 the budget session was abandoned for annual forty-five-day sessions.

SECTION 17

Impeachment by House. The House of Representatives shall have the sole power of impeachment, but in order to impeach, two-thirds of all the members elected must vote therefor.

This section was in the original constitution; there are no cases interpreting it.

SECTION 18

Trial of impeachment by Senate. All impeachments shall be tried by the Senate, and senators, when sitting for that purpose, shall take oath or make affirmation to do justice according to the law and the evidence. When the Governor is on trial, the Chief Justice of the Supreme Court shall preside. No person shall be convicted without the concurrence of two-thirds of the senators elected.

This section, unchanged from the original constitution, provides for the Senate to try impeachments, and it requires a two-thirds majority of the senators elected for conviction. There are no cases interpreting it.

SECTION 19

Officers liable for impeachment—Judgment—Prosecution by law. The Governor and other State and Judicial officers, except justices of the peace, shall be liable to impeachment for high crimes, misdemeanors, or malfeasance in office; but judgment in such cases shall extend only to removal from office and disqualification to hold any office of honor, trust or profit in the State. The party, whether convicted or acquitted, shall, nevertheless, be liable to prosecution, trial and punishment according to law.

This section, which is unchanged from the original constitution, makes the governor and "other State and Judicial officers" subject to impeachment for high crimes, misdemeanors, or malfeasance in office. It also provides that a party in an impeachment may be prosecuted according to law, whether convicted or acquitted. There is no case law on this section.

SECTION 20

Service of articles of impeachment. No person shall be tried on impeachment, unless he shall have been served with a copy of the articles thereof, at least ten days before the trial, and after such service he shall not exercise the duties of his office until he shall have been acquitted.

This section was in the original constitution; there have been no officials impeached.

SECTION 21

Removal of officers. All officers not liable to impeachment shall be removed for any of the offenses specified in this article, in such manner as may be provided by law.

This section was in the original constitution. It provided for the Legislature to enact statutes specifying procedures by which officials not liable to impeachment may be removed from office. A statute enacted to implement this section provided: "All others not liable to impeachment shall be subject to removal for high crimes, misdemeanors, or malfeasance in office as in this chapter provided" (formerly U.C.A. 77-7-1). The defendant challenged the phrase "malfeasance in office" as being unconstitutional because it was so indefinite. The Utah Supreme Court held that the term was not so vague as to be invalid; it is commonly understood as requiring an intentional act or omission which amounts to a crime or involves a substantial breach of trust imposed on an official by his office (*State v. Guerts*, 1961). Conviction of a county official for failure to file a federal income tax return (an offense not connected to his performance in his office) was held by the Utah Supreme Court not to be a basis for removal from office in *State v. Jones* (1965). Current statutes on removal from office provide that officials may be removed in a civil proceeding initiated by a public official or by a party other than the state (U.C.A. 77-6-1 et seq.).

SECTION 22

Reading of bills—Bill to contain only one subject—Bills passed by majority. Every bill shall be read by title three separate times in each house except in cases where two-thirds of the house where such bill is pending suspend this requirement. Except general appropriation bills and bills for the codification and general revision of laws, no bill shall be passed containing more than one subject, which shall be clearly expressed in its title. The vote upon the final passage of all bills shall be by yeas and nays and entered upon the respective journals of the house in which the vote occurs. No bill or joint resolution shall be passed except with the assent of the majority of all the members elected to each house of the Legislature.

This section requires three readings of each bill by title, limits bills to one subject, mandates recording of yeas and nays in the journals on final passage, and requires approval by a majority of all those elected in each house for passage of a measure. The current section now covers items addressed in two sections of the original constitution. The first section required an enacting clause, assent by a majority of all members (not just those voting), three readings (not just by title) before passage, a final vote by yeas and nays, and reenactment of laws revised or amended. In the 1972 revision of the Legislative article, the enacting clause provision was dropped, and the three readings were required only by title. The final yeas and nays were to be recorded in the journal. The single-subject provision was moved to this section as part of an amendment approved in 1972.

Single-subject requirements were common to state constitutions when Utah's document was written; they were justified as preventing "logrolling" among legislators, clarifying the scope of the bill, notifying the public of all the subjects covered by legislation, and holding legislators responsible to the public.

The single-subject provision generally has been interpreted broadly by the Utah Supreme Court. In 1915 the court held that this provision should be applied to serve its purpose in preventing the combination of incongruous subjects and should be liberally construed in favor of upholding the enactment (*Salt Lake City v. Wilson,* 1915). Later courts have continued generally to favor liberal construction. The provision should not hamper the lawmaking power in adopting comprehensive measures covering a subject where several branches may have some direct connection with the principal subject treated (*State v. McCornish,* 1921; *State v. Barlow,* 1944). And the title does not have to be an index to the act; the subject matter of the act should be reasonably related to the title and all parts of the act be reasonably related to each other (*State v. Twitchell,* 1959). If there is subject matter in a bill not clearly expressed in the title, the act is not unconstitutional as to subject matters which are clearly expressed in the title, if the act would be complete and capable of being enforced with such provisions eliminated (*State v. Hoffman,* 1937).

Despite the liberal interpretations in previous cases, the newly formed Constitutional Revision Commission concluded in 1969 that revisions of entire articles of the constitution could be challenged without constitutional language specifically exempting them from the single-subject rule. A "Gateway" amendment allowing revision of entire articles as a single amendment was accepted by the voters in 1970 and placed in Article XXIII.

SECTION 23

Regulation of income taxes. (Enacted in 1972, repealed and transferred to Article XIII, section 12(2) in 1982.)

SECTION 24

Presiding officers to sign bills. The presiding officer of each house, not later than five days following adjournment, shall sign all bills and joint resolutions passed by the Legislature, certifying to their accuracy and authenticity as enacted by the Legislature.

This section was amended in the 1972 revision of the Legislative article, deleting a requirement for the signing to be recorded in the journal, and adding the phrase, "certifying to their accuracy and authenticity as enacted by the Legislature." The Utah Supreme Court has held that the presiding officers of the two houses do not have discretionary power to refuse to sign a bill passed by his/her house. If such an officer neglected to sign a bill through oversight, and the bill could be ascertained to have been enacted properly, it could be published as part of the regular session laws (*Dean v. Rampton,* 1975).

SECTION 25

Publication of acts—Effective dates of acts. All acts shall be officially published, and no act shall take effect until sixty days after the adjournment of the session at which it passed, unless the Legislature by a vote of two-thirds of all the members elected to each house, shall otherwise direct.

This section provides for the effective date of legislation sixty days after the end of the session in which it was passed, except for bills passed by a two-thirds majority. This section was amended in the 1972 revision to eliminate a provision that no law could take effect until it was published. A challenge under this section to a retroactive tax increase failed when the Utah Supreme Court held in *Mecham v. State Tax Commission* (1966) that there was nothing in the constitution to prevent such a retroactive law.

SECTION 26

Private laws forbidden. No private or special law shall be enacted where a general law can be applicable.

This section in the original constitution was a lengthy one. It attempted to list virtually every kind of special law the constitutional convention delegates wanted forbidden to future legislators. The list of eighteen items included granting divorces, punishing crimes, and granting privileges to individuals or corporations. The section was reduced to the current version in the major revision of the article approved by voters in 1972. The original article clearly reflected the constitutional convention's concern with special favors to some and is a companion piece to Article I, section 24, which requires that "All laws of a general nature shall have uniform operation." These provisions express the feeling that laws should not promote special treatment and should be administered even-handedly, as well as a reaction to the corruption of some mid-nineteenth-century Legislatures.

The Utah Supreme Court has defined a special law as one relating to particular persons, places, or things, or to entities not particularized but arbitrarily selected or distinguished from the general group of similar entities for the purpose of conferring privileges or imposing peculiar disabilities or burdensome duties on the exercise of a common right (*Utah Farm Bureau Insurance Co. v. Utah Insurance Guaranty Association,* 1977). General laws apply to, and operate uniformly, on all members of any class of persons, places, or things (*State v. Kallas,* 1939).

The difficulty with general laws is that individuals, groups, or institutions may need to be treated differently in order to deal realistically with them. This problem leads to classification of such individuals or entities by law. Cities in Utah are classified according to population, as provided in Article XI, section 5, a practice upheld in 1922 in *Salt Lake City v. Salt Lake County* (1922). But not all classifications have met with Utah Supreme Court approval; a classification must be natural and have some regard to the character of the legislation (*Board of Education v. Hunter,* 1916). A statute limiting the practice of cosmetology to women and girls, for example, did not survive a court test in *Leetham v. McGinn* (1989). The Utah Supreme Court upheld a statute exempting benevolent associations from a premium tax in *Blue Cross and Blue Shield v. State* (1989), stating that a classification would be sustained if facts can reasonably be conceived which would justify the distinctions or differences in state policy between different persons.

SECTION 27

Lotteries not authorized. The Legislature shall not authorize any game of chance, lottery or gift enterprise under any pretense or for any purpose.

This section prohibits games of chance or lotteries, which have been defined by the Utah Supreme Court. The section was part of the original constitution as section 28, before the 1972 revision. Under this provision, games of skill are not considered an illegal lottery. Games requiring a valuable consideration for participation are lotteries. Lotteries involve a prize, distribution of prizes by chance, and valuable consideration required to be eligible for a prize. A grocery chain's bingo game was held not to constitute an illegal lottery, since the game card was distributed free upon request in *Albertson's Inc. v. Hansen* (1979). An act permitting pari-mutuel betting at the race track was held not to violate his section in *Utah State Fair Association v. Green* (1926). With the proliferation of state lotteries in recent years—Utah being one of only two states prohibiting them—there have been pressures to change this provision. The Legislature has been notably reluctant to change it, partly because of the quiet but firm opposition of the majority Church of Jesus Christ of Latter-day Saints (Mormon) to all forms of gambling.

SECTION 28

Special privileges forbidden. The Legislature shall not delegate to any special commission, private corporation or association, any power to make, supervise or interfere with any municipal improvement, money, property or effects, whether held in trust or otherwise, to levy taxes, to select a capitol site, or to perform any municipal functions.

This section protects cities and towns from having their municipal or taxing functions delegated by the Legislature to a special commission or similar organization. It was in the original constitution as section 29; it was transferred in 1972. The Utah Supreme Court's interpretation of this clause, commonly known as the "ripper" clause, has focused on two elements: first, whether or not the entity exercising the authority is a special commission, and second, whether or not the authority exercised by the entity can be considered a municipal function. Boards or commissions created by the Legislature generally are considered to be special commissions, although the meaning of this term is not always clear. The state Public Service Commission, which regulates utilities, was held to be a special commission in *Logan City v. Public Utilities Commission* (1928). The court has held that this provision only limits the creation of those entities which assume *municipal* functions but which are not municipalities. A special commission is only constitutionally impermissible when it is given powers of purely municipal concern (*Tribe v. Salt Lake City Corporation,* 1975). In recent cases, the court has used a balancing test to determine whether or not a specific activity was a municipal function. It has weighed the relative abilities of the state and municipal governments to perform the function, the degree to which the performance of the function affects the interests of those beyond the boundaries of the municipality, and the extent to which the legislation will intrude upon the ability of the people within the municipality to control through their elected officials the substantive policies that affect them uniquely (*City of West Jordan v. Utah State Retirement Board,* 1988; *Utah Associated Municipal Power Systems v. Public Service Commission,* 1990).

SECTION 29

Lending public credit forbidden—Exception. The Legislature shall not authorize the State, or any county, city, town, township, district or other political subdivision of the State to lend its credit or subscribe to stock or bonds in aid of any railroad, telegraph or other private individual or corporate enterprise or undertaking, except as provided in Article X, Section 5.

This section limits the ability of the Legislature to authorize the state or its political subdivisions to lend credit or subscribe to stock or bonds of any private enterprise. It was formerly section 31 in the original constitution. It was placed there after a sometimes bitter partisan debate in the constitutional convention over the wisdom of providing state subsidies or other assistance to the industries delegates hoped to attract to the new state. Delegates opposed to such state aid to private businesses pointed out that several states had incurred huge debts by pledging state credit to railroad companies that eventually went bankrupt. The issue of subsidies (or bounties, as the delegates called them) was dropped, but to guard against abuses of the state's credit, the delegates accepted this section. In 1974 an amendment that would have permitted the state to lend its credit "only to aid in the establishment or expansion of private industry within the state" was submitted to the voters. Opponents raised the old fears of jeopardizing the state's fiscal integrity, and it was defeated.

The Utah Supreme Court has heard fourteen cases in which it was contended that section 29 had been violated. In thirteen of them, it was asserted that there was a lending of credit in aid of private enterprise. In the first seven cases decided, the court concluded that there was no direct aid to private enterprise; instead, a public purpose was served. In a 1961 case, *Utah State Land Board v. Utah State Finance Commission,* purchase by a state agency of well-established corporate securities in the investment of public funds was held not to violate the constitution. In the next six cases, the court held that there was no actual lending of credit; they involved issuance of revenue bonds payable only out of the revenues of the projects. In 1986 the use of state-appropriated funds by the state-funded Utah Technology Finance Corporation (UTFC) for a limited partnership interest in a venture fund designed to provide small, high-technology businesses with startup capital was challenged in *Utah Technology Finance Corporation v. Wilkinson.* The court held that the act creating UTFC did not violate this section insofar as it forbids the lending of the state's credit; its loans to fledgling high-tech businesses did not make the state a guarantor of their debts. The purchase of the limited partnership interest in the venture fund, however, the court deemed to be "clearly the subscription to stock in aid of private enterprise" forbidden by section 29. In recent years this issue has generated much controversy, and there have been efforts to delete it as an outmoded provision for an era in which stimulation of new industry is seen by some as vital to the state. Thus far they have not been successful.

In 1996 voters approved the addition of the last phrase, "except as provided in Article X, Section 5" to permit the state to guarantee the debt of school districts.

SECTION 30

Continuity in government.
(1) Notwithstanding any general or special provisions of the Constitution, in order to insure continuity of state and local government operations when such operations are seriously disrupted as a result of natural or man-made disaster or disaster caused by enemy attack, the Legislature may:

(a) provide for prompt and temporary succession to the powers and duties of any elected or appointed public office, the incumbents of which may become unavailable for carrying on the powers and duties of such offices; and

(b) adopt measures necessary and proper for insuring the continuity of governmental operations including, but not limited to, the financing thereof.

(2) Subsection (1) does not permit these temporary public officers to act or these temporary measures to be contrary to the Constitution and applicable law.

This section, added to the constitution in 1964, provides for continuing operation of state and local governments in case of a natural or man-made disaster or in time of enemy attack. The most recent amendment to this section was approved by voters in 1990, adding to the conditions under which the Legislature might provide for temporary officers and adopt measures to insure the continuity of governmental operations. The previous section, adopted in 1972, gave the Legislature "the power and immediate duty" to take these measures in periods of emergency "resulting from disaster caused by enemy attack." It made no provision for governmental disruption by natural or man-made disaster, as the current version does. The 1990 amendment also made action by the Legislature discretionary rather than mandatory.

SECTION 31

Additional compensation of legislators. For attendance at meetings of interim committees established by law to function between legislative sessions, members of the Legislature shall receive additional per diem compensation and mileage at a rate not to exceed that provided in this Constitution for regular legislative sessions.

This section was added in the 1972 revision of the article to provide constitutional authority for payment of per diem compensation and mileage expenses to legislators serving on committees that function between sessions. These committees, which study policy issues assigned to them in order to provide information for the next regular session, are considered particularly important to a part-time Legislature. The amount of compensation is determined by the citizens' salary commission, as provided in section 9 of this article.

SECTION 32

Appointment of additional employees—Legal counsel.
(1) The Legislature may appoint temporary or permanent nonmember employees for work during and between sessions.
(2) The Legislature may appoint legal counsel which shall provide and control all legal services for the Legislature unless otherwise provided by statute.

This section was added to the constitution in the 1972 article revision to clarify the right of the Legislature to hire permanent staff and to have its own legal services independent of the Office of the Attorney General. The original section was amended in 1992 by dropping the term "independent counsel" and substituting "unless otherwise provided by statute" for "except as the Legislature by law shall authorize performance thereof by the attorney general." Some changes in style also were made.

Attorneys general throughout the state's history generally have maintained that their office should provide legal services for state government. In 1992 the Judicial Department article (Art. VIII, sec. 12) and the Executive Department article (Art. VII, sec. 5) were amended to permit the judiciary and the governor to obtain separate legal services. Now all of the three departments have the constitutional right to obtain their own legal counsel.

SECTION 33

Legislative auditor appointed. The Legislature shall appoint a legislative auditor to serve at its pleasure. The legislative auditor shall have authority to conduct audits of any funds, functions, and accounts in any branch, department, agency or political subdivision of this state and shall perform such other related duties as may be prescribed by the Legislature. He shall report to and be answerable only to the Legislature.

This section provided for appointment of a legislative auditor and described the duties of the office and its accountability only to the Legislature. Although there was (and is) a state auditor in the Executive Department, the Legislative article revision approved by the voters in 1972 included this provision for an auditor accountable to the Legislature and with a broader set of functions. The audits by the Office of the Legislative Auditor General may reach beyond traditional financial audits, as the Legislature may desire. Audits may be conducted to—among other purposes—determine whether administrators have adhered to legislative intent in agency operations, to assess the efficiency of an agency in performing its functions, or to measure an agency's performance against intended objectives.

Article VII

Executive Department

The executive branch of Utah state government has undergone dramatic changes since the mid-1960s, when serious attention began to be focused on its shortcomings. As originally written on the eve of statehood, the Executive Department article copied the plan used by other states at the time. There were six independently elected officials at the head of government; they were thought by some constitutional convention delegates to have very little to do in the new state and, in effect, be part-time officials.[32] Consequently, much of the time spent debating the article was taken up with the salaries of these officials. Some were given positions on the numerous boards and commissions created to administer state functions. Among the multi-member bodies designated in the constitution were a Board of Pardons, Board of State Prison Commissioners, Board of Insane Asylum Commissioners, Board of Reform School Commissioners, State Board of Education, State Board of Equalization, Board of Labor, Conciliation, and Arbitration, and most powerful of all, a Board of Examiners to pass on all financial claims against the state. As new agencies were created, some were headed by boards or commissions rather than single executives accountable to the governor.

A long-time critic of the design of Utah's Executive Department has argued that "politically independent executive offices fragment gubernatorial control . . . and make fair and intelligent citizen assessment of Executive Branch

[32] *Proceedings of the Convention,* 2: 1027–31.

responsibility impossible."[33] Other executive branch reformers spearheaded movements as early as 1921 to create a more coherent governmental structure but had little success. In 1941 Governor Herbert B. Maw recommended elimination of scores of agencies and consolidation of departments, and some of his recommendations were enacted into law, but they did not attack the fundamental problems of agencies headed by commissions or reduce the financial powers of the Board of Examiners.[34] In 1965 the Legislature created a twelve-member Commission on the Organization of the Executive Branch of the Government (which was promptly dubbed the "Little Hoover Commission" after the federal commission headed by former President Herbert Hoover). This Commission found that there were 156 separate officials, departments, boards, commissions, councils, and committees in state government, rendering the executive branch unmanageable.[35] The Little Hoover Commission report sparked hopes for fundamental changes, and reformers managed in 1966 to place a proposal for a constitutional convention to revise the entire constitution on the ballot. This proposal was overwhelmingly defeated, but the impetus for change in the executive and legislative branches remained.

A Constitutional Revision Commission, charged with examining the constitution an article at a time, was created, and it suggested several changes in the Executive Department article in 1974; voters refused to accept them. Several years of study by the Constitutional Revision Commission resulted in a large package of constitutional changes in the Executive Department article that were approved by the voters in 1980. Further changes in the article were made in another revision approved in 1992. Proponents of more centralized government and more powers for the governor find these changes modest. But they have resulted in the elimination of the Board of Examiners, which wielded great power and frequently fostered dissension between political rivals. These changes also encouraged statutory changes to consolidate agencies and make Utah government more manageable and efficient. They have not, however, succeeded in eliminating high-level elected officials and giving the governor the independent power to organize the Executive Department, which many reformers advocate.

SECTION 1

Executive Department officers—Terms, residence, and duties.

(1) The elective constitutional officers of the Executive department shall consist of Governor, Lieutenant Governor, State Auditor, State Treasurer, and Attorney General.

---

[33] John J. Flynn, "Constitutional Difficulties of Utah's Executive Branch and the Need for Reform," *Utah Law Review* 1996 (September): 355.

[34] Ibid., 365–66.

[35] Report of the Commission on the Reorganization of the Executive Branch of Government, 1961.

(2) Each officer shall:

(a) hold office for four years beginning on the first Monday of January next after their election:

(b) during their terms of office reside within the state; and

(c) perform such duties as are prescribed by this Constitution and as provided by statute.

The original 1896 Constitution provided that the Executive Department "shall consist of" the governor, secretary of state, state auditor, state treasurer, attorney general, and superintendent of public instruction. They were to serve four-year terms and to reside and keep the public books, records, and papers at the seat of government. In 1950 voters approved removal of the superintendent of public instruction from the list of Executive Department officials, and provided for selection by the State Board of Education (Art. X, sec. 3). In 1980 they dropped the secretary of state and added a lieutenant governor to the section. The lieutenant governor assumed some of the duties of the former secretary of state, in the electoral process, for example; other duties were assumed by other departments of government. The requirement for officials to live at the seat of government was dropped in favor of residence within the state. In 1992 the requirement to keep the public books, records, and papers as provided by law was also removed.

SECTION 2

Election of officers—Governor and Lieutenant Governor elected jointly.

(1) The officers provided for in Section 1 shall be elected by the qualified voters of the state at the time and place of voting for members of the Legislature. The candidates respectively having the highest number of votes cast for the office voted for shall be elected. If two or more candidates have an equal and the highest number of votes for any one of the offices, the two houses of the Legislature at its next session shall elect by joint ballot one of those candidates for that office.

(2) In the election the names of the candidates for Governor and Lieutenant Governor for each political party shall appear together on the ballot and the votes cast for a candidate for Governor shall be considered as also cast for the candidate for Lieutenant Governor.

This section provides for the election of state officers listed in section one, for breaking a tie vote for officers, and for tandem election of the governor and lieutenant governor. The section was changed in 1980 to provide for the governor and lieutenant governor to run together on the ballot, from the same political party, in order to avoid potential conflicts and enhance a cooperative relationship between the two offices. In practice, the governor selects the lieutenant governor candidate, who is then endorsed by the state party convention.

SECTION 3

Qualifications of officers.
(1) To be eligible for the office of Governor or Lieutenant Governor a person shall be 30 years of age or older at the time of election.
(2) To be eligible for the office of Attorney General a person shall be 25 years of age or older, at the time of election, admitted to practice before the Supreme Court of the State of Utah, and in good standing at the bar.
(3) To be eligible for the office of State Auditor or State Treasurer a person shall be 25 years of age or older, at the time of election.
(4) No person is eligible to any of the offices provided for in Section 1 unless at the time of election that person is a qualified voter and has been a resident citizen of the state for five years next preceding the election.

This section states the age, voting status, and residency qualifications for holding the office of governor, lieutenant governor, attorney general, state auditor, and state treasurer. Minor changes were made in this article in the revision approved in 1980, removing a reference to the territorial supreme court, and permitting the state auditor and state treasurer to succeed themselves in office. The original constitution had prohibited this, so in practice the two officers had traded offices every four years. In the 1992 revision, the minimum age for the auditor and treasurer were added, subsections were added, and stylistic changes were made.

SECTION 4

Governor commander-in-chief. The Governor shall be Commander-in-Chief of the military forces of the State, except when they shall be called into the service of the United States. The Governor shall have power to call out the militia to execute the laws, to suppress insurrection, or to repel invasion.

This section confirms the power of the governor as commander-in-chief of the state militia. It is unchanged from the original constitution, except for a change approved in 1980 to substitute "the Governor" for "he." This gender-neutral language was also inserted in several other sections.

SECTION 5

Executive power vested in Governor—Duties—Legal counsel.
(1) The executive power of the state shall be vested in the Governor who shall see that the laws are faithfully executed.
(2) The Governor shall transact all executive business with the officers of the government, civil and military, and may require information in writing from the

officers of the Executive Department, and from the officers and managers of state institutions upon any subject relating to the condition, management, and expenses of their respective offices and institutions. The Governor may at any time when the Legislature is not in session, if deemed necessary, appoint a committee to investigate and report to the Governor upon the condition of any executive office or state institution.

(3) The Governor shall communicate by message the condition of the state to the Legislature at every annual general session and recommend such measures as may be deemed expedient.

(4) The Governor may appoint legal counsel to advise the Governor.

This section vests the executive power of the state in the governor, describes the governor's role in directing executive department officials, requires a "state of the state" address to the Legislature at each general session, and permits appointment of legal counsel to advise the governor.

The Executive article revision approved in 1980 vested "the executive power of the state" in the governor. Unlike several other late-nineteenth-century western state constitutions that had multiple Executive Department officers but vested in the governor the "executive power," or "the supreme executive power," Utah's original constitution left the governor without this designation. Although this provision carries no specific grant of power, the promoters of this amendment felt it would add to the prestige of the office and distinguish the governor's responsibility from that of the other elected officials. The last subsection giving the governor the right to appoint legal counsel was approved in 1992; at the same election, the right to appoint counsel for the Judicial Department was given to the Judicial Council in Article VIII, section 12 (4). Since this power already had been granted to the Legislature in Article VI, section 32 (2), these additions permitted each of the three branches to obtain legal counsel independent of the Office of the Attorney General.

SECTION 6

Convening of extra sessions of Legislature. On extraordinary occasions, the Governor may convene the Legislature by proclamation, in which shall be stated the purpose for which the Legislature is to be convened, and it shall transact no legislative business except that for which it was especially convened, or such other legislative business as the Governor may call to its attention while in session. The Legislature, however, may provide for the expenses of the session and other matters incidental thereto. The Governor may also by proclamation convene the Senate in extraordinary session for the transaction of executive business.

This section, which is unchanged from the original 1896 Constitution, empowers the governor to call special sessions of the Legislature and to control the agenda of such sessions. The scope of the material to be covered in special sessions of the Legislature has been the subject of some litigation concerning the governor's control of the legislative business that shall be considered. The purpose of the session must be communicated to the Legislature by something more than a mere oral communication to certain senators, although not necessarily in writing (*State v. Scott,* 1943). In sustaining legislation enacted during a special session, the Utah Supreme Court will determine the purpose of the session from the entire context of the governor's message calling for the session. The governor may designate the subject for legislative action—and may suggest solutions to a policy problem, but he or she may not limit the means chosen by the Legislature to solve the problem, the court held in *State Tax Commission v. Preece* (1954). The state Senate is occasionally called into session to confirm the governor's appointments. Special sessions of both houses of the Legislature have become more frequent during recent years. This permits legislators to give more time to discuss matters on which consensus could not be reached during the regular session or to modify legislation that has created problems since it went into effect.

SECTION 7

Adjournment of Legislature by Governor. In case of a disagreement between the two houses of the Legislature at any special session, with respect to the time of adjournment, the Governor shall have power to adjourn the Legislature to such time as the Governor may think proper if it is not beyond the time fixed for the convening of the next Legislature.

Minor changes in style were made in this section as part of the revision of this article approved in 1980.

SECTION 8

Bills presented to Governor for approval and veto—Items of appropriation—Legislative session to consider vetoed items.

(1) Each bill passed by the Legislature, before it becomes a law, shall be presented to the Governor. If the bill is approved, the Governor shall sign it, and thereupon it shall become a law. If the bill is disapproved, it shall be returned with the Governor's objections to the house in which it originated. That house shall enter the objections upon its journal and proceed to reconsider the bill. If upon reconsideration the bill again passes both houses by a yea and nay vote of two-thirds of the members elected to each house, it shall become a law.

(2) If any bill is not returned by the Governor within ten days after it has been presented to the Governor, Sunday and the day it was received excepted, it shall become

a law without a signature. If legislative adjournment prevents return of the bill, it shall become a law unless the Governor within twenty days after adjournment files the objections to it with such officers as provided by law.

(3) The Governor may disapprove any item of appropriation contained in any bill while approving other portions of the bill. In such case the Governor shall append to the bill at the time of signing it a statement of the item or items which are disapproved, together with the reasons for disapproval, and the item or items may not take effect unless passed over the Governor's objections as provided in this section.

(4) If the Governor disapproves any bill or item of appropriation after the adjournment sine die of any session of the Legislature, the presiding officer of each house shall poll the members of that house on the matter of reconvening the Legislature. If two-thirds of the members of each house are in favor of reconvening, the Legislature shall be convened in a session that shall begin within 60 days after the adjournment of the session at which the disapproved bill or item of appropriation passed. This session may not exceed five calendar days and shall be convened at a time set jointly by the presiding officer of each house solely for the purpose of reconsidering the bill or item of appropriation disapproved. If upon reconsideration, the bill or item of appropriation again passes both houses of the Legislature by a yea and nay vote of two-thirds of the members elected to each house, the bill shall become law or the item of appropriation shall take effect on the original effective date of the law or item of appropriation.

This section establishes the right of the governor to veto bills (or items within appropriations bills) or let them become law without his or her signature, the right of the Legislature to override a veto during the session, and the right of legislators to convene (if two-thirds of the members approve) to consider overriding a veto of the governor after a session has ended.

In the Executive article revision approved in 1980, the governor was given ten days to veto a bill when the Legislature is in session and twenty days to exercise his veto power if the legislative session has ended. These extensions of time (the previous time limits were five days and ten days) were made to give the governor more time to consider the vast number of bills that are passed in the waning days of the legislative session. At the same time, the Legislature gained the right to override vetoes that occur after the ending of a session. Although such override sessions have been rare, legislators wanted the opportunity to "even the playing field" by having the opportunity to respond to vetoes. In practice, the presiding officers of the House of Representatives and the Senate are reluctant to call for such sessions unless a clear majority for an override exists. Minor stylistic changes were made in this section in the Executive article revision approved in 1992.

SECTION 9

Governor may fill certain vacancies. When any State or district office shall become vacant, and no mode is provided by the Constitution and laws for filling such vacancy, the Governor shall have the power to fill the same by granting a commission, which shall expire at the next election, and upon qualification of the person elected to such office.

This section, which has not been changed since statehood, gives the governor power to make temporary appointments to fill vacancies in elective state or district offices if there are no constitutional or statutory provisions for filling them. There are statutes providing for filling vacancies in most of the various departments of government.

SECTION 10

Governor's appointive power—Vacancies. The Governor shall nominate, and by and with consent of the Senate, appoint all State and district officers whose offices are established by this Constitution, or which may be created by law, and whose appointment or election is not otherwise provided for. If, during the recess of the Senate, a vacancy occurs in any State or district office, the Governor shall appoint some qualified person to discharge the duties thereof until the next meeting of the Senate, when the Governor shall nominate some person to fill such office. If the office of Lieutenant Governor, State Auditor, State Treasurer or Attorney General be vacated by death, resignation or otherwise, it shall be the duty of the Governor to fill the same by appointment, from the same political party of the removed person; and the appointee shall hold office until a successor shall be elected and qualified, as provided by law.

This section gives the governor the power to appoint, with the consent of the Senate, all state and district officers whose appointment or election is not otherwise provided for; to make temporary appointments when the Senate is not in session, and to fill vacancies in the Executive Department's constitutional offices. This provision has been held by the Utah Supreme Court to mean that the governor has the power to fill a vacancy when an elected state official fails to qualify for the office (*State ex rel. Stain v. Christensen,* 1934). An office is not held to be vacant when an office holder has a leave of absence or a temporary disability or disqualification (*Critchlow v. Monson,* 1942; *State ex rel. Jugler v. Grover,* 1942).

Except for an amendment in 1980 requiring replacement of constitutional officers with an appointee from the same political party, and changing the secretary of state to the lieutenant governor, this section is unchanged from the original constitution.

SECTION 11

Vacancy in office of Governor—Determination of disability. In case of the death of the Governor, impeachment, removal from office, resignation, or disability to discharge the duties of the office, or in case of a Governor-elect who fails to take office, the powers and duties of the Governor shall devolve upon the Lieutenant Governor until the disability ceases or until the next general election, when the vacancy shall be filled by election. If, during a vacancy in the office of Governor, the Lieutenant Governor resigns, dies, is removed, or becomes incapable of performing the duties of the office, the President of the Senate shall act as Governor until the vacancy is filled or disability ceases. If in this case the President of the Senate resigns, dies, is removed, or becomes incapable of performing the duties of the office, the Speaker of the House shall act as Governor until the vacancy is filled or disability ceases. While performing the duties of the Governor as provided in this section, the Lieutenant Governor, the President of the Senate, or the Speaker of the House, as the case may be, shall be entitled to the salary and emoluments of the Governor, except in cases of temporary disability.

The disability of the Governor or person acting as Governor shall be determined by either a written declaration transmitted to the Supreme Court by the Governor stating an inability to discharge the powers and duties of the office or by a majority of the Supreme Court on joint request of the President of the Senate and the Speaker of the House of Representatives. Such determination shall be final and conclusive. Thereafter, when the Governor transmits to the Supreme Court a written declaration that no disability exists, the Governor shall resume the powers and duties of the office unless the Supreme Court, upon joint request of the President of the Senate and the Speaker of the House of Representatives, or upon its own initiative, determines that the Governor is unable to discharge the powers and duties of the office. The Lieutenant Governor shall then continue to discharge these powers and duties as acting Governor. The Supreme Court has exclusive jurisdiction to determine all questions arising under this section.

This section details the process of replacing a governor in case of death, impeachment, removal from office, or disability. It clarifies the line of succession to the office in the event of a vacancy, and it provides a process for determination of a governor's disability. This provision was added to the constitution in the Executive article revision in 1980, replacing a provision in the original 1896 Constitution that simply stated the line of succession. In the earlier version, the secretary of state (now not a constitutional office) would assume the powers of a governor who was impeached, removed from office, unable to discharge the duties of his office, or absent from the state. There was no provision for determining the disability of a governor who did not acknowledge his or her disability, or for determining when the disability no longer existed. Besides providing methods of determining disability and placing jurisdiction over disputes under this section in the Utah Supreme Court, this new provision recognizes that with modern methods of communication, a governor who is out of the state can still function in the office. Formerly, whenever a governor was out of the state, the secretary of state or lieutenant governor became acting governor and could make decisions with the force of law.

SECTION 12

Board of Pardons and Parole—Appointment—Powers and procedures—Governor's powers and duties—Legislature's powers.

(1) There is created a Board of Pardons and Parole. The Governor shall appoint the members of the board with the consent of the Senate. The terms of office shall be as provided by statute.

(2) (a) The Board of Pardons and Parole, by majority vote and upon other conditions as provided by statute, may grant parole, remit fines, forfeitures and restitution orders, commute punishments, and grant pardons after convictions, in all cases except treason and impeachments, subject to regulations as provided by statute.

(b) A fine, forfeiture, or restitution order may not be remitted and a commutation, parole, or pardon may not be granted except after a full hearing before the board, in open session, and after previous notice of the time and place of the hearing has been given.

(c) The proceedings and decisions of the board, the reasons therefor in each case, and the dissent of any member who may disagree shall be recorded and filed as provided by statute with all papers used upon the hearing.

(3) (a) The Governor may grant respites or reprieves in all cases of convictions for offenses against the state except treason or conviction on impeachment. These respites or reprieves may not extend beyond the next session of the board. At that session, the board shall continue or determine the respite or reprieve, commute the punishment, or pardon the offense as provided in this section.

(b) In case of conviction for treason, the Governor may suspend execution of the sentence until the case is reported to the Legislature at its next annual general session, when the Legislature shall pardon or commute the sentence, or direct its execution. If the Legislature takes no action on the case before adjournment of that session, the sentence shall be executed.

This section provides for establishment by statute (U.C.A. 77-27-2 et seq.) of a Board of Pardons and Parole, its members appointed by the governor with the consent of the Senate. It permits the governor to grant temporary respites or reprieves (except for treason or conviction on impeachment)—but only until the next meeting of the Board, when the governor's decision may be either confirmed or overruled. The original 1896 Constitution provided for a Board of Pardons, consisting of the governor, justices of the Utah Supreme Court, and attorney general, with the same powers (except for parole) found in the current section. It also limited the governor's pardoning power by providing that respites and reprieves could not extend beyond the next session of the Board of Pardons. The Utah Supreme Court justices were included on the original Board, despite arguments in the constitutional convention that the justices were unlikely to pardon anyone whose conviction they had upheld while on the bench.[36] Since this arrangement was specified until otherwise provided by law, the composition and selection of the Board has been changed by the Legislature over time. Until the mid-1980s, a part-time Board of Pardons was selected by the state Board of Corrections. In the article revision approved in 1992, this section was extensively revised, giving the governor the power to appoint members of a Board of Pardons and Parole with the consent of the Senate. The Board was specifically given the power of parole (which it had already been exercising), and the governor was relieved of a constitutional responsibility to report each case of remission of fine or forfeiture, reprieve, commutation, or pardon granted since the last report. The governor's limited pardoning power remains; it is effective only until the next meeting of the Board of Pardons and Parole, which now meets several times each month.

In *Cardisco v. Davis* (1937) the Utah Supreme Court held that the Board of Pardons had the jurisdiction and power to fix the time a person shall serve when sentenced under the indeterminate sentence law—despite a prisoner's complaint that he did not get an expected deduction of time to be served for good behavior while in prison. The Board's exclusive power to commute punishments and grant pardons after conviction was upheld in *Combs v. Turner* (1971). The Utah Supreme Court held that the trial court could not, by dismissing a complaint ten months after an offender was committed to prison, change the length of his sentence; it ruled that after conviction and sentencing, the Board of Pardons has exclusive power to commute punishments and grant pardons.

There appears to be some misunderstanding of the powers of this Board; with Utah's indeterminate sentence law, the amount of time served (within limits set by law, such as five to fifteen years) is determined by the Board. The governor's limited power to issue pardons and reprieves does not prevent opponents of executions from seeking a governor's pardon, even though such a pardon would be temporary and subject to a decision by the Board of Pardons and Parole. In high-profile capital cases, governors seem to be content to refer protesters against the death penalty to the Board with their appeals. The writers of the constitution intended to remove the pressure on governors by shifting the pardoning process from the governor to the Board, and they seem to have succeeded.[37]

SECTIONS 13, 14, AND 15

Repealed.

Section 13, which was the target of executive branch reform movements for decades, originally established a Board of State Prison Commissioners and a

---

[36] *Proceedings of the Convention,* 2: 1006–7.

[37] Ibid., 2: 1010–11.

Board of Examiners. The Board of State Prison Commissioners was eliminated in the 1980 Executive article revision. The Board of Examiners, which was empowered originally to examine all claims against the state, was composed in 1992 of the governor, attorney general, and state auditor, who often were of different political parties. There was frequent litigation interpreting the powers of the Board of Examiners before it was eliminated in the Executive article revision approved in 1992. Former sections 14 and 15 establishing the Board of Insane Asylum Commissioners and a Board of Reform School Commissioners were eliminated in the 1980 revision.

SECTION 14

Duties of Lieutenant Governor.

The Lieutenant Governor shall:

(1) serve on all boards and commissions in lieu of the Governor whenever so designated by the Governor,

(2) perform such duties as may be delegated by the Governor; and

(3) perform other duties as may be provided by statute.

The duties of the lieutenant governor to assist the governor and perform other statutory duties are established in this section. The section replaced former section 16, which provided for the duties of a secretary of state; it was added to the constitution in the 1980 revision of this section, and the office of secretary of state was eliminated. It was designed to strenthen the office, to allow the governor to delegate important responsibilities, and to foster a strong relationship between the governor and lieutenant governor by having the two run in tandem for election. The statutory duties of the lieutenant governor (U.C.A. 671a-1 et seq.), include some of the duties of the former secretary of state, including supervision of elections. When the designation of a secretary of state is required by local, state, federal, or international law, the lieutenant governor is designated (U.C.A. 67-1a-6). In the revision approved in 1992 there were minor stylistic changes in this section.

SECTION 15

Duties of State Auditor and State Treasurer.

(1) The State Auditor shall perform financial post audits of public accounts except as otherwise provided by this Constitution.

(2) The State Treasurer shall be the custodian of public moneys.

(3) Each shall perform other duties as provided by statute.

This section provides a brief description of the major duties of the state auditor and state treasurer and specifies that other duties will be provided by statute.

The 1980 Executive article revision changed former section 17 to provide that the state auditor perform financial post audits of public accounts, except as otherwise provided by the constitution. The Utah Supreme Court had previously held that the constitutional duties of the auditor include those which the territorial auditor was performing at the time of the adoption of the constitution, and the Legislature could not relieve the auditor of any of those duties, such as approving warrants, before they can be paid by the Finance Department (*Preece v. Rampton,* 1972). A similar case held that the constitutional duties of the treasurer were those which the territorial treasurer was performing at the adoption of the constitution, and the Legislature may not relieve him of any of those constitutional duties (*Allen v. Rampton,* 1969). Duties of the state treasurer include keeping an account of all revenues received and disbursed and investment of the various state funds to provide a safe source of additional income. The general duties of the state treasurer as custodian of state funds are found in U.C.A. 67-4-1 et seq.

The functions and duties of the state auditor are found in U.C.A. 67-3-1 et seq.; he or she is required, among other duties, to audit each state fund on a regular basis, to see that all revenues to the state are collected, and to establish uniform accounting systems. (See commentary on the legislative auditor, Article VI, section 33.)

SECTION 16

Duties of Secretary of State. Repealed.

SECTION 16

Duties of Attorney General. The Attorney General shall be the legal adviser of the State officers, except as otherwise provided by this Constitution, and shall perform such other duties as provided by law.

The original constitution was amended in the revision approved in 1980 to add the words "except as otherwise provided by this Constitution." Until this revision, there was uncertainty as to the ability of state agencies to obtain counsel outside the Office of the Attorney General. A successful challenge to the Legislature's right to appoint its own counsel in *Hansen v. Legal Services Committee of the Utah State Legislature* (1967) led to a constitutional amendment in 1972 permitting the Legislature to obtain legal advice from its own counsel. Constitutional authorization for independent counsel for the governor and the judiciary followed in the amendment of the Executive and Judicial articles approved in 1992. In the meantime, in *Hansen v. Utah State Retirement Board* (1982), the Utah Supreme Court ruled that the Utah State Retirement Board, the University of Utah hospital, the State Industrial Commission, and the Utah State Insurance Fund were not Executive Department agencies, and the attorney general did not have exclusive authority to act as their legal adviser.

In the same case, the court held that the director of the Department of Administrative Services and the state treasurer *are* state officers within the meaning of this section, and it is within the authority of the attorney general to act as legal adviser to those officers when they perform Executive Department functions. On the other hand, the court held that when these two officials perform duties for state agencies which are not Executive Department agencies, it is not within the constitutional authority of the attorney general to act as legal adviser to them. The term "state officers" clearly does not include the officials of all state agencies, but the court did not enunciate a clear standard for distinguishing between "Executive Department" agencies and those that are not. The three agencies in the case, as well as several other agencies and boards, perform functions that are quasi-legislative, quasi-judicial, or similar functions of private businesses, and they have been given some independence from the control of the Executive Department (in salaries paid to officials, for example). Their accountability to the Legislature, in view of their semiprivate status, has been questioned by some legislators. In the *State Retirement Board* case, it should be noted, the Legislature had previously authorized the three non–Executive Department agencies that were defendants to hire independent counsel. The duties of the attorney general are found in U.C.A. 67-3-1 et seq.

In recent years, the governor has used the power to appoint an attorney as a full-time legal adviser and also has occasionally employed outside counsel to deal with some high-profile cases in which he had a particular interest.

SECTION 17

Duties of Superintendent of Public Instruction. Repealed.

This section was repealed in an amendment that made several changes in the Education article (Art. X). This official was designated as the executive officer of the State Board of Education in Article X, section 3.

SECTION 18

Compensation of state and local officers.

(1) the Governor, Lieutenant Governor, State Auditor, State Treasurer, Attorney General, and any other state officer as the Legislature may provide, shall receive for their services a fixed and definite compensation as provided by law.

(2) (a) The compensation provided for in Subsection (1) shall be in full for all services rendered by those officers in any official capacity or employment during their terms of office.

(b) An officer may not receive for the performance of any official duty any fee for personal use, but all fees fixed by the Legislature for the performance by any of them of any official duty shall be collected in advance and deposited with the appropriate treasury.

(c) The Legislature may provide for the payment of actual and necessary expenses of those officers while traveling in the performance of official duties.

This section provides for fixed compensation for state officers as full payment for their services, forbids collection of fees for personal use, and permits the Legislature to compensate officers for necessary travel expenses.

The original constitution had a section containing substantially the same provisions regarding salaries and other compensation for services and travel expenses. It fixed the salaries of the governor and other Executive Department officers, until otherwise provided by law. Since then, salaries have been raised periodically by legislative action. To provide a method for systematic determination of appropriate salaries, the Legislature established an Executive and Judicial Compensation Commission in 1981 (U.C.A. 67-8-1 et seq.). This Commission has six members; one appointed by the governor, one by the president of the Senate, and one by the speaker of the House of Representatives; these three appoint two more members, and the State Bar Commission appoints one. No member can be an employee of the executive, legislative, or judicial branch. The Commission regularly reviews executive and judicial salaries and recommends salary schedules to the Legislature. Minor changes in wording in this section were made by amendments approved in 1980 and 1992.

SECTION 19

Grants and commissions. All grants and commissions shall be in the name and by the authority of the State of Utah, sealed with the great Seal of the State, signed by the Governor, and countersigned by such officer as provided by law.

This section provides for the governor's signature and affixing of the state seal to all grants and commissions; it was amended in the revision approved in 1980 to remove the provision for the secretary of state to countersign grants and commissions and to provide for countersignature by an officer as provided by law.

SECTION 20

The Great Seal. There shall be a seal of the State, which shall be called "The Great Seal of the State of Utah," and shall be kept by such officer as provided by law.

This section provides for a seal of the state, which currently is kept by the lieutenant governor. This section was formerly section 22, which was amended in the revision approved in 1980 to eliminate reference to the seal of the Territory of Utah and the secretary of state as keeper of the seal.

SECTION 21

United States officials ineligible to hold state office. No person, while holding any office under the United States' government, shall hold any office under the State government of Utah.

This section, formerly section 21, was designed to prevent the holding of two incompatible full-time offices. It was amended in the revision approved in 1980 to eliminate a provision that "the governor shall not be eligible for election to the senate of the United States during the term for which he shall have been elected Governor." The Utah Supreme Court has held that a justice of the Supreme Court did not forfeit his office by being called into the United States Army as a reserve officer, at least where he disavows any right to collect any salary as judge (*Critchlow v. Monson,* 1942).

SECTION 22

The Great Seal. Repealed in part and transferred to section 20.

SECTION 23

United States officials ineligible—Governor not eligible for Senate. Repealed in part and transferred in part to section 21.

SECTION 24

Temporary succession to public offices in emergency. Repealed.

The provisions of this section regarding emergency powers were declared unconstitutional in *Lee v. State* (1962) and were eliminated in the article revision approved in 1980.

Article VIII

Judicial Department

Utah's original Judicial Department article, written on the eve of statehood by a constitutional convention, was designed to fit the pattern common to other state court systems at that time. It contained twenty-eight detailed sections, including the composition of judicial districts, a prohibition against hiring relatives, and a mandate for the Utah Supreme Court to prepare a syllabus for each judgment or decree. By the time the state reached its centennial year in 1996, this article had been amended in 1944 and 1946 to permit legislative changes in district courts and judges' salaries, and in 1968 to provide for mandatory retirement of judges.

By the early 1980s, it seemed that a thorough study of the article was overdue, and the Constitutional Revision Commission took on the task. The result was a complete revision of the article, which was approved by the Legislature and by voters in 1984. This revision, which took effect in 1985, resulted in the repeal of ten sections that were considered outdated or unnecessary, including sections requiring that judges be conservators of peace, that decisions be in writing, and that judges prepare a syllabus of each case covering each point adjudicated. Other sections prescribing one form of civil action and setting the salaries of judges were also eliminated. Sections on courts of record and on mandatory retirement and removal of judges from office were repealed in part and reenacted in part to other sections of the article. The objective of the 1984 revision was to create a modern, unified court system and an independent judiciary.

The original Judicial Department article provided for a three-judge supreme court, trial courts in seven judicial districts, justices of the peace (commonly known as J.P. courts), and "such other courts inferior to the Supreme Court as may be established by law." There was a right of appeal to the supreme court from final judgments of the district courts. Judges could be removed by a two-thirds vote of both houses of the Legislature. They were required to be members of the bar and "learned in the law."

In practice, the judiciary became dependent on the political process. Judges ran on political party tickets and were exposed to some of the same political pressures as other office holders. Good judges were swept out of office in political landslides, and, until recent years, there was a strong correlation between the political affiliation of supreme court justices and the dominant political party.[38] Gradual changes have been made over the years to enhance the independence of the judiciary; judges of all courts except the justice courts are appointed by the governor from a nonpartisan slate produced by a bipartisan nominating commission, and they stand unopposed in a retention election after serving for a few years. Although the Utah judiciary was remarkably free of scandals, a Judicial Conduct Commission was created to deal with complaints about judicial behavior and to enhance accountability.

The revision approved in 1984 provided constitutional authority to establish a unified court system under a Judicial Council, with centralized administration, rulemaking, and budgeting for all courts of record. It also gave greater flexibility to the Legislature in changing the court system to meet the needs of a rapidly growing and shifting population. Eliminating a right of appeal to the Utah Supreme Court permitted the establishment of a Court of Appeals to reduce the supreme court's increasing case load. The revised article provided for judges to face periodic retention elections without opposition (a modified Missouri Plan using nominating commissions but permitting attorneys to challenge sitting judges had been established prior to 1985). It also removed the threat of removal by a two-thirds vote of each house of the Legislature (they are still subject to impeachment) and established a Judicial Conduct Commission to hear complaints against judges.

SECTION 1

Judicial powers—Courts. The judicial power of the state shall be vested in a Supreme Court, in a trial court of general jurisdiction known as the district court, and in such other courts as the Legislature by statute may establish. The Supreme

[38] Stephen W. Julien, "The Utah State Supreme Court and Its Justices, 1896–1976," *Utah Historical Quarterly* 14 (Summer 1976): 272–73.

Court, the district court, and such other courts designated by statute shall be courts of record. Courts not of record shall also be established by statute.

This section establishes the Utah Supreme Court and district courts, along with other courts that may be established, as courts of record; it also authorizes establishment of courts not of record by statute. Before 1984, the judicial power of the state was "vested in the Senate sitting as a court of impeachment, in a supreme court, in district courts, in justices of the peace, and such other courts inferior to the Supreme Court as may be established by law." The justice of the peace courts had constitutional status, even though they were (and are) not courts of record. The state Senate still has the power to try impeachment cases of judicial officers—among others (Art. VI, secs. 18 and 19)—but this is not considered part of the plenary judicial power noted in Article V, Distribution of Powers (*In re Handley's Estate,* 1897).

The justice of the peace courts were established to provide court access close to the people throughout the state. The district courts established in the 1896 Constitution usually served multi-county districts (some still do); there was clearly a need for courts closer to the people in widely scattered communities, to settle disputes and handle some misdemeanor cases. Criticisms of the "J.P." courts, usually presided over by lay judges, mounted over the years, but they had staunch defenders and enough political power to resist moves to abolish them. The court reorganization following the 1984 Judicial Department article revision permitted counties and cities to create justice courts with limited jurisdiction to handle some misdemeanors, traffic violations, small claims, and some preliminary hearings.

Juvenile courts were established by the Legislature in 1907 to take a less rigidly legal approach to the problem of young offenders. To enhance their role of rehabilitation and treatment, these courts were placed in the state Department of Public Welfare in 1941. Two decades later, the constitutionality of this arrangement was challenged, and it was struck down by the Utah Supreme Court. It held the juvenile court to be an integral part of the Judicial Department (*In re Woodward,* 1963). As a result, the Juvenile Court Act of 1965 created a separate and independent state juvenile court within the state judicial system, with jurisdiction over all violations by juveniles of federal, state, or local laws.

While some cities had justice of the peace courts, others had created city courts to handle some criminal offenses. In the 1970s, the increasing case load of the district courts prompted creation of another set of trial courts, the circuit courts. Cities were persuaded to give up their city courts, and cases formerly handled by them went to the circuit courts. Circuit courts also heard some cases that previously had gone to district courts. By the early 1990s, it appeared that the court system would be more efficient by gradually abolishing the circuit courts and creating more district courts. This consolidation process has now been completed.

Before the 1984 revision, the constitution created a right of appeal to the Utah Supreme Court from all final judgments of the district courts. The need for an intermediate appellate court became critical in the early 1980s when the supreme court accumulated a staggering backlog of cases. After the Judicial article revision, the seven-judge Court of Appeals was created and given jurisdiction over some cases formerly heard by the higher court. It hears appeals from the district courts in domestic relations cases, in criminal cases not involving first-degree or capital felonies, and in other matters provided by statute. The supreme court can send to the Court of Appeals any case over which it has original or appellate jurisdiction, except those dealing with matters specifically assigned to it by law.

To help reduce the caseloads of judges in the district courts, court commissioners, similar to the magistrates found in federal courts, were established in the district courts. Commissioners at first heard and made recommendations to the judges in such areas as domestic relations and juvenile matters. In 1991 they were empowered by the Legislature to enter final judgments and impose sentences in criminal cases with the consent of the defendant. In 1994 this statute was struck down to the extent that it purported to vest the ultimate power of courts of record in persons not duly appointed as Article VIII judges and held accountable according to constitutional procedures. The Utah Supreme Court approved use of court commissioners, referees, and other assistants for various other purposes, but not for exercising judicial powers. It did not, however, make this decision retroactive, nor did it clarify and define core judicial functions in the civil context (*Salt Lake City v. Ohms,* 1994; *Holm v. Smilovitz,* 1992).

The restructuring of the trial court system resulted in a constitutional change in the criminal trial jury. In 1996 voters approved a change in the number of jurors required in section 10 of the Declaration of Rights (Art. I). The number of jurors required is determined by the seriousness of the offense, rather than by the court in which the offender is tried, so that the size of juries in the district courts will be determined by the nature of the offense charged. (See commentary on Article I, section 10.)

SECTION 2

Supreme court—Chief justice—Declaring law unconstitutional—Justice unable to participate. The Supreme Court shall be the highest court and shall consist of at least five justices. The number of justices may be changed by statute, but no change shall have the effect of removing a justice from office. A chief justice shall be selected from among the justices of the Supreme Court as provided by statute. The chief justice may resign as chief justice without resigning from the Supreme Court. The Supreme Court by rule may sit and render final judgment either en banc or in divisions. The court shall not declare any law unconstitutional under this constitution or the Constitution of the United States, except on the concurrence of a majority of all justices of the Supreme Court. If a justice of the Supreme Court is disqualified or otherwise unable to participate in a cause before the court, the chief justice, or in the event the chief justice is disqualified or unable to participate, the remaining justices, shall call an active judge from an appellate court or the district court to participate in the cause.

This section provides for a minimum of five supreme court justices, election of a chief justice, a majority of the court to declare a statute unconstitutional, and for temporary seating of a judge to participate in the absence of a justice. The original state constitution provided for three supreme court judges to be elected at large by voters of the state. There was an option to increase the court to five judges after 1905. The number was increased to five in 1917; at the same time, the term of the judges was increased from six to ten years. The judge having the shortest time remaining became the chief judge. After the 1984 revision, the judges were designated as justices in the constitution, and they were empowered to elect the chief justice for a four-year term as provided by statute (U.C.A. 78-2-1).

The provision for disqualification or inability to participate has been interpreted by the court to include illness, a physical disability, or other condition incapacitating a justice, a personal interest in the particular case, or the death of a member. It also includes the temporary absence of a justice to serve in the armed forces (*Critchlow v. Monson,* 1942; *State ex rel. Jugler v. Grover,* 1942).

SECTION 3

Jurisdiction of supreme court. The Supreme Court shall have original jurisdiction to issue all extraordinary writs and to answer questions of state law certified by a court of the United States. The Supreme Court shall have appellate jurisdiction over all other matters to be exercised as provided by statute, and power to issue all writs and orders necessary for the exercise of the Supreme Court's jurisdiction or the complete determination of any cause.

This section sets forth the original and appellate jurisdiction of the Utah Supreme Court. Much of this section was contained in section 4 before the 1984 revision, including a specific listing of the writs the court could issue. The authority to answer questions of state law certified by a United States court had been denied in 1981 in *Holden v. N.L. Industries* (1981), and it was specifically granted in the new section 3.

In a series of cases where state prisoners attempted to appeal their conviction by using writs of *habeas corpus,* the court ruled in 1972 that *habeas corpus* could not be used by defendants after the time for appeal from their conviction had expired (*Zumbrunnen v. Turner,* 1972). In *Currier v. Holden* (1993), however, the ninety-day statute of limitation period was held to be unconstitutional in violation of Article I, section 11 (open courts).

SECTION 4

Rulemaking power of supreme court—Judges pro tempore—Regulation of practice of law. The Supreme Court shall adopt rules of procedure and evidence to be used in the courts of the state and shall by rule manage the appellate process. The Legislature may amend the rules of procedure and evidence adopted by the Supreme Court upon a vote of two-thirds of all members of both houses of the Legislature. Except as otherwise provided by this constitution, the Supreme Court by rule may authorize retired justices and judges and judges pro tempore to perform any judicial duties. Judges pro tempore shall be citizens of the United States, Utah residents, and admitted to practice law in Utah. The Supreme Court by rule shall govern the practice of law, including admission to practice law and the conduct and discipline of persons admitted to practice law.

This section establishes the rulemaking power of the Utah Supreme Court (subject to amendment by the Legislature), the power of the court to authorize judges pro tempore, and the power to govern the practice of law. The section was added to the constitution in the 1984 revision as part of the movement to centralize and clarify the responsibility for the rules and procedures of the state courts. It made possible uniformity of rules of procedure and evidence among the several districts, subject to amendment by a two-thirds vote of both houses of the Legislature. It also placed in the supreme court responsibility for governing the practice of law. There was no section on rules and procedures in the constitution dealing with these matters before the adoption of this section.

Until 1943 the Legislature held the authority over rulemaking but delegated the power to make procedural rules to the supreme court; it retained, however, the power to supersede these rules. From 1951 until the 1984 revision, the court's rulemaking responsibilities were expanded to include evidentiary rules; this power was given constitutional status in the 1984 revision—but not before the Legislature added the legislative veto. This creates, in effect, a check on the court's rulemaking power, and the line between substantive and procedural rules (or between matters appropriate for statutory treatment and others better left to court rulemaking) is not always clear.[39]

The power of the Utah Supreme Court to govern the practice of law has been held to include control over the procedures used to discipline State Bar members.

---

[39] Lisa Watts Baskin, "The Judicial Rules Review Committee," *Voir Dire* 1 (Winter 1996): 30–31; Kent R. Hart, "Court Rulemaking in Utah Following the 1985 Revision of the Utah Constitution," *Utah Law Review* 1992 (No. 1): 168–74.

This includes the power to strike unfair and inappropriate language from the State Bar rules (*In re Crandall,* 1989). It also includes the power to discipline attorneys (*In re McCune,* 1986).

The supreme court is constitutionally obligated to review the Judicial Conduct Commission's proceedings, but it has no authority to undertake initial review of matters related to compliance with the judicial canons of ethics.

SECTION 5

Jurisdiction of district court and other courts—Right of appeal. The district court shall have original jurisdiction in all matters except as limited by this constitution or by statute, and power to issue all extraordinary writs. The district court shall have appellate jurisdiction as provided by statute. The jurisdiction of all other courts, both original and appellate, shall be provided by statute. Except for matters filed originally with the Supreme Court, there shall be in all cases an appeal of right from the court of original jurisdiction to a court with appellate jurisdiction over the cause.

This section, written in the 1984 revision, designates state courts as courts of original and appellate jurisdiction, as provided by statute. It also provides that, except for matters filed originally with the Utah Supreme Court, there shall be in all cases an appeal of right to a court with appellate jurisdiction. This section permits the Legislature to make changes in the appeals process as the court system and the case loads change. It eliminated specific provisions formerly found in sections 7, 8, and 9, such as listing specific writs the district courts could issue. It also eliminated the district courts' "general control" over inferior courts and tribunals within their respective jurisdictions, which now is vested in the supreme court, through adoption of rules to be used in the courts (sec. 4), and the Judicial Council (sec. 12).

The meaning of "original jurisdiction" of the district courts was defined in a 1941 case as *not* meaning that there is a right for a case to be tried there unless specifically prohibited by law (*State v. Johnson,* 1941). The original section, unchanged until the 1984 revision, specified original jurisdiction of the district courts "in all matters civil and criminal, not excepted in this Constitution, and not prohibited by law." Since the original constitution was written, juvenile and circuit courts were added to the system, and their jurisdiction was provided by statute.

The right of appeal is preserved, but the Legislature designates the court to which a party in a lower court may appeal. The Court of Appeals now hears many cases which had a right of appeal to the supreme court until 1985. It currently hears appeals from district and juvenile courts, reviews appeals in criminal cases not involving first-degree or capital felonies, and other cases defined in statutes (U.C.A. 78-2a-3).

The Utah Supreme Court reviews judgments of lower courts involving federal or state constitutional questions, cases involving first-degree or capital felonies, and other cases over which the Court of Appeals does not have appellate jurisdiction. It also hears appeals of formal adjudication proceedings which originate with the Public Service Commission; the State Tax Commission; the Board of Forestry, Fires, and State Lands; the Board of Oil, Gas, and Mining; the School and Institutional Trust Lands Board of Trustees; and the State Engineer. It also reviews actions reviewed by the director of the Department of Natural Resources. The supreme court has discretion in granting or denying a petition of certiorari for review of a Court of Appeals decision. It may transfer to the Court of Appeals any case over which it has jurisdiction, except those matters specifically reserved by statute to the supreme court. This system has provided significant help to the Utah Supreme Court, which had a large backlog of cases before the Court of Appeals started functioning in 1987.

In cases at law appealed to the Utah Supreme Court, the review is limited to questions of law, and a jury verdict on a question of fact which is supported by any competent evidence will not be disturbed (*Rees v. Intermountain Health Care, Inc.*, 1991). In equity cases, the supreme court reviews the evidence but will upset the finding of a trial court only if the evidence clearly preponderates against the lower court's findings (*Dugan v. Jones*, 1986), or the court finds that the trial court has misapplied the law, or abused its discretion, so that an injustice has resulted (*Watson v. Watson*, 1992; *Sinclair v. Sinclair*, 1986).[40]

SECTION 6

Number of judges of district court and other courts—Divisions. The number of judges of the district court and of other courts of record established by the Legislature shall be provided by statute. No change in the number of judges shall have the effect of removing a judge from office during a judge's term of office. Geographic divisions for all courts of record except the Supreme Court may be provided by statute. No change in divisions shall have the effect of removing a judge from office during a judge's term of office.

This provision gives the Legislature the power to determine the number of judges and the geographic divisions of courts of record (except the supreme court). The original 1896 Constitution specified the boundaries of seven district courts "until otherwise provided by law." In 1944 voters approved an amendment specifically giving the Legislature the power to change the limits of any judicial district and to increase or decrease the number of districts, or the number

---

[40] Standards of review are explained in Norman H. Jackson, "Utah Standards of Appellate Review," *Utah Bar Journal* 7 (October 1994): 9–37.

of judges in each district, although no alteration or increase should have the effect of removing a judge from office. The 1984 revision had essentially the same provisions, except that it specifically exempts the supreme court from being subdivided. The state now has eight judicial districts served by consolidated district courts.

Former section 5 provided for seven judicial districts, with from one to three judges, each chosen by qualified electors for four-year terms. District judges were required to sit at the county seat of each county in their district at least four times a year.

SECTION 7

Qualifications of justices and judges. Supreme Court justices shall be at least 30 years old, United States citizens, Utah residents for five years preceding selection, and admitted to practice law in Utah. Judges of other courts of record shall be at least 25 years old, United States citizens, Utah residents for three years preceding selection, and admitted to practice law in Utah. If geographic divisions are provided for any court, judges of that court shall reside in the geographic division for which they are selected.

This section contains the age and residency requirements for judicial offices—thirty years of age and five years' residency for supreme court justices, and twenty-five years of age and three years' residency for judges of other courts of record. The qualifications for the judiciary after a 1944 amendment were found in sections 2 and 5; they had virtually the same requirements as this new section in the 1984 revision, except that they required active membership in the bar. The previous sections 2 and 5 also contained provisions for judges pro tempore and for holding district court sessions at least four times a year in each county.

SECTION 8

Vacancies—Nominating commissions—Senate approval.
(1) When a vacancy occurs in a court of record, the governor shall fill the vacancy by appointment from a list of at least three nominees certified to the governor by the Judicial Nominating Commission having authority over the vacancy. The governor shall fill the vacancy within 30 days after receiving the list of nominees. If the governor fails to fill the vacancy within the time prescribed, the chief justice of the Supreme Court shall within 20 days make the appointment from the list of nominees.
(2) The Legislature by statute shall provide for the nominating commissions' composition and procedures. No member of the Legislature may serve as a member of, nor may the Legislature appoint members to, any Judicial Nominating Commission.
(3) The Senate shall consider and render a decision on each judicial appointment within 60 days of the date of appointment. If necessary, the Senate shall convene itself

in extraordinary session for the purpose of considering judicial appointments. The appointment shall be effective upon approval of a majority of all members of the Senate. If the Senate fails to approve the appointment, the office shall be considered vacant and a new nominating process shall commence.
(4) Selection of judges shall be based solely upon consideration of fitness for office without regard to any partisan political considerations.

This section provides for appointment of justices and judges of courts of record by the governor after screening by a nominating commission and for confirmation by the state Senate. The nonpartisan nominating commissions are established by statute (U.C.A. 20A-12-102 through 105). This section was added to the article in the 1984 revision to give constitutional status to the bipartisan nominating process and to eliminate the Legislature's role in selection of nominating commission members. It provided a legislative voice in the process, however, by requiring Senate confirmation of the governor's appointees. An amendment approved in 1992 increased the time for the Senate to consider and render a decision on the governor's judicial nominees from thirty to sixty days.

The last part of the section, which requires selection "based solely upon consideration of fitness for office without regard for any partisan political considerations" was part of section 3 in the pre-1984 article. It was added in a 1944 amendment which attempted to emphasize judicial competence and remove partisanship from judicial elections. Not until 1952, however, did judges run in elections on a nonpartisan basis, and not until the 1984 revision did the nominating commission gain constitutional status.

The Legislature has established regional nominating commissions for district court vacancies (U.C.A. 20A-12–103). The governor appoints seven commissioners, including two from a list of ten nominees provided by the Utah State Bar; the chief justice serves as an ex officio, nonvoting member. No member of the Legislature may serve on a nominating commission; not more than four commissioners may be lawyers; and not more than four may be from the same political party. There is a separate but similar nominating commission for vacancies on the Utah Supreme Court and the Court of Appeals (U.C.A. 20A-12-102).

SECTION 9

Judicial retention elections. Each appointee to a court of record shall be subject to an unopposed retention election at the first general election held more than three years after appointment. Following initial voter approval, each Supreme Court justice every tenth year, and each judge of other courts of record every sixth year, shall be subject to an unopposed retention election at the corresponding general election. Judicial retention elections shall be held on a nonpartisan ballot in a manner provided by statute. If geographic divisions are provided for any court of record, the judges of those courts shall stand for retention election only in the geographic division to which they are selected.

This section, added in the 1984 revision of the article, provides constitutional status for unopposed retention elections for justices and judges. It was vigorously opposed by some critics, who saw this system as undemocratic and unfair. To answer charges that this would ensure virtually lifetime tenure without accountability, the Judicial Conduct Commission was established in this article (sec. 13). In addition, the judges' performance ratings, which are determined by polling lawyers, are printed in the Voter Information Pamphlet, and the Judicial Council will not certify a judge for a retention election if she or he does not have an approval rating above 70 percent. Recent criticism that this process is not specific enough has resulted in continuing efforts to get more information to the public by the press. For the 1996 election, the *Salt Lake Tribune* published its own scorecard on the judges, based on interviews with about a third of the state's practicing attorneys, rating judges from poor to excellent in each of six categories.[41]

SECTION 10

Restrictions on justices and judges. Supreme court justices, district court judges, and judges of all other courts of record while holding office may not practice law, hold any elective nonjudicial public office, or hold office in a political party.

This provision, which prohibits justices and judges of courts of record from practicing law or holding a public or political party office, was added in the 1984 revision to avoid conflicts of interest (or the appearance of such conflicts) for judges. The supreme court held in 1990 that offices in the Utah State Bar were not "elective nonjudicial public offices" within the meaning of this section (*In re Greenwood*).

SECTION 11

Judges of courts not of record. Judges of courts not of record shall be selected in a manner, for a term, and with qualifications provided by statute. However, no qualification may be imposed which requires judges of courts not of record to be admitted to practice law. The number of judges of courts not of record shall be provided by statute.

---

[41] Results published in *Salt Lake Tribune,* 20 October 1996.

This section provides for the qualification of judges of courts not of record (the justice courts) to be provided by statute, and it prohibits the Legislature from limiting these positions to persons admitted to the State Bar. These courts are established either by a county or by a city, although they are subject to regulation by the supreme court and the Judicial Council (U.C.A. 78-5-101 through 106). Most of the judges of the justice courts are not law-trained, and they were concerned about making legal training a requirement for these positions. Their concerns prompted the addition of this provision in the 1984 revision. Current requirements for justice court judges are United States citizenship, the age of twenty-five, a high school education, and demonstrated "maturity of judgment" (U.C.A. 78-5-137(3) and (4).

SECTION 12

Judicial Council—Chief justice as administrative officer—Legal counsel.

(1) There is created a Judicial Council which shall adopt rules for the administration of the courts of the state.

(2) The Judicial Council shall consist of the chief justice of the Supreme Court, as presiding officer, and other justices, judges, and other persons as provided by statute. There shall be at least one representative on the Judicial Council from each court established by the constitution or by statute.

(3) The chief justice of the Supreme Court shall be the chief administrative officer for the courts and shall implement the rules adopted by the Judicial Council.

(4) The Judicial Council may appoint legal counsel which shall provide all legal services for the Judicial Department unless otherwise provided by statute.

This section provides for the Judicial Council, which was created by the Legislature in 1973 to unify the policies and procedures of the trial courts of the state and to better provide for the needs of each court. It also provides for the membership of the council, designates the chief justice as the chief administrative officer for the courts, and authorizes appointment of legal counsel for the Judicial Department. The revised Judicial article in 1985 made the Judicial Council a constitutional body, responsible for adopting uniform rules for the administration of all the courts in the state. A previous constitutional provision had given the district courts "general control" over inferior courts and tribunals within their jurisdictions, an arrangement which provided no assurance of uniformity within the system.

In addition to the management of the judiciary, the Council also has the responsibility to set standards for judicial performance, court facilities, support services, and judicial and nonjudicial staff positions. The chief justice of the supreme court chairs the Council as chief administrative officer of the Judicial Department. The other members currently include a supreme court justice, a judge of the Court of Appeals, five district court judges, two juvenile court judges, three justice court judges, a representative of the Utah State Bar, and the state court administrator (U.C.A. 78-3-21(1).

The Council holds monthly meetings at the Administrative Office of the Courts in Salt Lake City, which gives other agencies and citizens an opportunity to present issues and concerns directly to the judiciary.

The Court Administrator Act, passed in 1973 and revised in 1986, provides for the appointment of a state court administrator. The administrator is assisted by deputy administrators, an appellate court administrator, trial court administrators and executives, as well as staff members in the Administrative Office of the Courts who deal with personnel management, research, information services, judicial education, and other matters needed to keep the court system functioning efficiently (U.C.A. 78-3-23 through 27). The Administrative Office of the Courts serves as staff to the Judicial Council and other boards and committees in the judicial system. There was no constitutional provision for an administrative body for the courts until the 1984 revision. There was no provision for legal counsel for the Judicial Department until this was added to the constitution in 1992, the same year the governor received constitutional authority to appoint legal counsel. The Legislature had been given constitutional authority to appoint its own legal counsel in 1972.

SECTION 13

Judicial Conduct Commission. A Judicial Conduct Commission is established which shall investigate and conduct confidential hearings regarding complaints against any justice or judge. Following its investigations and hearings, the Judicial Conduct Commission may order the reprimand, censure, suspension, removal, or involuntary retirement of any justice or judge for the following:

(1) action which constitutes willful misconduct in office;

(2) final conviction of a crime punishable as a felony under state or federal law;

(3) willful and persistent failure to perform judicial duties;

(4) disability that seriously interferes with the performance of judicial duties; or

(5) conduct prejudicial to the administration of justice which brings a judicial office into disrepute.

Prior to the implementation of any commission order, the Supreme Court shall review the commission's proceedings as to both law and fact. The court may also permit the introduction of additional evidence. After its review, the Supreme Court shall, as it finds just and proper, issue its order implementing, rejecting, or modifying the commission's order. The Legislature by statute shall provide for the composition and procedures of the Judicial Conduct Commission.

This section created the Judicial Conduct Commission to hear complaints against justices or judges for misconduct in office, failure to perform judicial duties, disability, or conduct prejudicial to the administration of justice. To provide for judicial accountability within the system, the Commission was established by the Legislature in 1977 and was given constitutional status in the 1984 revision. Until then, the constitution provided for removal of judges by conviction after impeachment (Art. VI, sec. 19) or by a concurrent vote of both houses of the Legislature (former Art. VIII, sec. 11). An affirmative vote of two-thirds of the membership of each house was required, and the vote, along with the "cause or causes" of removal would be entered in the journal of each house. No Utah judge has been impeached or removed by the Legislature.

The Judicial Conduct Commission has ten members. Two members are appointed by the speaker of the House of Representatives, two by the president of the Senate, two persons not members of the bar appointed by the governor, three members from the Board of Commissioners of the bar appointed by the Board, and one judge of a trial court of record selected by the Judicial Conduct Commission. After receiving a complaint and conducting an initial investigation, the Commission may issue a private reprimand or file a formal complaint to be reviewed en banc or by a three-judge panel. After a hearing, the Commission may recommend removal, suspension, involuntary retirement, or reprimand—subject to review by the Utah Supreme Court (U.C.A. 78-7-27(1). All proceedings are confidential until they reach the supreme court.

The Judicial Conduct Commission's tenure has not been without controversy. Complaints about judges have increased dramatically during the last decade, making it difficult for the Commission to deal with them swiftly. The confidentiality of cases until they come before the Utah Supreme Court creates an atmosphere of secrecy and sparks criticism that complaints enter a "black hole" after being filed with the Commission.[42] The secrecy curtain parted a bit when the supreme court refused in 1996 to close hearings to consider public sanctions against two justice court judges. Over the protests of the two judges, the court refused to close their hearings, a move applauded by local news media.

Increased staff and funding were provided by the Legislature in 1995 to meet the increased demand. The confidentiality requirement, designed to protect judges from unfounded complaints, probably will continue to leave the public with the impression that the judiciary is slow to deal with its own problems. By 1996 only one judge had been publicly reprimanded since the Commission was founded.

---

[42] Denise Dragoo, "The Judicial Conduct Commission Comes of Age," *Utah Bar Journal* 7 (August-September 1995): 8.

SECTION 14

Compensation of justices and judges. The Legislature shall provide for the compensation of all justices and judges. The salaries of justices and judges shall not be diminished during their terms of office.

The original state constitution had a similar provision, but it provided that judges' salaries should not be "increased or diminished during the time for which they are elected." It also had another section which set salaries of supreme court and district court judges at $3,000 per annum ($1,000 more than the governor) and mileage, "payable quarterly out of the State treasury" until otherwise provided by law. An argument in the constitutional convention over whether judges should pay mileage costs out of their salaries was settled when the unfairness of the proposal to judges in geographically large districts with widely scattered venues was explained to delegates at the convention. The Judicial article was shaped by the convention's lawyer-delegates, who argued that higher salaries were necessary to attract the best lawyers to the bench.[43] Some of these delegates later served as judges after statehood.

In 1946 this section (then section 12) was amended to eliminate the words "or increased." This permitted salaries to be raised beyond the $3,000 yearly which was still specified in the constitution. In 1984, the two sections on judges' compensation were repealed and rewritten as the current brief provision. The Judicial Council has a citizen advisory committee that makes periodic studies and recommendations on judicial salaries to the Executive and Judicial Compensation Commission. After consideration of these findings, judicial salaries are set by the Legislature in the annual budget.

SECTION 15

Mandatory retirement. The Legislature may provide standards for the mandatory retirement of justices and judges from office.

In 1968 a new section in the Judicial article provided that the Legislature "may provide uniform standards for mandatory retirement and for removal of judges from office" (former section 28). Any legislation implementing the section was to be applicable only to conduct occurring subsequent to the effective date of such legislation, and any determination requiring the retirement or removal of a judge from office was subject to review by the Utah Supreme Court.

Subsequently, the Legislature passed a law providing mandatory retirement ages of seventy for judges and seventy-two for justices of the supreme court.

[43] *Proceedings of the Convention,* 2: 1375–87.

When a judge who was reelected at the age of seventy-four challenged the statute, the supreme court upheld the law and ruled that the judge was not entitled to assume office (*Nelson v. Miller*, 1971).

In the 1984 revision, the 1968 provision on retirement and removal from office was repealed. Section 13 on the Judicial Conduct Commission and section 15 on mandatory retirement were written to cover removal from office. In 1996 a new retirement law was passed by the Legislature. It specifies mandatory retirement at age seventy-five, except for judges currently serving; they may complete their terms (U.C.A. 49-6-801).

SECTION 16

Public prosecutors. The Legislature shall provide for a system of public prosecutors who shall have primary responsibility for the prosecution of criminal actions brought in the name of the State of Utah and shall perform such other duties as may be provided by statute. Public prosecutors shall be elected in a manner provided by statute, and shall be admitted to practice law in Utah. If a public prosecutor fails or refuses to prosecute, the Supreme Court shall have power to appoint a prosecutor pro tempore.

This section permits counties to provide for the election of a public prosecutor to prosecute criminal actions within the county. There was no comparable provision in the Judicial article prior to 1984. Before then, the elected county attorneys served as prosecutors in criminal cases, along with their responsibility for civil matters and advisory role to county officials. After the adoption of this amendment, the Legislature authorized county governing bodies to create countywide state prosecution districts (U.C.A. 17-18-1.9). The statute also permitted two or more counties to create and maintain a state prosecution district by interlocal agreement, sharing the services of a district prosecutor. Only Salt Lake County has created a prosecution district and provided for an elected district attorney to prosecute criminal cases.

SECTION 17 THROUGH 27

Repealed.

SECTION 28

Repealed in part and transferred.

Article IX

Congressional and Legislative Apportionment

This article was generated in the 1895 constitutional convention by a committee dominated by the rural counties. The result was similar to that in other western states where scattered populations far from the seat of government demanded that their voices be heard in the Legislature. The struggle over this article involved several arguments—using the federal analogy of the counties' status in relation to the state, the need of legislators to have a compact geographic area to cover, and the example of other states that had used geographic factors to guarantee representation to sparsely populated, rural counties.[44] The result was that the more heavily populated urban counties capitulated; each county was guaranteed at least one representative, and the original House and Senate district boundaries were written "until otherwise provided by law" into the constitution. Although the original article (in section 2) called for revision and adjustment of the apportionment for senators and representatives following each federal census "according to ratios to be fixed by law," legislators found this too difficult to do. Rural-county legislators clung to the power they had been granted in the Constitution and ignored its mandate for periodic changes. Between 1896 and 1921 several bills proposing reapportionment failed to gain approval. A 1921 apportionment act increased the number of senators to twenty and the number of representatives to fifty-five. Another increase in membership was made in a

[44] Arguments during debate on this article are in *Proceedings of the Convention,* 2: 831–55.

1931 apportionment act to lessen the pain of drawing boundaries that might cost members their seats.

Several attempts at reapportionment between 1931 and 1954 were unsuccessful. In 1954, voters in the urban "Wasatch Front" counties defeated a proposed constitutional amendment that would have provided at least one senator for each county and would have made the rural-urban division of seats even less favorable to the urban counties. Following this defeat, the Legislature passed a reapportionment act that kept the provision for at least one House seat per county but apportioned the Senate by population. This act was upheld by the Utah Supreme Court in *Parkinson v. Watson* (1955), perpetuating a malapportioned Legislature.

Finally, a federal court forced the Legislature to act. In *Baker v. Carr* in 1962 the U.S. Supreme Court had brought the issue of reapportionment into its jurisdiction. It established the standard of essential equality of voters under the U.S. Constitution in *Gray v. Sanders* (1963). In *Wesberry v. Sanders* (1964) the Court struck down population disparities in congressional districts under the equal protection clause of the Fourteenth Amendment, and in *Reynolds v. Sims* (1964) the Court mandated that both houses of a state Legislature have equal population districts. The Court's rejection of a combination of both population-and geographic-based districts for Colorado's Legislature in *Lucas v. Forty-Fourth General Assembly of the State of Colorado* (1964)—a plan which had been approved by a referendum—emphasized its determination not to compromise on this issue and gave Utah's apportionment article and its new statute no hope for survival.

When Utah's newly enacted law landed before a three-judge federal district court in 1963, the Utah court was faced with large disparities in representation. One senator represented 55,000 inhabitants and another just 10,000; a mere 25.3 percent of the state's population could elect a majority of the state Senate.[45] The 1963 law was struck down, along with the constitution's requirement of one representative for each county, in *Petuskey v. Clyde* (1964). Utah's Reapportionment Act of 1965 was upheld by the same three-judge court in *Petuskey v. Rampton* (1965). Since then, the Legislature has reapportioned congressional and legislative districts following each federal census, using computer-generated data provided by the Office of Legislative Research and General Counsel, according to the current Utah statute (U.C.A. 36-1-1 et seq.).

SECTION 1

Apportionment. At the session next following an enumeration made by the authority of the United States, the Legislature shall divide the state into congressional, legislative, and other districts accordingly.

---

[45] Cited in *Petuskey v. Clyde,* 234 F.Supp. 960 (1964), at 969.

This section provides for the Legislature to establish districts for election of members of the U.S. Congress and members of the Legislature. The original section 1 referred only to the election of a representative at large to the Congress. Apportionment of the Legislature originally was addressed in section 2; it called for apportionment of Senate and House districts according to ratios to be fixed by law. When this article was revised in 1988, section 2 was repealed, and apportionment for both congressional and legislative districts was addressed in the current section 1.

At the time of statehood, Utah was entitled to only one representative to the U.S. Congress, but section 1 provided that "when a new apportionment shall be made by Congress, the Legislature shall divide the State into congressional districts accordingly." Not until 1910 did the U.S. Census show the population growth that entitled Utah to a second representative, and not until after the 1980 census did the representation increase to three. This provision mandating the Legislature to divide the state into districts did not translate into a mandate for equal population in the districts, however. Substantial equality of population was not achieved until after the U.S. Supreme Court cases in the 1960s and 1970s, notably *Wesberry v. Sanders* and *Reynolds v. Sims* in 1964. The constitution was not changed at that time, but the Legislature reapportioned representation to follow federal court guidelines.

SECTION 2

Number of members of Legislature. The Senate shall consist of a membership not to exceed twenty-nine in number, and the number of representatives shall never be less than twice nor greater than three times the number of senators.

The original section 2 provided for a state census every ten years, beginning in 1905 (which was not done), and for the reapportionment of the state Senate and House of Representatives after every federal census (which also was not done). The original section 2 was repealed in the 1988 revision, and the requirement for legislative redistricting was moved into section 1. An amended section 3 was then renumbered as section 2.

The former section 3 stipulated a Senate of eighteen members and a House of forty-five members. In the 1988 revision, this was changed to provide for a limit of twenty-nine Senate members and a House membership that could number from twice to three times the number of senators. Part of the former section 3 had been held unconstitutional in *Petuskey v. Clyde* in 1964.

The current Legislature has a Senate membership of twenty-nine, established in U.C.A. 36-1-1(3), and the House has seventy-five members, specified in U.C.A. 36-1-4(3).

SECTION 3

Repealed and transferred.

SECTION 4

Repealed.

This article was repealed in the 1988 revision. It had contained provisions for senatorial districts that were held unconstitutional in *Petuskey v. Clyde* in 1964. The part of this section that listed the counties making up each Senate and House district was also repealed.

Article X

Education

Utah's Education article reflects some of the tensions and religious conflicts of the state's territorial past, as well as the struggles in its first century of statehood to provide adequate schools for a burgeoning school population. During the territorial period, Utah's "common" schools were poorly financed, often held in Mormon church buildings, and marked by a curriculum liberally sprinkled with Mormon religious doctrine. Few had any tax revenues to provide financial stability; most depended on tuition paid by parents.[46] Despite the pleas for school appropriations by territorial governors (all non-Mormons who had come from outside the territory after 1857) the Legislative Assembly refused to change the system of decentralized, locally controlled schools. Failure of the federal government to keep its promise to provide land sections for support of the schools also contributed to the chronic lack of funds.[47] Brigham Young's frequently voiced opposition to territorial financing—and the secularization of schools that he feared would follow—dictated the course of education in Utah until his death in 1877.[48]

---

[46] Stanley S. Ivins, "Free Schools Come to Utah," *Utah Historical Quarterly* 22 (October 1954): 329, 331; John Clifton Moffitt, *The History of Public Education in Utah* (Provo, Utah: Author, 1946), 121.

[47] Frederick S. Buchanan, *Culture, Class and Accommodation: Public Schooling in Salt Lake City, 1890–1994* (Salt Lake City: Smith Research Associates/Signature Books, 1996), 11.

[48] Ibid., 331, 335, 336.

Meanwhile, Catholic and Protestant schools had been gaining a foothold in the Territory. These schools, established to serve a growing non-Mormon population and to attract and "Christianize" Mormon children, provided competition with better-trained teachers that attracted some Mormon children to their classrooms. Although this contributed to the religious tensions that divided Mormon and non-Mormon Utahns, it increased the pressures for a more adequate educational structure for the Territory.[49] Finally, in 1890, the act providing territorial support for free schools through the elementary grades (Laws of the Territory of Utah, Ch. 8, sec. 1) was passed.

In 1895, the Territory was also supporting the University of Utah, which had been founded as the University of Deseret in 1850 but was virtually dormant for lack of funding from 1852 through 1869, and the Utah State Agricultural College (now Utah State University), a land-grant college founded in 1888. When the constitution was framed, the Territory was in an economic depression triggered by the Panic of 1893, and the major concern in debates on the Education article was with financing the schools. Some delegates envisioned a high-quality school system that would attract students from throughout the nation.[50] More practical delegates pointed out that the territorial school fund could not assure even a minimum school year for elementary grades in all the counties, and only two cities had been able to afford high schools; trying to create a Harvard in the West was "an iridescent dream."[51] Keen competition among several Utah cities for state institutions fueled heated controversies over the location of the schools for the deaf and blind, as well as the unification of the university and the agricultural college. Uniting the college and university clearly could save money, but the bitterness of the fight over location of a combined institution doomed this sensible proposal. Neither the Salt Lake City delegates (where the university was located) nor the Cache County delegates (the college was in the county seat at Logan) would give up, and the location of each finally was written into the constitution.

Considering the contentions of the past over schools, and the territorial polarization along religious lines, the Education article that emerged from the convention was remarkable for its emphasis on the essentials required in the Enabling Act: an open, nonsectarian public school system, provision for a permanent State School Fund, a ban against religious or partisan tests for teachers or students in the public schools, and a prohibition of public funding for any academic institution "controlled in whole, or in part by any church, sect or denomination whatever" (now reworded in sec. 8).

Since statehood, there have been many amendments to the original Education article and to sections of the Revenue and Taxation article (Art. XIII) pertaining

---

[49] Charles S. Peterson, "A New Community: Mormon Teachers and the Separation of Church and State in Utah's Territorial Schools," *Utah Historical Quarterly* 48 (Summer 1980): 311.

[50] Delegate Charles C. Goodwin, *Proceedings of the Convention,* 2: 1253–54.

[51] Delegate Brigham H. Roberts, ibid., 2: 1364.

to school financing. These amendments have changed the structure, funding, and governance of the education system and have provided for increasing state support and equalization of funding throughout the state. Extensive changes were made in a revision approved in 1986 and others in a revision approved in 1996. They will be discussed in the commentary on each section.

SECTION 1

Free nonsectarian schools. The Legislature shall provide for the establishment and maintenance of the State's education systems including: (a) a public education system, which shall be open to all children of the state; and (b) a higher education system. Both systems shall be free from sectarian control.

This section currently describes two education systems to be established by the Legislature, both free from sectarian control. The Enabling Act for Utah statehood required the establishment of nonsectarian public schools, which was mandated in this section, as it originally read: "The Legislature shall provide for the establishment and maintenance of a uniform system of public schools, which shall be open to all the children of the State, and be free from sectarian control." The term "public schools" did not differentiate between the college-level schools and the elementary and secondary schools. Section 8 of the original constitution vested control of this system in the State Board of Education. The University of Utah and Utah State Agricultural College were given constitutional status in section 4, and over the years the two schools established de facto independence from control by the State Board of Education.

As more state colleges were created or acquired from the Mormon church between 1896 and 1957, each with its own financial needs, the issue of coordination and control of all the higher education institutions moved onto the legislative agenda. In 1957 the Legislature established a Coordinating Council of Higher Education to coordinate budgeting and exercise some control over programs and curricula at the various institutions. Since the institutions of higher education were rapidly expanding and competing individually for state funds, some legislators felt that a more powerful governing body for these institutions was needed. In 1969 the Legislature abolished the Coordinating Council and created by law—without changing the constitution—the Utah State Board of Higher Education to govern the nine institutions of the Utah System of Higher Education. The constitutionality of this arrangement soon was questioned, in view of the constitution's definition at that time of the "public school system" to include elementary and secondary schools, the college and university, and "such other schools as the Legislature may establish" (former Art. X, sec. 2). A "friendly" lawsuit by the State Board of Education (which at that time was designated in section 8 to "govern and control the public school system") to clarify the issue resulted in a decision by the Utah Supreme Court upholding the separation of "public" and "higher" education in the 1969 act (*State Board of Education v. State Board of Higher Education,* 1973). The constitutional ambiguity was removed when the Education article was extensively rewritten and the changes were approved by voters in 1986. The revision included the amendment of section 1 to establish the two separate educational systems. The provision for freedom from sectarian control was retained. Following this amendment, the next three sections of this article were amended to define the two education systems and their governance, and the code was revised; Title 53A now covers public education, and Title 53B pertains to higher education.

This section means that all children must have the opportunity to attend the grade or class of school for which they are suited by previous training or development. It does not mean, the Utah Supreme Court held in *Logan City School District v. Kowallis* (1938), that every school building is open to every school child in the state. Since schools are provided by the school district in which a student resides, students may not attend school in another district without the permission of the district they wish to attend.

SECTION 2

Defining the public education system and the higher education system—Fees in secondary schools allowed. The public education system shall include all public elementary and secondary schools and such other schools and programs as the Legislature may designate. The higher education system shall include all public universities and colleges and such other institutions and programs as the Legislature may designate. Public elementary and secondary schools shall be free, except the Legislature may authorize the imposition of fees in the secondary schools.

This section defines what shall constitute the public education system and the higher education system, designates which schools shall be free, and authorizes fees for secondary schools. This section originally defined a public school system to include all schools from kindergarten through high school, the agricultural college and university, and "such other schools as the Legislature may establish." The common schools (originally grades one through eight) were to be free; other schools were to be supported as provided by law. High schools were to be free in first-and second-class city school districts and in others as designated by the Legislature. The support of free high schools, however, would have to be provided by local taxation if the school district's share of the state school fund was inadequate to maintain all the free schools in the district. As other school districts began to establish high schools, voters in 1906 and 1910 approved amendments to this section to provide support for high schools from the Uniform School Fund (now defined in section 5). In the revision approved in 1986, this section was changed to provide an exception to free schools; imposition of fees in the secondary schools was authorized.

SECTION 3

State Board of Education. The general control and supervision of the public education system shall be vested in the State Board of Education. The membership of the board shall be established and elected as provided by statute. The State Board of Education shall appoint a State Superintendent of Public Instruction who shall be the executive officer of the board.

In a major revision of the Education article approved by voters in 1986, the provision for the State Board of Education and superintendent of public instruction, formerly found in section 8, was moved to section 3. The provisions of former section 3 on the Uniform School Fund and the State School Fund were moved to section 5.

In the original state constitution, the State Superintendent of Public Instruction was one of the elected officials of the Executive Department. This arrangement continued, despite many efforts to make the office appointive and "take it out of politics," until 1950, when voters approved an amendment providing for the appointment of the superintendent by the State Board of Education.

The State Board of Education has general control and supervision of the public school system but does not govern, manage, or operate school districts, institutions, and programs, except as authorized by statute. It may, however, adopt rules and policies in accordance with its responsibilities under the constitution and state laws and may "interrupt" disbursements of state aid to any district which fails to comply with rules adopted by the board (U.C.A. 534A-1-401 (1) and (2)). It is required to establish minimum standards for public schools, including certification of educators, school productivity, and cost effectiveness measures (U.C.A. 53A-1-402). The board consists of fifteen members elected from state school board districts and may include an appointed (nonvoting) student board member. A list of three of five candidates is selected by nominating committees for each district on a nonpartisan basis; the governor then selects two candidates for placement on the general election ballot. The state also has forty school districts with locally elected boards that operate the schools under the general direction of the Legislature and the State Board of Education.

SECTION 4

Control of higher education system by statute—Rights and immunities confirmed. The general control and supervision of the higher education system shall be provided for by statute. All rights, immunities, franchises, and endowments originally established or recognized by the constitution for any public university or college are confirmed.

After the long battle in the constitutional convention over combining the University of Utah and the Utah State Agricultural College (now Utah State University), the supporters of the two institutions had two provisions written into the original constitution. One section (then section 4) confirmed the location of each institution, along with the rights, immunities, franchises, and endowments they then possessed. Another section (then section 5) mandated that proceeds of the sale of lands reserved by the U.S. Congress in 1855 for the University of Deseret (now University of Utah) and lands granted for higher education in the Enabling Act of 1894 be preserved in permanent funds, the interest to be used for the support and maintenance of these institutions.

The issue of providing more centralized control of Utah's institutions of higher education—which by 1969 had grown from two universities to include seven more colleges and technical colleges—was addressed by the Legislature in that year by creating the Utah System of Higher Education. Not until nearly two decades later were the names of the two universities removed from the constitution and the Legislature empowered to provide for "general control and supervision" of the higher education system—which it had done in 1969. Since then, the system has been governed by a Board of Regents appointed by the governor, and each institution has a board of trustees to oversee its operations under the general policies of the Board of Regents.

The amended article approved in 1986 retained the original constitution's recognition of "rights, franchises, and endowments" of state universities and colleges. The rights and franchises assured to the two state universities were determined by the territorial laws in force at the time the constitution was adopted, the Utah Supreme Court held in *University of Utah v. Board of Examiners* (1956). In this case, the university sought a declaratory judgment defining these rights, and specifically asked that these rights and immunities be defined to prevent the Board of Examiners from interfering with the management and control of the property and affairs of the university by its Board of Regents. The district court held that the university was a constitutional corporation free from control of the Legislature, administrative bodies, commissions, agencies, and officers of the state. The Utah Supreme Court reversed this judgment, holding that the University of Utah was not an autonomous constitutional corporation free from legislative control but was subject to laws enacted relating to the university's purposes and government, and to financial and auditing controls.

SECTION 5

State School Fund and Uniform School Fund—Establishment and use—Debt guaranty.

(1) There is established a permanent State School Fund which shall consist of revenue from the following sources:

(a) proceeds from the sales of all lands granted by the United States to this state for the support of the public elementary and secondary schools;

(b) 5% of the net proceeds from the sales of United States public lands lying within this state;

(c) all revenues derived from non-renewable resources on state lands, other than sovereign lands and lands granted for other specific purposes;

(d) all revenues derived from the use of school trust lands;

(e) revenues appropriated by the Legislature; and

(f) other revenues and assets received by the fund under any other provision of law or by bequest or donation.

(2) The State School Fund principal shall be safely invested and held by the state in perpetuity. Only the interest received from investment of the State School Fund may be expended for the support of the public education system as defined in Article X, Section 2 of this constitution. The Legislature may make appropriations from school trust land revenues to provide funding necessary for the proper administration and management of those lands consistent with the state's fiduciary responsibilities towards the beneficiaries of the school land trust. Unexpended balances remaining from the appropriation at the end of each fiscal year shall be deposited in the State School Fund. A portion of the interest earnings of the State School Fund, in an amount equal to the total balance in the State School Fund at the close of each calendar year multiplied by the annual rate of inflation for the preceding year, as determined by the state treasurer, shall be retained in the State School Fund and added to the principal. The State School Fund shall be guaranteed by the state against loss or diversion.

(3) There is established a Uniform School Fund which shall consist of revenue from the following sources:

(a) interest from the State School Fund remaining after deduction of the amount retained in the State School Fund to protect the fund against losses due to inflation:

(b) revenues appropriated by the Legislature; and

(c) other revenues received by the fund under any other provision of law or by donation.

(4) The Uniform School Fund shall be maintained and used for the support of the state's public education system as defined in Article X, Section 2 of this constitution and apportioned as the Legislature shall provide.

(5) (a) The state may guarantee the debt of school districts created in accordance with Article XIV, Section 3, and may guarantee debt incurred to refund the school district debt. Any debt guaranty, the school district debt guaranteed thereby, or any borrowing of the state undertaken to facilitate the payment of the state's obligation under any debt guaranty shall not be included as a debt of the state for the purposes of the 1.5% limitation of Article XIV, Section 1.

(b) The Legislature may provide that reimbursement to the state shall be obtained from monies which otherwise would be used for the support of the educational programs of the school district which incurred the debt with respect to which a payment under the state's guaranty was made.

This section, much of which was part of section 3 in the original constitution, describes the two major school funds, their uses and sources of revenue, and it authorizes the state to guarantee the debt of school districts. The section has undergone many changes and additions. It has evolved, starting in 1900, into a comprehensive statement of the sources for public school finance, and it limits the use of revenue obtained by sale or lease of state and school trust lands. The section describes the revenue sources of the permanent State School Fund, which was created in the original constitution as a trust fund to build up an endowment for future school funding, and the Uniform School Fund, which was established in 1938 to finance the current operation of the public elementary and secondary schools. Since Utah's high birth rate has created the nation's highest ratio of school children to adult wage earners, and the state has a tradition of encouraging education, funding has always been a problem.[52] Supporters of education have disagreed over the dedication of certain revenues to the permanent State School Fund, but they have consistently fought for increasing state support of local school programs. Since the school districts provide about a fourth of the cost of their school programs through local property taxes, and property tax bases vary widely among the forty school districts, the poorer districts struggle to keep state support high and equalization provisions in place.

Subsection (1) describes sources of revenue for the State School Fund, most of which were provided in the original constitution. They included proceeds from the sale of lands granted by the United States for the support of elementary and secondary schools, 5 percent of the net proceeds of federal land sold in Utah, and revenues appropriated by the Legislature. Revenues from nonrenewable resources on state lands (such as oil, coal, and gas), which had been placed into the State School Fund, were appropriated by the Legislature for the Uniform School Fund for ongoing expenditures, an arrangement that was challenged in *Jensen v. Dinehart* in 1982. The Utah Supreme Court upheld the constitutionality of this practice, but in 1984 leaders concerned about future needs of the schools successfully sponsored an amendment to recapture these revenues for the permanent State School Fund.

In 1996 voters approved an amendment that added subsection (1) (f) providing for bequests or donations to the fund. Supporters hoped that future bequests could build up the fund, which was much smaller than similar funds in other western states.

[52] *State and Local Government in Utah* (Salt Lake City: Utah Foundation, 1992), 119.

Subsection (2) was modified by an amendment approved in 1994 which attempted to protect the permanent State School Fund from the ravages of inflation. It provided that a portion of the interest on this fund equal to the annual rate of inflation for the preceding year be retained in the State School Fund and added to the principal. The remainder of the interest was designated in subsection (3) (a) to be used in the Uniform School Fund for the operation of the public elementary and secondary schools as the Legislature shall provide.

Subsection (3) describes revenue sources for the Uniform School Fund, including a provision approved in 1994 for donations and other revenues, in addition to interest from the State School Fund and legislative appropriations.

In an effort to save interest costs for the state's school districts, a proposal that the state's high bond rating be used to guarantee the bonds of the districts was approved in 1996 as subsections (5)(a) and (b). This also required changes in Articles VI, XIII, and XIV.

SECTION 6

Separate control of city schools. Repealed.

This section, which was repealed in 1973, provided for separate school districts for cities of the first and second class.

SECTION 7

Proceeds of land grants constitute permanent funds. The proceeds from the sale of lands reserved by Acts of Congress for the establishment or benefit of the state's universities and colleges shall constitute permanent funds to be used for the purposes for which the funds were established. The funds' principal shall be safely invested and held by the state in perpetuity. Any income from the funds shall be used exclusively for the support and maintenance of the respective universities and colleges. The Legislature by statute may provide for necessary administrative costs. The funds shall be guaranteed by the state against loss or diversion.

This section formerly was section 5, which referred specifically to lands reserved for the benefit of the University of Utah and lands granted under the Enabling Act of 1894. Although these references were changed, the amendment approved by voters in 1986 still designates proceeds from sale of these lands to permanent funds and income from these funds to the support and maintenance of the state's universities and colleges. The Utah Supreme Court in 1953 held in *Conder v. University of Utah* that income from the federal land grants could be pledged to pay off a loan for construction of dormitories by the University of Utah, since buildings are a necessary part of a university, and their construction and repair are not excluded by the terms "support" and "maintenance."

SECTION 8

No religious or partisan tests in schools. No religious or partisan test or qualification shall be required as a condition of employment, admission, or attendance in the state's education systems.

The original state constitution, in section 12, banned religious or partisan tests for admission of teachers or students in state educational institutions. In the revision approved in 1986, the provision was moved to section 8. The text was changed to simplify it and broaden the protection to all employees, not just teachers.

SECTION 9

Public aid to church schools forbidden. Neither the state of Utah nor its political subdivisions may make any appropriation for the direct support of any school or educational institution controlled by any religious organization.

In the original state constitution this provision was section 13. It was included to emphasize the separation of church and state in education and to meet the Enabling Act's requirement for "public schools free from sectarian control." The same term was used in the final section of the Ordinance (Art. III). In the revision approved in 1986, this section was rewritten to simplify it and to make clear the concern with control by a religious organization. The word "direct" was added before support, which raises questions about possible future litigation to determine just what indirect support could be provided. Sponsors of the change argued that the original wording could prohibit contracts between the state and church schools that could benefit the state and pointed to federal court decisions that allow limited indirect aid to church schools. Opponents feared it would open the doors to pleas from church-owned schools for a share of scarce educational funding—as well as breach a carefully built barrier between church and state. The fact that the revision of this article was so extensive probably kept this issue from getting much public attention in the 1986 election. Since then, however, it has not been tested in the courts.

The original section 9 (repealed in the 1986 revision) prohibited the Legislature or the Board of Education from prescribing textbooks in the elementary and secondary schools. This created a potential loss of coordination between the State Board of Education's prescribed curriculum and related textbooks.

SECTION 10

Institutions for deaf, dumb, and blind. Property—Fund. Repealed.

This section was repealed in the 1986 revision. It provided for institutions which are now established by statute (U.C.A. 53A-25-101 and U.C.A. 53A-25-201). Repeal was considered appropriate because of increased use of community-based alternatives to these institutions.

SECTION 11

Metric system. Repealed.

This section, which required schools to teach the metric system, was in the original constitution but almost completely ignored during its entire history. It was repealed in the 1986 revision.

SECTIONS 12 AND 13

These sections, which banned religious or partisan tests in schools and public aid to religious schools, were reworded and renumbered as sections 8 and 9.

Article XI

Counties, Cities, and Towns

Utah has three general-purpose units of local government—counties, cities, and towns—as well as special districts and townships that have specific, limited functions. Utah's local government article contains only a part of the body of constitutional and statutory law that defines the structure and powers of the state's local governments. When the constitution was written in 1895, there were twenty-seven counties (now there are twenty-nine), organized under the Provisional State of Deseret or later under the Organic Act that created the Territory of Utah in 1850. There were also numerous cities, organized under either individual charters prior to 1888 or by general law after that time, and school districts scattered throughout the Territory.[53]

Most of the framers of Utah's Constitution were familiar with the operation and the needs of local governments, having served as mayors, council members, members of the county courts that governed counties, or in other city or county offices. As a consequence, they had firm opinions on the rights of local governments and the need to protect the independence and the assets of local units.

Several other articles contain important provisions that define the powers of local governments; they are described in the commentary on each pertinent section. The Legislative Department article (Art. VI) has several sections that

---

[53] Eugene E. Campbell, "Governmental Beginnings," in Richard D. Poll et al., eds, *Utah's History* (Provo, Utah: Brigham Young University Press, 1978), 163–64.

apply to local governments, including the initiative and referendum on local ordinances (sec. 1); the "general law" provision to prevent legislative meddling in local affairs (sec. 26); the "ripper clause" (sec. 28), preventing delegation to any special commission the power to supervise or interfere with any municipal functions; and a section preventing the lending of credit or subscription to stock or bonds in aid of a private enterprise by local governments (sec. 29).

Article XIII (Revenue and Taxation) has a profound effect on local governments, since the exemptions provided in section 2 affect their property tax revenue stream. Section 10 authorizes taxation of property owned by corporations and persons by local governments; statutes provide authority for other taxes, such as the sales tax. Section 5 prohibits the Legislature from imposing taxes for the purpose of any county, city, town, or other municipal corporation, but it permits political subdivisions to share their revenues with other political subdivisions. General obligation debts of cities and counties require a vote of their citizens. (See commentary on Article XIV, section 3.)

Special districts (except for school districts) did not gain constitutional status until approval in 1974 of a new section in the Public Debt article (Art. XIV, sec. 8), although many were created by statute before then. They provided a variety of services, including metropolitan water services, neighborhood redevelopment, and public transit. Now a rapidly growing part of local government, a dozen types of special districts meet a wide range of needs.[54] Special service districts are authorized in section 8 to levy taxes and bond (as provided by statute) for constructing and operating necessary facilities (sections 1(b) and (c)). Cities are protected from being included in any special district created by a county without their permission in section 8(3). Special district statutes are found in U.C.A. Title 17A. (See commentary on Article XIV, section 8.)

Until 1996, townships did not exist as political subdivisions of the state; the term was used to describe geographic areas surveyed by the federal government. In response to citizens of areas outside incorporated cities who wanted a voice in local planning and zoning, as well as protection against annexation to cities, the 1996 Legislature passed a law creating a new form of government within counties called townships. Created after an election of voters within a designated area, each township had a planning and zoning board to express the views of its citizens in regard to county land-use planning for the area. Because of some difficulties with the law, the Legislature repealed the original statute in 1997 and reconstituted the townships, with the power to make recommendations on planning and zoning to the county governing body (U.C.A. 17-27-200.5 et seq.).

Only five amendments to Article XI have been presented to voters. Three proposals were defeated: an amendment allowing the Legislature to change county

[54] For a listing of current types of districts see "Special Districts in Utah," Utah Constitutional Revision Commission Report, 20 June 1997; also *State and Local Government in Utah*, 253–57.

boundaries without a vote of the citizens in 1908, municipal home rule in 1920, and permission for metropolitan government in 1966. Two amendments have been approved: municipal home rule in 1932, and optional forms of county government in 1972.

SECTION 1

Existing counties, precincts, and school districts recognized. The several counties of the Territory of Utah, existing at the time of the adoption of this Constitution, are hereby recognized as legal subdivisions of this State, and the precincts, and school districts, now existing in said counties, as legal subdivisions thereof, and they shall so continue until changed by law in pursuance of this article.

This section provides for recognition of counties as legal subdivisions of the state, and for school districts and precincts as legal subdivisions of counties. It was in the original constitution and has not been changed. When the constitution was written there were twenty-seven counties; two were formed later from existing counties. Corporate powers of county governments are found in U.C.A. 17-11-1 et seq. Precincts are subdivisions of counties for voting or other purposes, not subdivisions of cities (even though county justice court precincts may be within cities), the Utah Supreme Court ruled in *Evans v. Christensen* 1978.

SECTION 2

Removal of county seats. No County Seat shall be removed unless two-thirds of the qualified electors of the county, voting on the proposition at a general election, shall vote in favor of such removal, and two-thirds of the votes cast on the proposition shall be required to re-locate a county seat. A proposition of removal shall not be submitted in the same county more than once in four years.

This section, unchanged from the original constitution, requires a vote of two-thirds of the registered voters of a county to remove a county seat from a city. It requires approval by two-thirds of those voting on a proposal to relocate a county seat to another municipality. This process is established in U.C.A. 17-11-1 and 2, which provides for a petition of removal signed by qualified voters equal in number to a majority of the votes cast at the preceding general election to be presented to the county legislative body (commission or council). An election on the question then requires a two-thirds vote for removal. The limit of such elections to once in four years was added to keep local competition for the county seat from undue disruption of county government.

SECTION 3

Changing county lines. No territory shall be stricken from any county unless a majority of the voters living in such territory, as well as of the county to which it is to be annexed, shall vote therefor, and then only under such conditions as may be prescribed by general law.

This section provides for annexation of one county to another or part of a county to another county. It was in the original constitution and has not been changed. When the constitutional convention considered this section, some delegates wanted to add a provision for sharing the debt of the county losing the territory. Others wanted to prescribe a minimum of 4,000 or 5,000 for the population of a new county or a minimum amount of property valuation.[55] They were outvoted by delegates who preferred a simpler section, leaving details to future Legislatures.

The statute covering annexation of one county by another (U.C.A. 17-2-1) provides that a majority of legal voters in the county that wishes to be annexed to a different county may petition the county they want to join. At a subsequent election, a majority of the voters in each county must approve the annexation. If residents in *part* of a county desire to join another county, they petition the governing bodies of both counties involved—the one in which they are located, and the county they wish to join—to call an election. A majority of voters in each county must approve the annexation (U.C.A. 17-2-6). An amendment to this statute in 1996 provided an exception to this process for citizens of a municipality that extends into an annexing county divided by a county line originally defined by a stream, river, or body of water. In this case, the annexation is approved if it gains a majority of those voting in just the area to be annexed (rather than the whole county), and also a majority of the votes in the county to which it will be annexed. The 1996 amendment was designed to make it easier for residents in a city that over time has grown across county lines to bring all the city's residents together in one county.

New counties may be created under U.C.A. 17-3-1 et seq. by a petition of one-fourth of the voters in an area designated for a new county, as well as one-fourth of the voters in the remaining area of a county. A majority of the qualified voters in each of these areas must approve, in an election, the creation of the new county. No new counties have been formed since Daggett County was created in 1917.

SECTION 4

Optional forms of county government—Precinct and township organizations. The Legislature shall by general law prescribe optional forms of county government

[55] *Proceedings of the Convention*, 1: 399.

and shall allow each county to select, subject to referendum in the manner provided by law, the prescribed optional form which best serves its needs, and by general laws shall provide for precinct and township organizations.

This section provides that the Legislature shall by general law prescribe optional forms of county government and for precinct and township organizations. It was changed in 1972 from the original section, which provided for establishment of a system of county government that was to be uniform throughout the state. The form prescribed for all counties prior to 1972 was the commission form, where legislative and executive functions are performed by a three-member commission elected at large from the entire county. Many students of local government felt that county government was sometimes unrepresentative (all three commissioners could be from one part of the county) and lacking in appropriate checks on legislative and executive actions. In 1972 voters approved a change to the present wording, and the Legislature responded with a process for either the county legislative body or 25 percent of the county's voters to propose by petition a change to one of three general county government plans (U.C.A. 17-35a-9 through 11) and one of four management arrangements (U.C.A. 17-35a-12). A specific plan must be proposed at an election, at which a majority vote is required to effect a change. Only two counties, Cache and Grand, have voted to change; both have adopted a community council form of government.

SECTION 5

Municipal corporations—To be created by general law—Right and manner of adopting charter for own government—Powers included. Corporations for municipal purposes shall not be created by special laws. The Legislature by general laws shall provide for the incorporation, organization and classification of cities and towns in proportion to population, which laws may be altered, amended or repealed. Any incorporated city or town may frame and adopt a charter for its own government in the following manner:

The legislative authority of the city may, by two-thirds vote of its members, and upon petition of qualified electors to the number of fifteen per cent of all votes cast at the next preceding election for the office of the mayor, shall forthwith provide by ordinance for the submission to the electors of the question: "Shall a commission be chosen to frame a charter?" The ordinance shall require that the question be submitted to the electors at the next regular municipal election. The ballot containing such question shall also contain the names of candidates for members of the proposed commission, but without party designation. Such candidates shall be nominated in the same manner as required by law for nomination of city officers. If a majority of the electors voting on the question of choosing a commission shall vote in the affirmative, then the fifteen candidates receiving a majority of the votes cast at such election, shall constitute the charter commission, and shall proceed to frame a charter.

Any charter so framed shall be submitted to the qualified electors of the city at an election to be held at a time to be determined by the charter commission, which shall be not less than sixty days subsequent to its completion and distribution among the electors and not more than one year from such date. Alternative provisions may also be submitted to be voted upon separately. The commission shall make provisions for the distribution of copies of the proposed charter and of any alternative provisions to the qualified electors of the city, not less than sixty days before the election at which it is voted upon. Such proposed charter and such alternative provisions as are approved by a majority of the electors voting thereon, shall become an organic law of such city at such time as may be fixed therein, and shall supersede any existing charter and all laws affecting the organization and government of such city which are now in conflict therewith. Within thirty days after its approval a copy of such charter as adopted, certified by the mayor and city recorder and authenticated by the seal of such city, shall be made in duplicate and deposited, one in the office of the secretary of State and the other in the office of the city recorder, and thereafter all courts shall take judicial notice of such charter.

Amendments to any such charter may be framed and submitted by a charter commission in the same manner as provided for making of charters, or may be proposed by the legislative authority of the city upon a two-thirds vote thereof, or by petition of qualified electors to a number equal to fifteen percent of the total votes cast for mayor on the next preceding election, and any such amendment may be submitted at the next regular municipal election, and having been approved by the majority of the electors voting thereon, shall become part of the charter at the time fixed in such amendment and shall be certified and filed as provided in case of charters.

Each city forming its charter under this section shall have, and is hereby granted, the authority to exercise all powers relating to municipal affairs, and to adopt and enforce within its limits, local police, sanitary and similar regulations not in conflict with the general law, and no enumeration of powers in this constitution or any law shall be deemed to limit or restrict the general grant of authority hereby conferred; but this grant of authority shall not include the power to regulate public utilities, not municipally owned, if any such regulation of public utilities is provided for by general law, nor be deemed to limit or restrict the power of the Legislature in matters relating to State affairs, to enact general laws applicable alike to all cities of the State.

The power to be conferred upon the cities by this section shall include the following:

(a) To levy, assess and collect taxes and borrow money, within the limits prescribed by general law, and to levy and collect special assessments for benefits conferred.

(b) To furnish all local public services, to purchase, hire, construct, own, maintain and operate, or lease, public utilities local in extent and use; to acquire by condemnation, or otherwise, within or without the corporate limits, property necessary for any such purposes, subject to restrictions imposed by general law for the protection of other communities; and to grant local public utility franchises and within its powers regulate the exercise thereof.

(c) To make local public improvements and to acquire by condemnation, or otherwise, property within its corporate limits necessary for such improvements; and also to acquire an excess over than [that] needed for any such improvement and to sell or lease such excess property with restrictions, in order to protect and preserve the improvement.

(d) To issue and sell bonds on the security of any such excess property, or of any public utility owned by the city, or of the revenues thereof, or both, including, in the case of public utility, a franchise stating the terms upon which, in case of foreclosure, the purchaser may operate such utility.

The first paragraph of this section, except for the last sentence, was in the original constitution. It provides that municipal corporations (cities and towns) shall be created and classified by general law. The last sentence introduces the provision for establishing a "home rule" charter for cities, an option added to the section in 1932. In the following paragraphs, the section describes the "home rule" process, including initiation of a charter proposal, framing a charter, submission of the charter document to the voters, the amending process, and the powers conferred on the cities by this section.

The pattern of creating city governments by general laws, rather than by special legislative charters, was well established by the latter part of the nineteenth century throughout most of the nation. Legislative charters for cities had been the pattern in Utah until 1888, when the Territory changed to the use of general laws for incorporating municipalities. During the constitutional convention some delegates felt that the larger cities should have their own charters, but this plan failed to convince a majority, and the delegates decided that general laws—with classification of cities according to population—would permit each city's needs to be met.[56]

This section gives charter cities the authority to exercise all powers relating to municipal affairs but does not exclude them from the operation of general laws applicable to all cities. Changes in the charter must be proposed by the legislative authority of the city by a two-thirds vote or by a petition signed by 15 percent of the city's qualified voters; a majority of the voters voting on the proposition at the next regular municipal election must approve them.

Part of this section following this sentence: "The power to be conferred upon the cities by this section shall include the following:" is somewhat ambiguous. The powers subsequently described appear to be those that are given to all cities, but they were put into the constitution as part of the amendment that permitted charter cities, and some legal experts on local government construe it as applying

[56] Ibid., 1: 401–3.

only to cities that operate under a home rule charter. Although this question has not been interpreted by the courts, it is clear that the powers described are those generally exercised by all cities.

Only three cities have adopted city charters since the charter cities amendment was approved in 1932, and two of the three have abandoned it. Making changes in the charters can be cumbersome, and the availability of optional plans since 1977 provided citizens with an easier way to change their form of government.

Until 1977 the forms of government prescribed by the Legislature were mandatory for all cities and towns, and only charter cities could deviate from them. The mandatory forms in the pre-1977 statute (U.C.A. 10-3-102 to 106) provided a commission form for first and second class cities, and a council with one member designated as mayor for third class cities and towns. An act providing optional forms of municipal government was passed in 1977 (U.C.A. 10-3-1202 through 1206), permitting cities to choose from council-mayor and council-manager plans—in addition to the forms previously required. Since then, several cities have changed to these forms.

Utah municipalities now have three possible designs for their governments: the original commission or council forms designated prior to 1977, one of the optional forms created by statute, or a form specified in a charter designed for a city.

Utah cities are classified according to population into four classes, the largest applying only to Salt Lake City and the smallest to municipalities of fewer than 800 residents (U.C.A. 10-2-301). The Utah Supreme Court held in 1988 in *City of West Jordan v. Utah State Retirement Board* (1988) that the classification of municipalities according to population is not a general ban on their classification on other grounds, but it establishes guidelines and limits on the Legislature's power by requiring that cities in each class be treated the same. The population classification only applies to laws that classify municipalities for the purpose of defining their powers and functions and directs that such laws must make distinctions between the powers of various municipalities on the basis of population only. In the same case, the court observed that the power granted by the constitution to chartered cities is no greater than the power the Legislature may confer on unchartered municipalities by general law; the powers of chartered cities, however, are directly conferred by the constitution and may not be controlled by the Legislature except as to matters reserved to the Legislature by the constitution.

Utah municipalities and counties have been given by the Legislature a general police power—the power to promote and protect the health, welfare, safety, and morals of their citizens. Cities, for example, were given the power by statute (U.C.A. 10-8-84) to pass laws "necessary and proper to provide for the safety and preserve the health, and promote the prosperity, improve the morals, peace and good order, comfort, and convenience of the city and its inhabitants."

Counties had a similar statute. Until 1980, these statutes generally were interpreted narrowly, upheld by the courts or struck down according to Dillon's Rule. This rule of statutory construction restricted local governments to powers *specifically* granted, necessarily inferred from powers granted, or *essential* to accomplishing the objectives of the government involved. In *State v. Hutchinson* (1980), the Utah Supreme Court upheld a Salt Lake County election ordinance by interpreting the general welfare statute (U.C.A. 17-5-77, now 17-5-263) as an independent, substantive source of regulatory power. The majority in *Hutchinson* declared Dillon's Rule "archaic, unrealistic, and unresponsive to the current needs of both state and local governments," arguing that this rule effectively nullified the legislative grant of general police power to the counties. The *Hutchinson* interpretation has not been overruled, but the Legislature can preempt local ordinances (such as a recent Salt Lake City gun-control ordinance), by mandating that local governments not pass ordinances more restrictive than a state statute. Some critics feel that the *Hutchinson* decision may have unintended consequences for the balancing of countervailing interests, by giving local government too much power and possibly neglecting minority interests.[57] The Legislature retains, however, the power to restrict the autonomy of local governments, except for the constitutional restraints noted above.

SECTION 6

Municipalities forbidden to sell waterworks or rights. No municipal corporation, shall directly or indirectly, lease, sell, alien or dispose of any waterworks, water rights, or sources of water supply now, or hereafter to be owned or controlled by it; but all such waterworks, water rights and sources of water supply now owned or hereafter to be acquired by any municipal corporation, shall be preserved, maintained and operated by it for supplying its inhabitants with water at reasonable charges: Provided, That nothing herein contained shall be construed to prevent any such municipal corporation from exchanging water-rights, or sources of water supply, for other water-rights or sources of water supply of equal value, and to be devoted in like manner to the public supply of its inhabitants.

This section, which is unchanged from the original constitution, forbids municipal corporations (cities and towns) from disposing of their water resources by any means, but it permits exchange of water rights or sources for others of equal value. It was passed by a unanimous vote of those present in the constitutional convention. The term "reasonable charges" generated some debate, since

---

[57] Kaiulani Poderick, "*State v. Hutchinson*—redefining the Scope of Local Regulatory Power," *Utah Law Review* 1981 (No. 3): 627.

Delegate Samuel Thurman feared it might prevent cities from giving water to their residents free of charge if they were able to do so.[58]

This section does not preclude forfeiture by a city of its water rights by nonuse, the Utah Supreme Court held in *Nephi City v. Hansen* (1989). It did not prevent Salt Lake City from granting the state free use of water as an inducement for moving the state capitol to the city, since the grant was made before statehood, and since the city did not relinquish its water rights (*Salt Lake City v. State,* 1968). An agreement whereby a city agreed to furnish a town with a certain amount of culinary water in exchange for irrigation water did not violate this section, although the contract was construed as requiring the city to furnish water regardless of its own needs in *Genola Town v. Santaquin City* (1941).

---

[58] *Proceedings of the Convention,* 1: 672–73.

Article XII

Corporations

The Corporations article in the original constitution contained twenty sections—some which delegates acknowledged would more appropriately be statutes. It was written in an era when states felt compelled to curb the growing power of trusts and monopolies. The era was also marked, however, particularly in the emerging states of the West, with a deep desire to attract the capital from the eastern states that could turn the West's assets into economic prosperity. Still another concern in Utah was that its infant industries be strengthened and preserved from both the rapacious trusts and the evil of overregulation by government. Meeting all these objectives in the Corporations article and the Labor article (Art. XVI)[59] was a daunting task. Hours were consumed in oratory promoting provisions "to prevent great corporations with millions and perhaps scores of millions behind their backs invading our territory, laying a paralyzing hand upon the resources which . . . ought to be left for the people."[60] Fear of the great trusts of the Gilded Age was mixed with a realistic understanding that Utah clearly needed financial resources from outside the new state "for the benefit of

[59] See commentary on Labor article (Art. XVI), section 2, which provides for a board of labor, conciliation, and arbitration.

[60] Delegate Brigham H. Roberts, *Proceedings of the Convention*, 2: 1553.

the general whole."[61] Adding to the problems in drafting this article was the fact that some measures designed to thwart monopolies—such as limiting enterprises to one line of business—would strangle the growth of some of Utah's cooperative businesses, which were then expanding horizontally.[62]

Despite the fact that over the years the federal government assumed responsibility for "trust-busting," regulation of railroads, banking, and other functions covered in this article, it was only amended twice, in 1940 and 1982, until voters approved a major revision that stripped away all but six sections and changed five of the remaining sections in 1992. In that year voters approved changes resulting from a detailed study of the article by the Constitutional Revision Commission. Some of the articles that were repealed refer to businesses regulated by the federal government, to offices that no longer exist, and to activities that are now covered by statutes and substantial case law. General laws for corporations are covered in U.C.A. 16-10a-101 et seq. Statutes governing public utilities, including railways, are found at U.C.A. 54-1-1 through 54-13-6.

SECTION 1

Corporations formation. Corporations may be formed under general laws but may not be created by special acts.

This section was in the original constitution, and it was not changed until the article was revised in 1992. At that time "shall" in the first sentence was changed to "may," and a lengthy sentence stating that the Legislature had the power to regulate corporations by law was deleted. The Utah Supreme Court in *Utah Farm Bureau Insurance Co. v. Utah Insurance Guaranty Association* (1977) defined a general law as one that operates uniformly upon all members of a class subject to the legislation. The court also noted that legislative classification is permitted, but the class created must be founded on some natural, intrinsic, or constitutional distinction. In *Utah Technology Finance Corp. v. Wilkinson* (1986), the court held that the corporation created by the Utah Technology and Innovation Act (U.C.A. 9–2-701 et seq.) was a public corporation created by the Legislature to serve public purposes and this section did not apply.

SECTIONS 2 AND 3

Repealed.

---

[61] Delegate John R. Murdock, ibid., 2: 1473. The lengthy debates on the Corporations article are covered in various parts of the *Proceedings of the Convention*; major issues generally are covered in 2: 1464–76; 2: 1547–84; and 2: 1588–1604.

[62] Delegate Edward Snow, ibid., 2: 1547.

These sections required corporations in existence at the time of statehood in 1896 to register and forbade the Legislature to extend franchises or charters existing under state laws.

SECTION 4

Suits. All corporations may sue and be sued, in all courts, in like cases as natural persons.

This section was changed in the 1992 revision to delete a lengthy first sentence defining the meaning of the term "corporations," and make stylistic changes in the remaining sentence.

SECTIONS 5, 6, AND 7

Repealed.

Section 5 dealt with stock issuance and proscribed "fictitious increase" of stock or indebtedness. Section 6 prohibited corporations organized outside Utah from transacting business within the state on conditions more favorable than those prescribed by law for similar corporations organized under state law. Section 7 forbade leasing or alienating any franchise so as to relieve the liabilities of the lessor.

SECTION 8

Consent of local authorities necessary to use of streets. No law shall be passed granting the right to construct and operate a street railroad, telegraph, telephone or electric light plant within any city or incorporated town, without the consent of the local authorities who have control of the street or highway proposed to be occupied for such purposes.

This section was placed in the constitution to give municipalities some control over the placement of railroad tracks or public utility plants within their borders. It has remained unchanged from the original wording. This does not include the power of cities to regulate rates charged by street railways; that power is retained in the state, the Utah Supreme Court held in *Murray City v. Utah Light & Traction Co.* (1920) and *Union Pacific Railroad v. Public Service Commission* (1943).

SECTIONS 9, 10, AND 11

Repealed.

Section 9 required corporations doing business in the state to maintain a place of business and an authorized agent in the state. Section 10 limited the business of a corporation to those expressly authorized in its charter or articles of incorporation. Section 11 stated that the right of the Legislature to take the property and franchises of corporations by eminent domain should never be abridged.

SECTION 12

Common carriers. All common carriers shall provide services without discrimination.

This section in the original constitution designated all railroad and other transportation companies as common carriers subject to legislative control, and it required such companies to receive and transport each others' passengers and freight without discrimination or unnecessary delay. It was designed to prevent discriminatory practices among railroads, such as charging different rates for various coal companies serving the same market, or refusing to serve certain companies. The language was simplified in the 1992 revision.

SECTIONS 13–18

Repealed.

Sections 13 through 16 were repealed in the 1992 revision. Section 13 prevented consolidation of stock, property, or franchises of competing railroads. Section 14 defined rolling stock and other movable property of railroads as personal property liable to taxation, execution, and sale. Section 15 mandated the Legislature to establish reasonable rates and prevent discrimination in rates. Section 16 forbade corporations from bringing private armies to preserve the peace or suppress domestic troubles (referring to Pinkerton private armies used in strike breaking). In 1982 voters approved the repeal of section 17, which prohibited officials of corporations chartered by any municipality from holding office in that city or town. In 1992 voters approved the repeal of section 18, which established liability of bank stock holders for double the amount of their capital stock.

SECTION 19

Blacklisting forbidden. Each person in Utah is free to obtain and enjoy employment whenever possible, and a person or corporation, or their agent, servant, or employee may not maliciously interfere with any person from obtaining employment or enjoying employment already obtained from any other person or corporation.

This section was originally designed to prevent employers from exchanging black lists, which would keep workers from getting jobs in any area where these lists circulated. The section was rewritten in the 1992 revision. The words "hindering in any way" were removed, along with the declaration that malicious interference would be a crime. A narrower anti-blacklisting section was placed in the Labor article, referring specifically to railroad companies or other corporations. (See Art. XVI, sec. 4.) In *United Association of Journeymen Local 57 v. Bechtel Power Corp.* (1987) the Tenth Circuit Court of Appeals held that the U.S. District Court lacked jurisdiction; plaintiff's blacklisting claims under Utah law were not preempted by the federal Labor Management Relations Act (29 U.S.C. sec. 185). Blacklisting of employees is made a felony by statute (U.C.A. 34-24-2).

The Utah Supreme Court held in *State v. Packard* (1952) that the freedom to work might be limited by reasonable regulations, such as professional licensing and the regulation of hours, wages, and workplace safety for the common good, but only with clearly expressed standards.

SECTION 20

Free market system as state policy—Restraint of trade and monopolies prohibited. It is the policy of the state of Utah that a free market system shall govern trade and commerce in this state to promote the dispersion of economic and political power and the general welfare of all the people. Each contract, combination in the form of trust or otherwise, or conspiracy in restraint of trade or commerce is prohibited. Except as otherwise provided by statute, it is also prohibited for any person to monopolize, attempt to monopolize, or combine or conspire with any other person or persons to monopolize any part of trade or commerce.

This section declares the policy of the state to be in favor of a free market system without monopolies, trusts, or other barriers to free competition. The original section 20, which had not been changed until the 1992 revision, was repealed at that time, and this wording was substituted for it. Originally, the section concentrated on declaring price-fixing by "individuals, corporations, or associations" as unlawful and against public policy, and it mandated that the Legislature pass laws for the enforcement of this policy. The revision emphasizes the broad policy preference for a free market economy and expands the list of antitrust activities to include monopolies, restraint of trade, and conspiracy. The revision was modeled largely after federal antitrust laws. The definition of a monopoly, the activities covered, and the prosecution for unlawful trade practices are covered in U.C.A. 76-10-912 et seq. An "attempt to monopolize" is defined as "action taken without a legitimate business purpose and with a specific intent of destroying competition or controlling prices to substantially lessen competition, or creating a monopoly, where there is a dangerous probability of creating a monopoly." Several regulated businesses, such as public utilities and securities dealers, banking, and insurance have limited exemptions under this section. The antitrust laws are construed not to forbid the existence and operation of labor, agricultural, or horticultural organizations "instituted for the purpose of mutual help and not having capital stock or conducted for profit" (U.C.A. 76-10-915 (2)).

Article XIII

Revenue and Taxation

The Revenue and Taxation article is the most frequently amended article in Utah's Constitution. It has been the subject of study over the years by numerous special committees, commissions, and task forces, all seeking a relatively painless way to pay for the increasing costs of government, ensure fairness among taxpayers, and minimize the political damage to legislators who are forced to deal with these issues.

The framers of Utah's Constitution, which was written during the depression that followed the Panic of 1893, were acutely aware of the need to provide for a frugal government and minimal taxation. Property subject to taxation was to be taxed initially for state purposes at five mills on each dollar (.005 percent), and this rate was to be lowered as the value of property in the state rose. It was not to be raised without a vote of citizens who had paid a property tax, and the rate was never to exceed eight mills. Delegates to the constitutional convention feared that the threat of high taxes during such hard times would threaten approval of the constitution at the ratifying election to be held in the fall of 1895.

The original document reflected the new state's dependence on the property tax, and this tax still seems to be the most politically sensitive revenue source—although property taxes now pay for only about one-fourth of the costs of Utah state and local government.[63] This article has been changed by more than a dozen amendments granting exemptions, and by several amendments dealing with appraisal of properties subject to taxation. This article also has been changed to include new ways of raising revenue, including taxes on sales, income, natural resource extraction, and motor fuel. It has been changed several times to provide a stable revenue source for the increasing needs of Utah's educational systems; other changes have been made to "earmark" specific revenue sources for certain functions. The net result is a tax code that has become increasingly more complex (U.C.A. 59-1-101 through 59-23-8).

SECTION 1

Fiscal year. The Legislature shall establish the fiscal year of the state.

The original constitution established a fiscal year of the first day of January "unless changed by the Legislature." The Legislature changed the fiscal year in 1905 from 1 January to 1 December, and changed it again in 1925 from 1 December to 1 July; it has now established a fiscal year that begins on 1 July and ends on 30 June (U.C.A. 63-13-1). This section was amended in 1996 to change the presumption of the original constitution that the fiscal year begins on 1 January.

SECTION 2

Tangible property to be taxed—Value ascertained—Exemptions—Remittance or abatement of taxes of poor—Intangible property—Legislature to provide annual tax for state.

(1) All tangible property in the state, not exempt under the laws of the United States, or under this Constitution, shall be taxed at a uniform and equal rate in proportion to its value, to be ascertained as provided by law.

(2) The following are property tax exemptions:

(a) the property of the state, school districts, and public libraries;

(b) the property of counties, cities, towns, special districts, and all other political subdivisions of the state, except that to the extent and in the manner provided by the Legislature the property of a county, city, town, special district or other political subdivision of the state located outside of its geographic boundaries as defined by law may be subject to the ad valorem property tax;

---

[63] Jewell J. Rasmussen, *History of Utah's First Century of Taxation and Public Debt: 1896–1995* (Salt Lake City: Bureau of Economic and Business Research, University of Utah, 1996), 145.

(c) property owned by a nonprofit entity which is used exclusively for religious, charitable, or educational purposes;

(d) places of burial not held or used for private or corporate benefit; and

(e) farm equipment and farm machinery as defined by statute. This exemption shall be implemented over a period of time as provided by statute.

(3) Tangible personal property present in Utah on January 1, held for sale or processing and which is shipped to final destination outside this state within twelve months may be deemed by law to have acquired no situs in Utah for purposes of ad valorem property taxation and may be exempted by law from such taxation, whether manufactured, processed or produced or otherwise originating within or without the state.

(4) Tangible personal property present in Utah on January 1, held for sale in the ordinary course of business and which constitutes the inventory of any retailer, or wholesaler or manufacturer or farmer, or livestock raiser may be deemed for purposes of ad valorem property taxation to be exempted.

(5) Water rights, ditches, canals, reservoirs, power plants, pumping plants, transmission lines, pipes and flumes owned and used by individuals or corporations for irrigating land within the state owned by such individuals or corporations, or the individual members thereof, shall be exempted from taxation to the extent that they shall be owned and used for such purposes.

(6) Power plants, power transmission lines and other property used for generating and delivering electrical power, a portion of which is used for furnishing power for pumping water for irrigation purposes on lands in the state of Utah, may be exempted from taxation to the extent that such property is used for such purposes. These exemptions shall accrue to the benefit of the users of water so pumped under such regulations as the Legislature may prescribe.

(7) The taxes of the poor may be remitted or abated at such times and in such manner as may be provided by law.

(8) The Legislature may provide by law for the exemption from taxation: of not to exceed 45% of the fair market value of residential property as defined by law; and all household furnishings, furniture, and equipment used exclusively by the owner thereof at his place of abode in maintaining a home for himself and family.

(9) Property owned by disabled persons who were disabled in the line of duty during any war, international conflict, or military training in the military service of the United States or of the state of Utah and by the unmarried surviving spouses and minor orphans of such disabled persons or of persons who during any war, international conflict, or military training in the military service of the United States or the state of Utah were killed in action or died in the line of duty as a result of such service may be exempted as the Legislature may provide.

(10) Intangible property may be exempted from taxation as property or it may be taxed as property in such manner and to such extent as the Legislature may provide, but if taxed as property the income therefrom shall not also be taxed. Provided that if

intangible property is taxed as property the rate thereof shall not exceed five mills on each dollar of valuation.

(11) The Legislature shall provide by law for an annual tax sufficient, with other sources of revenue, to defray the estimated ordinary expenses of the state for each fiscal year. For the purpose of paying the state debt, if any there be, the Legislature shall provide for levying a tax annually, sufficient to pay the annual interest and to pay the principal of such debt, within twenty years from the final passage of the law creating the debt.

This section provides for an equal and uniform rate of taxation of all tangible property not exempted under United States law or the state constitution, according to its value as provided by law. Eight subsections provide for exemptions from the property tax or authorize the Legislature to provide by law for exemptions. This section also provides that intangible property such as stocks and bonds may be taxed as property, or the income from it may be taxed—but not both. This provision, approved by voters in 1930, paved the way for the adoption of the income tax the following year. The final subsection mandates the Legislature to provide taxes to defray the expenses of the state, plus a tax sufficient to retire each state debt within twenty years from the time it was created by law.

Section 2 now combines section 2 and part of section 3 from the original constitution. In the original section 2 the word "property" was defined to include "moneys, credits, bonds, stocks, franchises and all matters and things (real, personal, and mixed) capable of private ownership" but forbade taxation of the stocks of any company or corporation when the property of such company or corporation was taxed. In the original section 3 there was a short list of exemptions: property of the United States, of the state and its political subdivisions, public libraries, lots with the buildings thereon used exclusively for either religious worship or charitable purposes, and public burial places. In addition, the strong sentiment in the constitutional convention for promoting agriculture is shown in the exemption of ditches, canals, and flumes owned by individuals or corporations used exclusively for irrigating lands.

Beginning in 1900, when the Legislature was authorized to remit or abate the taxes of the indigent poor, there had been a steady stream of amendments authorizing full or partial exemption from the property tax. By 1970 voters had amended this section to exempt—or authorized the Legislature to exempt—the following: water rights, irrigation reservoirs, pumping plants, transmission lines, and pipes used for irrigation; property stored within the state for shipment outside the state within a year; ordinary business, manufacturing, or farm inventories; power plants, power transmission lines, and other property used for generating and delivering electrical power for pumping irrigation water, to the extent that it is used for this purpose; $2,000 in value of homes, homesteads, and household furnishings used in maintaining a family home; an amount not to exceed

$3,000 in property owned by disabled war veterans or their unmarried widows or minor orphans. The latter applied also to the widows or orphans of persons killed in action or who died as a result of military service. The original exemption of property owned by the United States was repealed in 1946 (along with the same provision in Article III), on the grounds that the federal government could exempt its own property and that certain businesses operating on federal property might logically be subject to taxation.

After 1970, when passage of the Gateway Amendment (Art. XXIII, sec. 1) made possible more changes in a single amendment, study of this section produced several changes. In 1982 voters approved a substantial revision of the entire Revenue and Taxation article proposed by the Constitutional Revision Commission. Subsection (1) was amended by including the words "a uniform and equal rate." Subsection (2) had several changes. It was amended to exempt property owned by a nonprofit entity used exclusively for religious, charitable, or educational purposes. It was also amended to limit the exemption of property of political subdivisions by permitting the Legislature to tax property owned outside of its geographical boundaries. This was intended to permit taxation of a large power plant located in western Utah that is owned by a consortium of municipal governments. Another subsection provided that intangible property might be taxed as property (with the income therefrom exempted) or it could be exempted from taxation as property.

An amendment to section 2, subsection (8) was of vital interest to homeowners, who had seen the valuation of their homes increase rapidly in the inflation of the 1970s. It permitted the Legislature to provide by law for the exemption from taxation of up to 45 percent of the fair market value of residential property as defined by law. This was opposed by some major industrial and business interests, of course, because it shifted part of the property tax burden from homeowners to nonresidential property owners. In 1986 voters narrowly defeated a provision to exempt nonprofit hospitals and nursing homes from the property tax, but they approved an exemption for farm equipment and farm machinery, to be implemented over a period of years. In 1996 voters approved an amendment changing the exemption of property owned by disabled persons from those who served during "any war" to those disabled or killed in the line of duty during "any war, international conflict, or military training" in the military service of the United States or the state of Utah—as the Legislature may provide.

Although the number of exemptions has increased during the last few decades, the discretion given the Legislature in implementing them has been greater, by not specifying dollar amounts and by adding the phrase "as the Legislature may provide." The Revenue and Taxation code (U.C.A. Title 59) contains sections dealing with each exemption.

Court interpretations have determined the meaning of the charitable exemption provided in subsection (2)(c) for property owned by a nonprofit entity which is used exclusively for religious, charitable, or educational purposes.

In *Friendship Manor Corp. v. Tax Commission* in 1971 the Utah Supreme Court held that a housing facility for senior citizens was not exempt from taxation because residents were paying for all the services they received, and rents were not determined according to need, despite the fact that the facility was operated by a nonprofit corporation. In 1986 the court developed a "material reciprocity" test, holding that a housing complex for elderly and handicapped people that adjusted rents according to tenants' ability to pay, and did not collect enough rental income to cover costs, was entitled to the charitable use exemption (*Yorgason v. County Board of Equalization,* 1986).

The tax-exempt status of fraternal organization properties that house both social and charitable activities has been dealt with in individual cases. The Utah Supreme Court held in *Baker v. One Piece of Improved Real Property* (1977) that a fraternal organization's lodge property was not entitled to a tax exemption because the lodge's charitable expenditures amounted to an extremely small proportion of its total expenditures. The court held in *Loyal Order of Moose #259 v. County Board of Equalization* in 1982 that the exemption of a nonprofit corporation's real property was to be strictly construed, and the charitable use of the property must be exclusive. If a separate part of a building was used exclusively for charitable purposes, however, that part would qualify for an exemption.

In 1985 the court attempted to establish guidelines for this exemption in *Utah County ex rel. County Board of Equalization v. Intermountain Health Care, Inc.* It held that a hospital qualifies for a charitable exemption only if it meets the definition of charity—a gift to the community on an ongoing basis—or if its property is used exclusively for charitable purposes. It also outlined six guidelines for determining whether a hospital was using its property exclusively for a charitable purpose. The State Tax Commission issued a set of standards based on these guidelines which were to be used by county assessors and boards of equalization in determining the status of institutions claiming exemptions. These standards were upheld by the court in 1986 in *Yorgason v. County Board of Equalization,* a decision that sparked an unsuccessful attempt in 1986 to amend the constitution to specifically exempt from property taxation nonprofit hospitals and nursing homes. In *Howell v. County Board of Cache County* (1994), the Tax Commission's standards were challenged as going beyond the Commission's powers under subsection (2)(c). The constitutionality of the Tax Commission's standards was upheld as a valid exercise of powers granted in section 11 of this article in conformity with previous supreme court decisions. (See commentary under section 11.)

Under section 2, labor union property has been held not to house a charitable activity, since the union's primary purposes and activities were to benefit union members (*Salt Lake County v. Tax Commission,* 1983). A statute that rolled back the assessed value of all locally assessed real property to the 1978 level (to keep inflation from producing high property tax bills) was held to be in violation of sections 2 and 3 of this article in 1984 in *Rio Algom Corp. v. San Juan County.*

Although city property is exempted from taxes in section (2)(b), sewer charges to a school district were held to be payment for services, not taxes or assessments, in *Murray City v. Board of Education* (1964). The constitutional language covering exemptions is necessarily broad, requiring both statutory definitions and refinement by supreme court decisions.

SECTION 3

Assessment and taxation of tangible property—Livestock—Land used for agricultural purposes.

(1) The Legislature shall provide by law a uniform and equal rate of assessment on all tangible property in the state, according to its value in money, except as otherwise provided in Section 2 of this Article. The Legislature shall prescribe by law such provisions as shall secure a just valuation for taxation of such property, so that every person and corporation shall pay a tax in proportion to the value of his, her, or its tangible property, provided that the Legislature may determine the manner and extent of taxing livestock.

(2) Land used for agricultural purposes may, as the Legislature prescribes, be assessed according to its value for agricultural use without regard to the value it may have for other purposes.

This section is closely related to section 2, since it deals with the basis of property taxation—the valuation in money of the property to be taxed. It provides for a uniform and equal rate of assessment for all tangible property in the state, except "as otherwise provided in Section 2 of this Article." The base amount on which the tax is levied is as important as the rate of taxation in determining the tax bill of a property taxpayer; if all properties are assessed by the same method, a "uniform and equal rate of assessment" should result. But since some properties in Utah are assessed by county assessors and some (including mines and public utilities) by the State Tax Commission, disparities in assessments can be challenged as violating this section, as well as section 2.

This section originally included exemptions to the property tax. Exemptions now are found in section 2. Section 3 was first amended in 1900 to permit remission or abatement of the taxes of the indigent poor, and again in 1906 to exempt mortgages on both real and personal property from taxation. In 1938 voters approved the establishment of the Uniform School Fund, which distributes funds for operation of the elementary and secondary schools on a formula that equalizes funding between richer and poorer school districts. (See commentary on section 12 of this article.)

In the major revision of the Revenue and Taxation article approved in 1982, several provisions for specific rates of taxation, and a 75 percent limit on state support for the minimum school program were removed, giving more flexibility to the Legislature in tax and expenditure policies. The Legislature was allowed to determine the manner and extent of taxing livestock and to prescribe the assessment of agricultural land to protect it from being taxed on its value as residential property. Despite the efforts of the constitution's framers to create a "uniform and equal" rate of assessment on all tangible property in the state, pressures over the years have changed the constitutional provisions and the tax code on assessments (U.C.A. 59-2-103 et seq.) into a patchwork of exemptions and exceptions that benefit politically potent taxpaying groups.

In 1969 the Utah Supreme Court held that although absolute uniformity in assessment of property is not practicable, section 3 requires that values be reasonably uniform and equal (*Harmer v. State Tax Commission*). The Legislature by 1990 had developed by law different assessment levels for property tax purposes. Primary residential property was assessed at 80 percent of full market value, less a discount of 20 percent for "intangible values." All other property assessed by county assessors was listed at 80 percent of full market value, while all state-assessed property (such as mines and railroads) was listed at 100 percent of full market value. This created, in effect, a classification system for nonresidential properties that was challenged in 1990 in *Amax Magnesium Corp. v. Utah State Tax Commission*. The company, which was assessed by the State Tax Commission as a mining operation, argued that its assessment of 100 percent of market value violated sections 2 and 3 of Article XIII. The court agreed, and to solve the problem in the future, the Legislature placed all nonresidential property—whether assessed by the counties or the state, on an equal footing. Primary residential property, which is assessed by county assessors, may be allowed an exemption of up to 45 percent of its fair market value as provided in section 2 (8). Despite the many studies of Utah's revenue system designed to improve and stabilize its taxing policies, it is likely that both the constitutional and statutory provisions on assessments and exemptions will continue in the future to be studied and adjusted in response to new needs and political pressures.

SECTION 4

Mines and claims to be assessed—Basis and multiple—What to be assessed as tangible property. Repealed.

This section, which had been changed several times since 1896, was repealed in the 1996 general election. The Legislature recommended the repeal with the notation that this action was not intended to make substantive change in the existing statutes which describe the basis for assessing and taxing mining properties (U.C.A. 59-2-205 through 212).

SECTION 5

Local authorities to levy local taxes—Sharing tax and revenues by political subdivisions—Debt guaranty. The Legislature shall not impose taxes for the purpose of any county, city, town or other municipal corporation, but may, by law, vest in the corporate authorities thereof, respectively, the power to assess and collect taxes for all purposes of such corporation. Notwithstanding anything to the contrary contained in this Constitution, political subdivisions may share their tax and other revenues with other political subdivisions as provided by statute and the state may guarantee the debt of school districts and may guarantee debt incurred to refund the school district debt as provided in Article X, Section 5.

The first sentence of this section, which prohibited the Legislature from imposing taxes for the purpose of counties or municipalities, was part of the original state constitution. In the 1982 revision of the article, the provision which permits sharing of revenue by political subdivisions was added. In 1996 voters approved addition of the provision for guaranteeing the debt of school districts and debt incurred to refund the school district debt. This addition was needed to be consistent with the revision of the Public Debt article (Art. XIV), which permitted the state to guarantee debts of school districts.

When the Legislature imposed a new statewide tax levy to fund the costs of local property taxation assessment and collection, the tax was challenged as a state-imposed levy for local purposes. The Utah Supreme Court held, however, that this was not a state-imposed tax for county purposes in *Mountain States Telephone and Telegraph Co. v. Garfield County* (1991), and was not in violation of this section.

SECTION 6

Annual statement to be published. An accurate statement of the receipts and expenditures of the public moneys, shall be published annually in such manner as the Legislature may provide.

This section was in the original constitution and has not been changed. Such reports are issued annually by the state auditor.

SECTION 7

Rate of taxation on tangible property for general state purposes—Additional levy for support of public school system. Repealed.

Repeal of this section in 1986 removed the limit on the rate of taxation of tangible property and the 75 percent limit on state support of the elementary and secondary schools. Statutes and regulations in force at the time the repeal was approved, if not inconsistent with the amendment, were to remain in force.

SECTION 8

Officer not to make profit out of public moneys. The making of profit out of public moneys, or using the same for any purpose not authorized by law, by any public officer, shall be deemed a felony, and shall be punished as provided by law, but part of such punishment shall be disqualification to hold public office.

This section was in the original constitution and has remained unchanged. It has been interpreted to apply to officials who handle public property or funds (*Stone v. Stone,* 1967) and not to possible conflicts of interest, as in sale of janitorial supplies to the state by a firm co-owned by a member of the Legislature (*Brockbank v. Rampton,* 1968).

SECTION 9

State expenditure to be kept within revenues. No appropriation shall be made or any expenditure authorized by the Legislature if the expenditure of the State, during any fiscal year, shall exceed the total tax then provided for by law and applicable for the particular appropriation or expenditure, unless the Legislature making the appropriation shall provide for levying a sufficient tax to pay the appropriation or expenditure within the current fiscal year. This provision shall not apply to appropriations or expenditures to suppress insurrections, defend the State, or assist in defending the United States in time of war.

This section requires the state to balance revenues and expenditures during each fiscal year. The section was unchanged from the original constitution until voters in 1996 approved style changes and deletion of a reference to section 7 of this article, which had been repealed. This section reflects the constitution framers' determination to have a balanced budget, just as section 7 reflected their concern with future property tax levels and specified tax limits that could only be exceeded by a vote of citizens who paid property taxes. But the repeal of section 7 and elimination of the words "not exceeding the rates allowed in section seven of this article" leaves the constitution without a specific ceiling on rates of taxation, except for section 2(10) of this article. That section limits taxation of intangible property to five mills (.005) on the dollar if it is taxed as property.

SECTION 10

All property taxable where situated. All corporations or persons in this State, or doing business herein, shall be subject to taxation for State, county, school, municipal or other purposes, on the real and personal property owned or used by them within the Territorial limits of the authority levying the tax.

This section was in the original constitution and has not been amended. It has been interpreted to mean that "property owned" refers to the place where property is located, not where the owner may reside (*Murdock v. Murdock,* 1911). A law that provided for the additional tax generated by a redevelopment project to be used to pay for redevelopment purposes (rather than for functions of the county or other local governmental entities) did not violate this section (*Salt Lake County v. Murray City Redevelopment,* 1979).

SECTION 11

Creation of State Tax Commission—Membership—Governor to appoint—Terms—Duties—County boards—Duties. There shall be a State Tax Commission consisting of four members, not more than two of whom shall belong to the same political party. The members of the Commission shall be appointed by the Governor, by and with the consent of the Senate, for such terms of office as may be provided by law. The State Tax Commission shall administer and supervise the tax laws of the State. It shall assess mines and public utilities and adjust and equalize the valuation and assessment of property among the several counties. It shall have such other powers of original assessment as the Legislature may provide. Under such regulations in such cases and within such limitations as the Legislature may prescribe, it shall review proposed bond issues, revise the tax levies of local governmental units, and equalize the assessment and valuation of property within the counties. The duties imposed upon the State Board of Equalization by the Constitution and Laws of this State shall be performed by the State Tax Commission.

In each county of this State there shall be a County Board of Equalization consisting of the Board of County Commissioners of said county. The County Boards of Equalization shall adjust and equalize the valuation and assessment of the real and personal property within their respective counties, subject to such regulation and control by the State Tax Commission as may be prescribed by law. The State Tax Commission and the County Boards of Equalization shall each have such other powers as may be prescribed by the Legislature.

This section establishes the State Tax Commission, a bipartisan body to administer the tax laws. The Commission also assesses mines and public utilities. The section also establishes county boards of equalization. The original section established, "until otherwise provided by law," a State Board of Equalization consisting of the five main Executive Department officials. It also provided for county boards of equalization, consisting of the county commissions. The State Board of Equalization was charged with the duty to adjust and equalize the valuation of the real and personal property among the several counties; the county boards were to adjust and equalize these valuations within their counties. In 1930 voters approved a major change in this section. The State

Board of Equalization was replaced by a bipartisan State Tax Commission of four members to assume the duties of the former board to adjust and equalize the valuation and assessment of property among the several counties. It was also given the power to establish systems of public accounting, review proposed bond issues, revise the tax levies and budgets of local government units, and "such other powers of original assessment as the Legislature may provide." These powers grew by statutory enactment, including the power to hear some appeals from decisions of local taxing authorities (U.C.A. 59-1-201 et seq.). The Commission's role was, however, reduced in 1958 when voters approved an amendment that ended the power of the Commission to establish systems of public accounting.

In the first quarter century of statehood, the property tax financed approximately 90 percent of state and local government expenditures, so that correct and uniform valuation of property throughout the state was extremely important to assure fairness.[64] By the end of the 1920s, special commissions studying Utah's tax laws had pointed out that non-property-taxpayers were escaping most of the tax burden. Soon other taxes—on cigarettes, motor fuel, oleomargarine sales, and passenger and freight service—were enacted. These taxes did not require constitutional amendment to institute them or to change them, making them easier to establish and to change. The administration of these taxes also increased the work load of the State Tax Commission.

In 1930 voters approved several other important changes to the Revenue and Taxation article. To shift some of the burden from property owners, section 2 was changed to eliminate taxation of intangible property on an equal basis with tangible property—a change needed for adoption of an income tax in 1931. Other changes were made in the methods of assessing mines and mineral properties and in the structure of the State School Fund.

The Tax Commission's power to assess utilities has been held by the Utah Supreme Court to be exclusive; it may not be exercised by the Legislature or any other officer or board (*State ex rel. Public Service Commission v. Southern Pacific Co.*, 1938). The Utah Court of Appeals held in 1994 that the Tax Commission was not authorized to hear appeals from local taxing agency decisions unless empowered to do so by the constitution or statute (*Blaine Hudson Printing v. Utah State Tax Commission*).

In *Kennecott Corp. v. Salt Lake County Commission* (1985), the Utah Supreme Court held unconstitutional under this section a statute which permitted the district court to adjust mining assessments. A statute granting the district court jurisdiction to review by trial de novo (a new trial on the facts) Tax Commission decisions resulting from formal adjudicative proceedings was also held to violate

---

[64] Ibid., 22. Fees, inheritance taxes, and license taxes made up 8.6 percent of the revenues.

this section in *Evans and Sutherland Computer Corp. v. Utah State Tax Commission* in 1997.

As the tax base in Utah has grown and been diversified (a general sales tax was added in 1933), so has the work of administering the system. From time to time, studies suggest that the Tax Commission—one of the last remaining constitutionally established boards—should have its authority removed from the constitution, to provide flexibility in the administration of tax laws. Thus far, it remains a constitutional body.

SECTION 12

Stamp, income, occupation, license, or franchise tax permissible—Reference to United States laws in imposition of income taxes—Income or intangible property taxes allocated to public education system and higher education system.

(1) Nothing in this Constitution shall be construed to prevent the Legislature from providing a stamp tax, or a tax based on income, occupation, licenses, franchises, or other tax provided by law. The Legislature may provide for deductions, exemptions, or offsets on any tax based upon income, occupation, licenses, franchises, or other tax as provided by law pursuant to this section.

(2) Notwithstanding any provision of this Constitution, the Legislature, in any law imposing income taxes, may define the amount on, in respect to, or by which the taxes are imposed or measured, by reference to any provision of the laws of the United States as the same may be or become effective at any time or from time to time and may prescribe exemptions or modifications to any such provision.

(3) All revenue received from taxes on income or from taxes on intangible property shall be allocated to the support of the public education system and the higher education system as defined in Article X, Section 2 of this Constitution.

This section deals with three subjects. It enumerates several types of taxes that might be imposed by the Legislature and provides broad authority with the addition of "or other tax provided by law." Lawmakers are also authorized to determine deductions, exemptions, or offsets to these taxes without the need for constitutional amendment. It provides that the Legislature may simplify state income taxes by basing them on United States income taxes, with exemptions or modifications as the Legislature may provide. The third part of the section deals with allocating revenue produced by income taxes.

Part of subsection (1) permitting "a stamp tax, or a tax based on income, occupation, licenses, franchises, or mortgages" was in the original state constitution. In 1906 voters overwhelmingly approved the exemption of mortgages from taxation. The rest of the subsection broadening legislative powers was part of the extensive revision of the article approved in 1982.

In an effort to make filing state tax returns easier (or so its proponents argued), subsection (2), which permits the Legislature to base Utah's income tax on the federal income tax, was approved by voters in 1970. The third subsection addressed a perennial issue in Utah's school financing struggle. When the state income tax was enacted in 1931, 75 percent of the proceeds was earmarked for the support of a minimum state school program, the rest for the state General Fund. In 1946 voters approved the allocation of all revenue from taxes on income and intangible property to the support of the "public school system as defined in Article X, Section 2 of this Constitution, such portion consisting only of kindergarten schools, common schools and high schools" (then Art. XIII, sec. 7). The 1982 revision allocated income taxes to "the support of the public school system as defined in Article X, Sec. 2 of this Constitution"—leaving out the specific application to elementary and secondary schools. At that time, the Education article still included a college, a university, and "such other schools as the Legislature may establish" in its definition of "the public school system." In the Education article revision which was approved in 1986, the term "public school system" was abandoned, and two separate "education" systems were designated in Article X, section 2—a "public education system" and a "higher education system." The income tax revenue continued to support only elementary and secondary schools, even though an Attorney General's Opinion in 1990 (Opinion 90-39, 17 December 1990) stated that revenue from the income tax could be used for other than "public education," including "higher education," if authorized by the Legislature. In 1996 voters approved an amendment that settled the question by changing the wording in subsection 3 from "public school system" to "public education system" and "higher education system" as defined in the Education article. Although public education leaders had vigorously resisted efforts to share these revenues in the past, they did not oppose the 1996 amendment, having been assured that new statutes would protect their funding. (See commentary on Article X, section 2.)

SECTION 13

Revenue from highway user and motor fuel taxes to be used for highway purposes. The proceeds from the imposition of any license tax, registration fee, driver education tax, or other charge related to the operation of any motor vehicle upon any public highway in this state, and the proceeds from the imposition of any excise tax on gasoline or other liquid motor fuels used for propelling such vehicle, except for statutory refunds and adjustments allowed thereunder and for costs of collection and administration, shall be used exclusively for highway purposes as follows:

(1) The construction, improvement, repair and maintenance of city streets, county roads, and state highways, including but not restricted to payment for

property taken for or damaged by rights of way, and for administrative costs necessarily incurred for said purposes.

(2) The administration of a driver education program.

(3) The enforcement of state motor vehicle and traffic laws.

(4) Tourists and publicity expense in any single biennium not in excess of the lesser of the following: (a) .5 per cent of the total biennial revenues from motor fuel taxes, or (b) an amount equal to the 1959–1961 biennium.

This section was added to the constitution by a vote of the electors in 1962. It describes several—but not all—of the taxes and fees motor vehicle users must pay in Utah for the privilege of using roads and highways; it also describes the purposes for which this revenue may be used. The motor fuel tax was first levied in 1923, when it raised only a small amount of revenue. Since then, the Legislature has added several additional fees and charges to enhance the revenue stream in the Transportation Fund (U.C.A. 51-5-4(4)(b). The motor fuel tax now makes up approximately 6 percent of the total revenue for state and local governments.[65] After taking out the revenue designated in subsections (2), (3), and (4) and for administrative costs, 25 percent of the remaining net highway-user revenue is distributed to cities and counties for local road purposes, and 75 percent is allocated to the State Department of Transportation for state highway purposes.[66]

This section was sold to the voters in a campaign by major highway users as a measure to improve highways and make sure that the increasing revenues in this fund would not be diverted to uses other than those specified in the constitution. It is a classic example of constitutional "earmarking," a practice opposed by most government finance experts, but since it apparently benefits a large constituency—motor vehicle users—it is not likely to be changed.

SECTION 14

Tangible personal property tax exemption. Aircraft, watercraft, motor vehicles, and other tangible personal property, not otherwise exempt under the laws of the United States or under this Constitution, may be exempted from taxation as property by the Legislature. In the exercise of the discretion granted under this section, however, the Legislature may only exempt tangible personal property that is required by law to be registered with the state before it is used on a public highway, on a public waterway, on public land, or in the air. If the Legislature exempts tangible personal property from taxation under this section, it shall provide for uniform statewide fees or uniform statewide rates of assessment or levy in lieu of the tax on such property.

[65] Ibid., 145.

[66] Utah Foundation, *State and Local Government in Utah*, 97.

> The value of any tangible personal property exempted from taxation, however, shall remain and be considered as part of the state tax base for the purpose of determining debt limitations as set forth in Article XIV of this Constitution. The proceeds from such a tax or fee are not subject to Sec. 13 of this Article and shall be distributed to the taxing districts in which the exempted property is located in the same proportion as the revenue collected from real property tax is distributed to such districts.

This section permits the Legislature to exempt aircraft, watercraft, motor vehicles, and other tangible personal property used on public highways, lands, waterways, or air space from taxation as property, and to provide for such properties a uniform, statewide fee in place of the tax. The section was added to the constitution in 1984 after a similar provision was rejected ten years earlier. It was proposed to meet the problem of widely differing taxes levied from county to county on the same make and model of automobile. These rates were different because the different tax levies within each county are determined by the taxing units in the county, such as the county government, cities, school districts, and other special districts; the result is that rural counties with fewer needs for urban services and lower governmental costs have a lower overall tax levy. This led to some "tax shopping" by automobile or boat owners who owned property in counties with lower tax rates and licensed their motor vehicles and boats in the county that had lower taxes.

To implement this section, the Legislature provided for a uniform fee on tangible personal property required to be registered with the state.

Article XIV

Public Debt

SECTION 1

Fixing the limit of the state indebtedness—Exceptions. To meet casual deficits or failures in revenue, and for necessary expenditures for public purposes, including the erection of public buildings, and for the payment of all Territorial indebtedness assumed by the State, the State may contract debts, not exceeding in the aggregate at any one time, an amount equal to one and one-half per centum of the value of the taxable property of the State, as shown by the last assessment for State purposes, previous to the incurring of such indebtedness. But the State shall never contract any indebtedness, except as provided in Article XIV, Section 2, in excess of such amount, and all monies arising from loans herein authorized, shall be applied solely to the purposes for which they were obtained.

This section establishes the debt limit for Utah state government. Nothing was more certain in the Utah constitutional convention than a strict limit on the indebtedness of the future state. The territorial economy was mired in a depression sparked by the Panic of 1893 and the new state was required by the Enabling Act to assume a territorial debt of more than $750,000. In addition, several counties and cities carried heavy debt loads into statehood.[67] The convention debates

[67] Frank S. Moseley, "Constitutional Restrictions Upon Municipal Indebtedness," *Utah Law Review* 1966 (No. 2): 464.

were replete with horror stories about states that had hovered over the edge of bankruptcy—or toppled over the brink. A few delegates proposed limits on any debt, despite the obvious need for critical infrastructure for the new state. An eloquent lawyer delegate warned that future needs of the state could not be foreseen, and urged that the constitution set as a debt limit a small percentage of the value of all taxable property—which then totaled about $100 million.[68] This view did not prevail, however, and a limit of $200,000 was set, exclusive of the territorial debt. The original section also provided that when the territorial debt was paid, the state should not contract any debt in excess of $200,000, except under the conditions noted in section 2.

In 1910 voters approved a change in this section to limit the aggregate debt to 1.5 percent of taxable property. In 1920, and again in 1922, voters refused to raise the limit to 2 percent, and it remains at the original percentage, based on the full fair market value of taxable property in the state (U.C.A. 63B-2-106). In 1996, when the constitution was amended to permit the state to guarantee the debt of school districts, this section was reworded to refer to the exceptions to the debt limit in Article XIV, section 2.

In 1989 the Legislature passed the State Appropriations and Tax Limitation Act (U.C.A. 63-38c-101 through 402), which limited total state appropriations in each fiscal year to 1985 appropriations, plus an amount determined by a formula based on inflation, population increase, and personal income growth. A statutory debt limit was then tied to this amount in the act (U.C.A. 63-38c-402), setting a ceiling of 20 percent of the appropriations limit for general obligation bonding. This means that in 1996, for example, the state was only $243 million below the statutory debt limit, but it was $1.122 billion below the constitutional debt limit. The statutory limit, however, could be raised by a two-thirds vote of both houses of the Legislature.[69] To determine what types of debt by state agencies fall under the debt limits in this section, the Utah Supreme Court has decided several cases, drawing the line between general obligation debts and other debts that are not subject to the public debt limits. In 1950 the court held in *Spence v. Utah State Agricultural College* that bonds issued to finance construction of a student union building did not create a debt against the state because they would be paid solely from revenue derived from operation of the building. In *Conder v. University of Utah* (1953), the court held that the "restricted special fund" doctrine (restriction on municipalities' applying funds other than those derived from income to payment of revenue bonds) did not apply in this case. The university's agreement to pledge income from state land funds in addition to

[68] Charles C. Goodwin, *Proceedings of the Convention,* 2: 1118. Debates on the public debt issue are at 2: 1116–1141 and 1184–1201.

[69] *State of Utah Comprehensive Annual Financial Report: Fiscal Year 1996* (Salt Lake City: Utah State Division of Finance, 1996), vi, ix.

rents, student fees, and other sources mentioned in the statute made the bonds special obligations and not a pledge of state credit.

The constitutionality of a statute creating a state housing finance agency was upheld in *Utah Housing Finance Agency v. Smart* in 1977, because the agency could obtain funds by sale of notes, bonds, and other obligations, and the act specifically stated that debts of the agency could not become debts of the state.

SECTION 2

Debts for public defense. The State may contract debts to repel invasion, suppress insurrection, or to defend the State in war, but the money arising from the contracting of such debts shall be applied solely to the purpose for which it was obtained.

This section was in the original constitution, to provide for emergency situations that might rise. It has not been amended.

SECTION 3

Debts of counties, cities, towns, and school districts not to exceed revenue—Exception. No debt in excess of the taxes for the current year shall be created by any county or subdivision thereof, or by any school district therein, or by any city, town or village, or any subdivision thereof in this State; unless the proposition to create such debt, shall have been submitted to a vote of such qualified electors as shall have paid a property tax therein, in the year preceding such election, and a majority of those voting thereon shall have voted in favor of incurring such debt.

This section was in the original constitution and has not been amended. It was originally intended—along with section 4—to limit local governments in their use of public debt. This section requires a vote of property owners, placing the burden of debts on those whose property taxes would pay for them, and acting as a check on local officials. This was a common requirement in other states at the time and was an exception provided for in the Declaration of Rights (Art. I, sec. 4): "No property qualification shall be required of any person to vote, or hold office, except as provided in this Constitution." Although this exception remains in Article I and in this section, it has been ignored in practice since the U.S. Supreme Court's decisions in *Cipriano v. City of Houma* (1969) and *Phoenix v. Kolodziesjski* (1970) striking down property qualifications in some bond elections.

The litigation arising under sections 3 and 4 generally involves judicial determination of whether or not a particular debt falls under the limits of these sections and tests the various methods that have been devised over the years to stay within these limits. To avoid these constitutional debt limits, cities and counties may use revenue bonds to pay for projects—such as public housing—that produce income to repay the bonds; they do not come within constitutional debt limits. Or when cities and counties are near their constitutional debt limits and are unable to finance capital projects—such as water storage and distribution systems—out of current revenues, they sometimes create special service districts to build and operate such projects. The special service district then has a separate statutory debt limit.

The Utah Supreme Court held in *Barnes v. Lehi City* (1929) that this section does not apply to a contract to purchase a power plant where public property would be financed exclusively from revenue derived from the property—the special fund doctrine. The court held in *Lehi City v. Meiling* (1935) that a metropolitan water district was not a municipal corporation and hence not subject to a 4 percent debt limit. The court ruled in *Pearson v. Salt Lake County* (1959) that a bond issue financed by a special improvement tax levied only as a lien against adjoining real property was not a county debt contrary to the constitution; this tax was different from a tax for county or municipal purposes that would benefit all citizens. A long-term contract for water purchases by a city, the total amount being larger than one year's taxes, was held in *Barlow v. Clearfield City Corp.* (1954) not to violate this section, since taxes were to be levied annually to make the debt payments not covered by water revenues and other sources. Given the fact that general obligation bonds (which pledge the community's credit and are subject to the limits in sections 3 and 4) carry a lower interest rate than do bonds payable from specific revenues, many local officials prefer to go to the voters for authorization to issue these bonds rather than issue the more expensive revenue bonds.

SECTION 4

Limit of indebtedness of counties, cities, towns, and school districts. When authorized to create indebtedness as provided in Section 3 of this Article, no county shall become indebted to an amount, including existing indebtedness, exceeding two percentum. No city, town, school district, or other municipal corporation shall become indebted to an amount, including existing indebtedness, exceeding four per centum of the value of the taxable property therein, the value to be ascertained by the last assessment for State and County purposes, previous to the incurring of such indebtedness; except that in incorporated cities the assessment shall be taken from the last assessment for city purposes; provided, that no part of the indebtedness allowed in this section shall be incurred for other than strictly county, city, town or school district purposes; provided further, that any city of the first and second class when authorized as provided in Section three of this article, may be allowed to incur a larger indebtedness, not to exceed four per centum and any city of the third class, or town, not to exceed eight per centum additional, for supplying such city or town with water, artificial lights or sewers, when the works for supplying such water, light and sewers, shall be owned and controlled by the municipality.

This section goes along with section 3 to create a specific limit in the amount of debt voters may authorize for local governments. The present section is identical to the original section, except for an amendment approved by voters in 1910 which allowed 4 percent additional debt for water, artificial lights, or sewers in first and second class cities (the larger cities) and 8 percent additional for these improvements in cities of the third class and towns. This change recognized the need for a relatively heavier debt in the smaller municipalities to acquire infrastructure.

Most of the case law determining the kinds of debt that come within the limits of section 4 is essentially the same as that in section 3. The debt limit does not apply to redevelopment agencies; their bonds are paid with revenues generated by the bonded facility and taxes allocated to the agency (*Tribe v. Salt Lake City Corp.*, 1975 and *Salt Lake County v. Murray City Redevelopment*, 1979). The limit does not apply to money borrowed and short-term bonds issued for expenditures made in anticipation of taxes for the current year (*Dickinson v. Salt Lake City*, 1921). Municipal improvements must, however, be funded out of current year revenues or by debt authorized by voters and limited by this section (*Fjeldsted v. Ogden City*, 1933). Before 1947, statutes provided for assessment of all taxable property at its full cash value. In that year, to avoid the effect of inflated property values on taxes, the Legislature provided for assessment of all taxable property at 40 percent of its full cash value. A school district bond issue (which would have come within the 4 percent debt limit if based on the full value of property within the school district, but would exceed the debt limit if based on the 40 percent "assessed value") was challenged. The Utah Supreme Court held that the term "value" in the constitution means the full cash worth, not some percentage of that worth that might be designated as assessed value (*Board of Education v. Passey*, 1952).

SECTION 5

Borrowed money to be applied to authorized use. All moneys borrowed by, or on behalf of the State or any legal subdivision thereof, shall be used solely for the purpose specified in the law authorizing the loan.

This section, which is unchanged from the original constitution, limits the use of money derived from bonding to the purpose spcified by statute.

SECTION 6

State not to assume county, city, town, or school district debts—Exception. The State shall not assume the debt, or any part thereof, of any county, city, town, or school district, except as provided in Article X, Section 5.

This section was in the original constitution, unchanged until voters approved an exception in 1996. The exception permits the guarantee by the state of bonds issued by local school districts, in order to obtain lower interest rates. The Education article (Art. X, sec. 5) provides that the state may guarantee debt incurred to refund the school district debt. It also provides that "Any debt guaranty, the school district debt guaranteed thereby, or any borrowing of the state undertaken to facilitate the payment of the state's obligation under any debt guaranty shall not be included as a debt of the state for purposes of the 1.5% limitation of Article XIV, Section 1."

SECTION 7

Existing indebtedness not impaired. Nothing in this article shall be so construed as to impair or add to the obligation of any debt heretofore contracted, in accordance with the laws of Utah Territory, by any county, city, town or school district, or to prevent the contracting of any debt, or the issuing of bonds therefor, in accordance with said laws, upon any proposition for that purpose, which, according to said laws, may have been submitted to a vote of the qualified electors of any county, city, town or school district before the day on which this constitution takes effect.

This section was in the original constitution. It was designed to cover the transition from territorial status to statehood by preserving the status of indebtedness lawfully contracted by local governments under territorial law.

SECTION 8

Special service districts.
(1) The Legislature by general statute may authorize:
(a) any county, city, or town to establish special districts within all or any part of the county, city, or town to be governed by the governing authority of the county, city, or town, and each special district may provide water, sewerage, drainage, flood control, garbage, transportation, recreation, health care, and fire protection services or any combination of these services in accordance with that statute;
(b) any county, city, or town to levy taxes upon the taxable property in such special district for the purpose of acquiring, constructing, equipping, operating, and maintaining facilities required for any or all of such services; and
(c) any special district to issue bonds of the special district for the purpose of acquiring, constructing, and equipping any of these facilities without regard to the limitations of Sections 3 and 4 of this Article XIV but subject to such limitation on the aggregate amount of these bonds which may be outstanding at any one time as may be provided by statute.

(2) The authority to levy taxes upon the taxable property in these districts and to issue bonds of these districts payable from taxes levied on the taxable property in them shall be conditioned upon the assent of a majority of the qualified electors of the district voting in an election for this purpose to be held as provided by statute.
(3) Any such district created by a county may contain all or part of any incorporated municipality or municipalities but only with the consent of the governing authorities thereof.

This section provides a way to establish services that require substantial capital expenditures without regard to the debt limits of cities and counties in sections 3 and 4. It also permits counties or municipalities to create special service districts to address problems that may affect only citizens living in a part of a city or county. Voters approved the addition of this section in 1974 and amended it in 1990 to make a number of style changes and one substantive change, substitution of "health care" for "hospital" in subsection (1)(a). This was done to make possible a wider range of health services for special service districts. Although there is no debt limit that applies to all special districts, the Legislature may establish by law a debt limit for each type of district.

Article XV

Militia

SECTION 1

How constituted. The militia shall consist of all able-bodied male inhabitants of the State, between the ages of eighteen and forty-five years, except such as are exempted by law.

This section was in the original constitution and has not been changed. Militias were a common feature in nineteenth-century American constitutions, as they were in the early history of western territories. While the Mormon church membership was settled in Nauvoo, Illinois, the city boasted a citizen militia called the Nauvoo Legion. As difficulties between the Mormons and other citizens of the area became exacerbated, the charter of this organization was annulled by the state in 1845. Legion members either went west with the main companies of pioneers or enlisted in a U.S. Army unit known as the Mormon Battalion, which marched from Fort Leavenworth, Kansas to San Diego, California—ostensibly to take part in the Mexican War. These men formed a nucleus of experienced men out of which militia forces were created in the settlements "to preserve the peace and repel Indian depredations."[70] Nostalgically named the Nauvoo Legion, these militia units took part in numerous military engagements

[70] Hamilton Gardner, *History of the 222nd Field Artillery,* unpublished manuscript, quoted in Richard C. Roberts, *History of the Utah National Guard: 1894–1954* (Ph.D. diss., University of Utah, 1973), 1.

with the Native American tribes, as the Mormon colonizers pressed farther into the tribes' traditional lands.

The Mormon-dominated militia sometimes had uneasy relationships with the non-Mormon territorial officials. Finally, the Nauvoo Legion was abolished by congressional action in the Edmunds-Tucker Act of 1887. By 1894, with statehood in the offing, the territorial Legislature created the "organized militia" in the National Guard of Utah, with regular required drills, and a financial subsidy from the United States government. The same act of the Legislative Assembly provided for a militia consisting of every able-bodied male citizen (or those intending to become citizens) between the ages of eighteen and forty-five.

When the constitutional convention met in 1895, its membership included several veterans of the Nauvoo Legion, along with half a dozen veterans of the Civil War. There was no question that militia duty would be required for the able-bodied men of the new state to augment the National Guard if necessary; the age limits, duty for noncitizens, and exemptions were the only issues.[71] It was understood that the militia would not be activated for military duty in peacetime; the National Guard would have this responsibility, but the militia would provide a reserve for emergencies.[72] This is still the status of the unorganized militia, although the "organized militia" or National Guard can be called to serve by the president of the United States as well as the governor.

The militia is mentioned in two other articles of the constitution. The governor is designated as commander-in-chief of "the military forces of the State, except when they shall be called into the service of the United States," and has the power to call out the militia "to execute the law, to suppress insurrection, or to repel invasion" (Art. VII, sec. 4). The Elections and Right of Suffrage article provides that "No voter shall be obliged to perform militia duty on the day of election except in time of war or public danger" (Art. IV, sec. 4).

Since the constitutional provision for the militia is broad and general, the Legislature has provided by statute for its organization in two parts: the National Guard (consisting of a department of army and a department for air) and the unorganized militia (U.C.A. 39-1-1 et seq.). Both are under the command of the governor. The militia statute was amended by the Legislature in 1988 to provide for a militia consisting of all able-bodied *citizens* and all able-bodied *persons* of foreign birth who have declared their intention to become citizens, rather than the *male inhabitants* designated in this section. It also includes a long list of persons exempted, including judges, state officials, physicians, ministers of the gospel, and others employed in critical occupations.

---

[71] Debate in *Proceedings of the Convention,* 1: 815–18.

[72] Ibid., 1: 817.

SECTION 2

Organization and equipment. The Legislature shall provide by law for the organization, equipment and discipline of the militia, which shall conform as nearly as practicable to the regulations for the government of the armies of the United States.

This section was in the original constitution and has not been changed. The Legislature has provided by statute that "the numerical strength, composition, distribution, organization, arms, uniforms, equipment, training and discipline shall be prescribed by the governor in conformity with the laws and regulations of the United States and the laws of this state" (U.C.A. 39-1-2).

Article XVI

Labor

SECTION 1

Rights of labor to be protected. The rights of labor shall have just protection through laws calculated to promote the industrial welfare of the State.

This section, which has not been changed from the original constitution, was designed to show concern for laboring people by referring to laws to be passed at some time in the future. It expresses the purpose of the article, and it captures the spirit of the debates on labor during the constitutional convention. Although there was some sympathy for the problems of wage earners, the convention was dominated by professional men and entrepreneurs who were determined to create an economic atmosphere encouraging to industrial expansion and attraction of capital from the East. Several efforts were made to strike out the entire article as unnecessary, and to leave labor legislation to the Legislature.[73] A proposal to provide equal pay to men and women working at the same jobs, sponsored by a leading Republican delegate, encountered sardonic comments and a quick defeat.[74] A provision forbidding employment of youths under

[73] *Proceedings of the Convention,* 2: 1163–64.

[74] Proposed by George M. Cannon and defeated as "unenforceable," *Proceedings of the Convention,* 2: 1169–70.

eighteen in occupations "dangerous to limb and life" met the same fate.[75] Other measures designed to protect laboring men and women were adopted, however, in sections 3, 4, 5, 6, and 8.

SECTION 2

Board of labor. The Legislature shall provide by law, for a Board of Labor, Conciliation and Arbitration, which shall fairly represent the interests of both capital and labor. The Board shall perform duties, and receive compensation as prescribed by law.

After a spirited debate, this section was adopted by the constitutional convention, and it has not been changed. The main theme in the debate was the effect this provision could have on prospects for attracting much-needed capital to the new state. Proponents argued that it would show potential investors that the state was determined to promote good relations between capital and labor; opponents argued that there had been little labor strife in the Territory, and such a board would "send the wrong signal" to eastern investors.[76] Although a binding arbitration provision was ruled out, delegates concluded that the Board would be controlled by law and might perform a useful role in the future. Actually, this Board has not been established, but the Legislature has designated the Workforce Appeals Board as the labor relations board for the state (U.C.A. 34-20-3).

The Constitutional Revision Commission in the mid-1990s made a thorough study of the Labor article. It proposed replacing this section with a section authorizing the Legislature to provide for resolution of labor disputes through the use of mediation, conciliation, and binding arbitration, and for a board or commission to carry out such activities. The binding arbitration proposal was opposed by management and manufacturing interests, and the proposed revision was not considered by the Legislature.[77]

SECTION 3

Certain employment and practices to be prohibited.
The Legislature shall prohibit:

(1) The employment of children under the age of fourteen years, in underground mines.

(2) The involuntary contracting of convict labor.

(3) The political and commercial control of employees.

[75] Ibid., 2: 1174.

[76] Ibid., 2: 1033–45.

[77] See *Report of the Utah Constitutional Revision Commission, 1996,* Appendix D.

This section originally had four subsections; an amendment repealing one subsection and altering two others was approved by voters in 1980. The amendment reflected changes in women's employment and changing attitudes toward prisoners' work. Subsection (1) originally prohibited employment of women as well as children under fourteen in underground mines; by 1980 this was preempted by federal equal employment opportunity laws, and women were working in Utah underground mines, so the reference to women was deleted. Subsection (2) originally prohibited "the contracting of convict labor." The word "involuntary" was added to this subsection in the 1980 revision to prevent possible abuses of prisoners in sweatshop conditions. The original subsection (3) that was repealed prohibited "the labor of convicts outside prison grounds, except on public works under the direct control of the State." Although some delegates in the constitutional convention had argued that prisoners needed some kind of work, it was not clear just what types of work should be permitted by this section. The Utah Supreme Court in 1923 held in *Price v. Mabey* that the provision was intended to avoid contracting the labor of prisoners to manufacturers in unfair competition with free labor. The following year, the court held in *Utah Manufacturers Association v. Mabey* (1924) that a prison garment factory under control of prison officials did not have the elements of "contracting prison labor" forbidden by this section. By 1980, with the prison population increasing rapidly, a need to shift some prisoners to community correctional facilities and employment in the community, and a clear need for prisoners to have some kind of meaningful employment, the subsection was changed. The changes were designed to give constitutional protection to the establishment of employment within prisons under conditions where inmates could learn skills useful to them after their release. In addition, corrections officials were establishing community "half-way houses," where inmates in the last months of their sentences could work in local industries and ease their transition from prison. The current statute on prison labor encourages employment of "as many offenders as practicable" in correctional facilities to produce goods for sale to the state or its political subdivisions (U.C.A. 64-13-19).

The political and commercial control of employees prohibited in current subsection (3) was intended to prevent political harassment of employees and forced use of company stores, practices that were prevalent in "company towns" in the nineteenth century.

SECTION 4

Exchange of blacklists prohibited. The exchange of black lists by railroad companies, or other corporations, associations or persons is prohibited.

This section was in the original constitution and has not been amended. A similar but more detailed and expanded provision is also found in the

Corporations article (Art. XII, sec. 19). The practice of blacklisting employees by corporations—particularly railroad companies—was deplored by convention delegates. Some delegates, however, were skeptical of the possibility of enforcing anti-blacklisting laws. The Utah statute on blacklisting elaborates on this section by prohibiting anyone from causing to be "published or blacklisted, any employee discharged or voluntarily leaving the service of any person, company or corporation with intent and for the purpose" of preventing such employee from engaging in or securing similar or other employment (U.C.A. 34-24.1). The U.S. Tenth Circuit Court of Appeals held in *United Association of Journeymen Local 57 v. Bechtel Power Corp.* in 1987 that blacklisting claims under Utah law are not preempted by the federal Labor Management Relations Act. In *Worden v. Provo City* (1992) the federal district court for Utah held that to prevail on a claim of blacklisting the intent to blacklist must be shown.

SECTION 5

Injuries resulting in death—Damages. The right of action to recover damages for injuries resulting in death, shall never be abrogated, and the amount recoverable shall not be subject to any statutory limitation, except in cases where compensation for injuries resulting in death is provided for by law.

The original section provided a right of action to recover damages for injuries resulting in death without exception, and without a statutory limitation on the amount. In 1920 voters approved by a narrow margin the exception now in this section. The 1917 Legislature—noted as among the state's most progressive in enacting social legislation—had passed a Workmen's Compensation Act, now Workers' Compensation Act (U.C.A. 35A, Ch. 3). The 1920 amendment was intended to implement this act—to shift the burden of lawsuits from the employer and the dependents of workers to an insurance fund that would cover claims without proof of fault. The Utah Supreme Court held in 1980 that compensation under this act is limited by statute to dependents; it is not the same as damages. The purpose of this amendment was to abrogate some rights formerly held by people entitled to sue under the wrongful death statute (*Star v. Industrial Commission*, 1980; *Morill v. J & M Construction Co.*, 1981). The Legislature has made the right to compensation for an employee's injuries or death the exclusive remedy against the employer "in place of any and all other civil liability whatsoever, at common law or otherwise," except for cases under the Utah Occupational Disease Act (U.C.A. 35A, Ch. 3a).

SECTION 6

Eight hours a day's labor on public works—Health and safety laws. Eight hours shall constitute a day's work on all works or undertakings carried on or aided by the

State, county or municipal governments; and the Legislature shall pass laws to provide for the health and safety of employees in factories, smelters and mines.

This section, part of the original constitution, sets work standards for public employment and encourages future Legislatures to provide for the health and safety of employees in factories and mining industries. Working conditions in mines provided the impetus for this provision, which was proposed by a prominent mining entrepreneur (and later U.S. Senator), Thomas F. Kearns. The limit of eight hours a day on government works was vigorously debated. Its proponents noted that the territory was still in an economic depression, and limiting hours would spread the work among the thousands of unemployed workers. Opponents felt that some workers could not survive on the income from just eight hours' work and would be willing to work a longer day. The provision passed easily and became a long-standing benchmark in Utah labor law, despite the fact that it applied only to public employees.

This section and other sections of the Labor article were studied in the early 1990s by the Constitutional Revision Commission at the request of the Legislature. Although the Commission found routine noncompliance with the language in this section, and it was generally agreed that the removal of the eight-hour workday for public employees had no legal implications for the private sector, organized labor representatives felt the provision was symbolic of the ideal work situation and they opposed deletion of this section. The proposed amendment changing this provision was not considered by the Legislature.

SECTION 7

Legislature to enforce this article. The Legislature, by appropriate legislation, shall provide for the enforcement of the provisions of this article.

This section was in the original constitution and has not been changed. It seems to be redundant in view of Article I, section 26, which states that "The provisions of this Constitution are mandatory and prohibitory, unless by express words they are declared to be otherwise." There are, however, opportunities to challenge the scope of the legislative power, and this was the case with the early laws enforcing section 6. Utah's statute limiting hours of work in underground mines and smelters was challenged as an infringement on "liberty of contract" but upheld as a valid exercise of the state's police power by the U.S. Supreme Court in *Holden v. Hardy* (1898). The Court observed that the hazardous nature of this kind of work was widely recognized and that several states had passed laws for miners' protection.

SECTION 8

Minimum wage for women and minors—Comfort and safety laws. The Legislature may, by appropriate legislation provide for the establishment of a minimum wage for women and minors and may provide for the comfort, health, safety and general welfare of any and all employees. No provision of this constitution shall be construed as a limitation upon the authority of the legislature to confer upon any commission now or hereafter created such power and authority as the legislature may deem requisite to carry out the provisions of this section.

This section was added to the article in 1933 and has not been changed. It provides for passage of minimum wage laws for women and minors and for the general welfare of all employees, and it also gives the Legislature the power to create a commission to enforce labor laws. The Utah Supreme Court held in 1938 in *McGrew v. Industrial Commission* that the Legislature had the power to enact such legislation "at least as to women and minors" before the passage of this section. The legislative sponsors of this amendment in 1933, however, were concerned that such laws might not be constitutional, and they wanted to provide constitutional backing for minimum wage and hour legislation that had been passed in the 1933 session. Utah's current Minimum Wage Act (U.C.A. 34-40-102 et seq.) covers all private and public employees. The minimum wage is to be reviewed at least every three years, and whenever the federal minimum wage is changed, by the Department of Workforce Services. The minimum is raised periodically, but it may not exceed the federal minimum wage. The department may provide for separate minimum hourly wages for minors.

Article XVII

Water Rights

SECTION 1

Existing rights confirmed. All existing rights to the use of any of the waters in this State for any useful or beneficial purpose, are hereby recognized and confirmed.

The simplicity of this article, which has remained the same since the original constitution was written, belies the intense interest in the preservation and use of this vital resource that has marked Utah's entire history. After the Mormon pioneers entered the Salt Lake Valley in 1847 they quickly developed an irrigation system to make the desert habitable, or even to "blossom as the rose." The mountain streams that flowed from the canyons and turned the arid valley into farmland were—like the land itself—considered part of the community effort to build the kingdom of God on earth. Water and land were allocated by Mormon church leaders according to the needs of the settlers as part of a communitarian settlement.

After Utah gained territorial status in 1850, the territorial Legislature under the Organic Act developed civil governments, and in 1852 the responsibility for allocating and controlling waters was given to the governing bodies of the counties, the county courts (which consisted of a probate judge and several selectmen). In 1865 the Legislative Assembly provided for the establishment of irrigation districts with the power to tax for irrigation works, such as reservoirs. Canal companies owned by shareholders were formed to allocate use of the waters of the creeks. As in other western states, Utah followed the "prior appropriation" doctrine, the "first in time, first in right" rule that gives priority to the first person to divert water and subject it to beneficial use. This is in contrast to the riparian doctrine governing water rights in eastern states, where water rights arise out of ownership of land adjacent to the stream, and the user is to pass on to downstream users water that is substantially undiminished in quantity and quality.[78]

As in other aspects of economic life in the early territorial period, there was an emphasis on the needs of the community and the common good in the distribution and use of water. When times changed and success in private enterprises became the dominant economic aspiration in the Territory, water law reflected this shift in philosophy. An 1880 territorial law established water commissioners in each county with the authority to determine all claims of right to the use of water and issue certificates of water rights to parties found to possess vested water rights, and to record the certificates. This process confirmed the right of the existing cities and canal companies to water in the streams they had appropriated under the old water policies. Water company shares (which entitled the owners to a part of a stream flow) could be traded like any other piece of property and were no longer tied to the land.

The emphasis on private ownership of water rights clearly dominated the thinking of delegates to the constitutional convention in 1895 as they pondered two different systems in their neighboring states, Wyoming and Colorado.[79] In Colorado's 1876 Constitution, unappropriated water of natural streams was designated "the property of the public . . . dedicated to the use of the people of the State" but subject to future appropriation according to a system giving priority for domestic purposes (Art. XVI, secs. 5 through 8). Wyoming's 1890 Constitution declared that the water of natural streams was "the property of the state," confirmed the "prior appropriation" doctrine, and established a board of control and state engineer to supervise the appropriation and use of surface water (Art. VII, secs. 1 through 5).

The constitutional convention debate on the Water Rights article focused on assuring the sanctity of the private right to use water, and on confirmation of claims on this limited resource that were already in place—which probably doomed the Wyoming model from the start. Delegate Edward Snow warned that the Wyoming model would "confiscate the water rights of the Territory and place them under State control," and he urged that the future appropriations of water be left to the Legislature.[80] Delegate Lorin Farr, an early settler of the Territory, warned that "there will be lawsuit after lawsuit if there is not some way

[78] Ronald B. Robie, "Modernizing State Water Rights Laws: Some Suggestions for New Directions," *Utah Law Review* 1974 (Winter): 762.

[79] Gordon Morris Bakken, *Rocky Mountain Constitution Making*, 65–66.

[80] *Proceedings of the Convention*, 2: 1211–12.

settled to control that water." He urged that the convention provide for "a board or somebody in charge of this water."[81] This was not to be. In the end, existing rights to "any of the waters" in the state for useful or beneficial purposes were confirmed, and future disposition of unappropriated waters was left to the Legislature and the courts.

The dominant position of agricultural interests in the convention was evident in the debate on this article (nearly one-third of the delegates were farmers or ranchers), and the interest in protecting use of water for irrigation is clear not only in this article but in the Revenue and Taxation article, which exempts from taxation waterways used by individuals or corporations for irrigation (Art. XIII, sec. 2 (5)).

The Legislature in 1897 established the first specific statutory procedure for the future appropriation of water, which provided for filing of notice for use of a stream, then completing work to divert the water for beneficial use. This process was not exclusive; the right to unappropriated water could still be established by simply diverting and applying the water to beneficial use.[82] In the same year, the Office of the State Engineer was created.

As the federal government began to sponsor water development projects in the West, the Utah Legislature modernized state water policy by passing a statute that has—with several amendments over the years—become the state water code. This 1903 statute placed the supervision of water rights in the Office of the State Engineer. This act also required a hydrographic survey of the state to establish previous claims and provided for determination of future claims by the State Engineer.[83] This opened the way for the Strawberry Valley reservoir project in 1905. A long list of subsequent federal reclamation projects during the state's first century provided enormous benefits to agriculture and also boosted tourism and recreational activities. The federal dollars provided by these projects (along with other federal expenditures in the state) have long been a source of political capital for senators and representatives "bringing home the bacon."

The current statute on water and irrigation (U.C.A. 73-1-1 et seq.) follows the original Colorado constitutional model: "All waters in this state, whether above or under the ground are hereby declared to be the property of the public, subject to all existing rights to the use thereof" (U.C.A. 73-1-1). It goes on, however, to establish a system of water management much like that in the original Wyoming Constitution. It designates a state engineer appointed by the governor, by and with the consent of the Senate, to "secure the equitable and fair apportionment

---

[81] Ibid., 2: 1212–13.

[82] Wells A. Hutchins and Dallin W. Jensen, *The Utah Law of Water Rights* (Salt Lake City: State Engineer of Utah and Natural Resource Economics Division, U.S. Department of Agriculture, 1965), 14, 15.

[83] Richard W. Sadler and Richard C. Roberts, *The Weber River Basin: Grass Roots Democracy and Water Development* (Logan: Utah State University Press, 1994), 10.

and distribution of the water according to the respective rights of appropriators" (U.C.A. 73-2-1). The State Engineer has broad powers to protect water resources, to allocate water rights for unappropriated streams, and to approve the use of unappropriated public waters for "some useful and beneficial purpose" (U.C.A. 73-2-1, 73-2-16, 73-3-1, 73-3-8). Beneficial uses that have been recognized include domestic, livestock watering, irrigation, municipal, power generation, manufacturing, mining, and fish culture. In times of scarcity, domestic use has priority over use for all other purposes.[84] Until 1935, the statutes covered only surface waters; in that year the control of ground waters (underground water deposits or streams) was added.

Although the State Engineer has wide discretionary powers, the adjudication of conflicting claims and challenges to the State Engineer's decisions is vested in the district courts, which review in a trial de novo (an original hearing of facts).

The statutes on water and irrigation also provide for the Board of Water Resources within the Department of Natural Resources, an eight-member body appointed by the governor, with the advice and consent of the Senate (U.C.A. 73-10-1.5). Members represent eight different districts of the state. The Board administers the Water Resources Construction Fund, which consists of money from the sale or management of the 500,000 acres of land selected for the establishment of reservoirs under section 12 of the Utah Enabling Act, legislative appropriations, and charges against water and power users. The Board uses the fund to develop water conservation projects, to fund dam safety studies, and to upgrade dams according to a priority list established by the State Engineer. It also makes loans to cities and towns, metropolitan water districts, and other water districts for construction or improvement of water systems through the Water Resources Cities Water Loan Fund.

The Utah Supreme Court has held that prior rights to water are limited to quantities reasonably necessary for the purposes to which it is applied (*Little Cottonwood Water Co. v. Kimball*, 1930). The U.S. Supreme Court held in 1923 that percolating underground waters within public lands are open to appropriation for irrigation or other beneficial uses, subject only to reasonable use (*Snake Creek Mining & Tunnel Co. v. Midway Irrigation Co.*, 1923). Grazers of sheep may lawfully take water for grazing purposes unless the quality or quantity of the water claimed by another is appreciably diminished (*Adams v. Portage Irrigation, Reservoir & Power Co.*, 1937).

---

[84] Richard L. Dewsnup and Dallin W. Jensen, *A Summary-Digest of State Water Laws* (National Water Commission, 1973), 726.

Article XVIII

Forestry

SECTION 1

Forests to be preserved. The Legislature shall enact laws to prevent the destruction of and to preserve the forests on the lands of the State, and upon any part of the public domain, the control of which may be conferred by Congress upon the State.

This article was in the original constitution and has not been changed. Forest protection on public lands was part of the responsibility of the Department of State Lands, and since 1996 has been the responsibility of the Division of Forestry, Fire and State Lands. (See commentary on Article XX and U.C.A. 65A-8-1 et seq.)

The Division of Forestry, Fire and State Lands is charged with the prevention and spread of fire on nonfederal forest, range, and watershed lands; protecting nonfederal forest and watershed areas on conservation principles; and encouraging private landowners in preserving, protecting, and managing forest and other lands. The division also is responsible for controlling wildland fires, and counties are required to "abate the public nuisance" caused by uncontrolled fire on privately owned or county-owned forest, range, and watershed lands. The statute also provides for fire protection agreements and financial assistance to counties for fire suppression. A professional state forester, who is responsible to the director of the division, has the power to close areas that are found hazardous.

Article XIX

Public Buildings and State Institutions

This article in the original constitution was necessary because of the intense competition among several cities in the Territory for state institutions. It was repealed in 1988. The original article had three sections: section 1 transferred the institutions and property of the Territory to the state; section 2 provided for penal and other institutions "for the public good" to be established; and section 3 provided for the permanent location of state institutions. The seat of government and the state fair were located in Salt Lake City and the state prison in Salt Lake County. The institutions for the deaf and dumb and for the blind, as well as the state reform school, were located in Ogden. The state insane asylum (renamed the "state hospital" in 1930) was located in Provo. An amendment approved in 1946 removed the constitutional location of all the institutions except the seat of government and the state fair (although none of them was moved). In 1988 voters approved the repeal of all three sections and transferred to Article XXII (Miscellaneous) the provision for the seat of state government in Salt Lake City.

Article XX

Public Lands

SECTION 1

Land grants accepted on terms of trust. All lands of the State that have been, or may hereafter be granted to the State by Congress, and all lands acquired by gift, grant or devise, from any person or corporation, or that may otherwise be acquired, are hereby accepted, and declared to be the public lands of the State; and shall be held in trust for the people, to be disposed of as may be provided by law, for the respective purposes for which they have been or may be granted, donated, devised or otherwise acquired.

This section, which is unchanged from the original constitution, provides that all lands granted to or otherwise acquired by the state are to be held in trust for the people, subject to disposal for the purposes for which they were acquired. At the time of statehood, the Enabling Act of 1894 that contained the requirements for Utah to become a state included several land grants for specific purposes. Section 6 of the Enabling Act granted four specific sections out of every township of thirty-six square miles for the support of common schools. If these sections (numbers 2, 16, 32, and 36) had been disposed of by Congress prior to admission of the state, indemnity lands from other federal landholdings in the state were to be selected, with the approval of the Secretary of the Interior.

Section 7 of the Enabling Act provided that 100 sections of the unappropriated lands within the state were to be granted to the state for erecting public buildings at the capital of the state (when one was permanently located) "for legislative, executive, and judicial purposes."

Section 8 of the Enabling Act granted two townships previously authorized in 1855 for the establishment of the University of Utah for university purposes, and in addition granted 110,000 acres of land, including all saline lands, for the university. The State Agricultural College (now Utah State University) was granted 200,000 acres. Proceeds of the sale of any of these lands was to be safely invested in permanent funds, and the income was to be used exclusively for the two institutions. Section 9 of the Enabling Act provided that 5 percent of the proceeds from the sales of public lands within the state by the United States after statehood should constitute a permanent school fund; only the interest thereon should be used for the support of the common schools. Section 10 emphasized that the "interest only" from the permanent school fund should be used for educational purposes; it also specified that lands granted for these purposes should not be subject to preemption, homestead entry, or any other entry under the land laws of the United States, but should be surveyed for school purposes only.

Section 12 of the Enabling Act provided various land grants for special purposes, including permanent water reservoirs, an insane asylum, a university school of mines, a deaf and dumb asylum, state normal schools, an institution for the blind, and a miners' hospital. In addition, the U.S. penitentiary, with appurtenant lands, was granted to the state.

This article accepts the public lands described in the Enabling Act for the purposes for which they have been "granted, donated, devised or otherwise acquired." (See commentary to Article III (Ordinance) and to Article X (Education, sections 5 and 7).) The right and title to the unappropriated public lands and Indian lands by the United States is confirmed in Article III (Ordinance). A recent estimate of federal holdings in Utah (which includes, among other properties, defense establishments, forests, national parks, and monuments), is 63.4 percent of the total land area; in addition, Indian reservations cover 4.3 percent of the state. State properties (including trust lands) make up 10.5 percent, and privately held lands total just 21.8 percent of the state's land area.[85] The large amount of land owned by governments, particularly in economically struggling rural counties, keeps public land policies high on the state's political agenda.

Although the land grants at statehood were intended to create a financial base for support of education, it has been difficult to manage them efficiently. Most of these sections are scattered throughout the state in noncontiguous parcels among federal lands. Since much of Utah's land was not surveyed until 1869, some of these sections were occupied by settlers prior to that time. In an effort to consolidate these trust lands for more efficient management, Governor Scott

[85] Utah Office of Planning and Budget, "Estimated Land Ownership by County," 1997.

Matheson in 1980 proposed a massive land exchange with the federal government. This initiative, known as Project BOLD, has not been carried to fruition.[86]

Management of lands granted to the state originally was vested in the State Lands Commissioners, later in a State Land Board. In 1967 management was placed in the Division of State Lands, in the Department of Natural Resources. An administrative reorganization changed the name to the Division of State Lands and Forestry; in 1994 the Legislature changed the name to the Division of Sovereign Lands and Forestry and changed the responsibilities of the Division by creating a new agency to manage trust lands, and in 1996 the Division was renamed as the Division of Forestry, Fire and State Lands.

In 1994 the Legislature created a new, independent agency—the School and Institutional Trust Lands Administration—to manage the school and institutional trust lands separately from the other public lands. This agency is headed by a seven-person board appointed by the governor, which makes policy decisions regarding Utah's trust lands. (See commentary on Article III.) The new agency was created in response to criticism that the schools' trust lands were not being managed for the beneficiaries. There appeared to be conflicts between the different state interests in public lands, with some taking precedence over the trust, royalties not being paid at market rates, and abuses by federal agencies using the lands.[87] Critics claimed that the state's permanent school fund had been short-changed by previous sales and leases of the lands division at less than fair market value.[88]

The concerns of environmental interest groups, shared by some legal analysts, that financial return for the school fund should not be the only goal of the agency, clearly were not foremost in the minds of legislators when the new agency was created. The agency is directed to administer the trust for the exclusive benefit of the trust beneficiaries, not for the benefit of other agencies or the general welfare of the state (U.C.A. 53C-1-102). This was a statutory confirmation of the view of the Utah Supreme Court in *National Parks and Conservation Association v. Board of State Lands* (1993) that sections 6 and 10 of the Enabling Act, together with this article, mandate a trust for the support of the common schools, and the duty of the trustees is to "maximize the monetary return of school trust lands." The court rejected the argument that the fiduciary duty to act in the interest of the school fund did not apply to the use of the trust lands, citing a 1943 plurality opinion in *Duchesne County v. State Tax Commission* holding that the school land

---

[86] Kedric A. Bassett, "Utah's School Trust Lands: Dilemma in Land Use Management and the Possible Effect of Utah's Trust Land Management Act," Comment: *Journal of Energy Law and Policy* 9(1989): 195, n. 22.

[87] Lucinda Dillon, "Matters of Trust," *Deseret News*, 15 December 1996, B1 and B2.

[88] Lucinda Dillon, "Pall of Confusion Hangs over the Trust-land Issue," *Deseret News*, 18 December 1996, B1 and B2.

trust is limited in the purposes and uses thereof. U.S. Supreme Court opinions also have emphasized the purpose and limited use of school trust funds, including *Ervien v. United States* (1919), limiting use of school trust money for advertising that might enhance the value of the trust lands; and *Lassen v. Arizona ex rel. Arizona Highway Department* (1967), requiring compensation by the state highway department for construction of highways on school trust lands. Although critics of the "optimum revenue" approach seek a broader approach to balance current and future interests, it seems unlikely that the current course will be changed to accommodate a "comparative weighing of those interests."[89]

The Division of Forestry, Fire and State Lands administers the sovereign lands (lands below the ordinary high water mark of navigable bodies of water at the date of statehood) as part of the lands "otherwise acquired" that are noted in the Enabling Act. These lands were not expressly granted to the state; they became state lands upon admission of Utah on an equal footing with the original states. The state in its sovereign capacity was vested with the title to the beds of all navigable waters located within its boundaries at that time (*State v. Rolio,* 1927). In *Rolio,* a landowner adjacent to Utah Lake claimed title to the lake bed adjacent to land he had been granted by a federal patent in 1879. In denying the claim, the Utah Supreme Court observed that the title to lands under navigable waters had been held by the United States for the benefit of the whole people and in trust for future states. Title then vests in the states upon their admission into the Union, and these lands may be controlled and disposed of as the state may elect, subject only to the power of Congress to control such waters for the purposes of navigation in commerce among the states.

The Division of Forestry, Fire and State Lands issues mineral leases on all state lands except school and institutional trust lands, including state parks, and it provides for forestry and fire control (U.C.A. 65A-1-1 et seq.) Headed by a director, the division is advised by the Forestry, Fire and State Lands Advisory Council. It is mandated to administer state lands under "comprehensive land management policies using multiple use-sustained yield principles" (U.C.A. 65A-1-2). "Multiple use" is defined as management of resources to best meet present and future needs of the people of the state, and "sustained yield" means maintaining high-level output of the various renewable resources of land without impairment of the productivity of the land (U.C.A. 65A-1-1 (3) and (7)).

The Division, in its responsibility for implementing the general provisions of this article (along with the School and Institutional Lands Administration) faces continuing challenges in balancing economic interests within its constitutional constraints.

[89] Wayne McCormack, "Land Use Planning and Management of State School Lands," *Utah Law Review* 1982 (No. 3): 546–47.

Article XXI

Salaries

This article provided for public officers to be paid fixed and definite salaries, except for an exempted group, for which the Legislature would set fees for full compensation. Repeal of this article was approved by voters in 1992. By then there were constitutional provisions for salaries of legislators (Art. VI, sec. 9), state officials (Art. VII, sec. 18), and judges and justices (Art. VIII, sec. 14). The specific amounts to be paid these officials were taken out of the constitution and provisions made for the determination of future salaries.

The original article contained two sections. Section 1 provided that all state, district, city, county, town, and school officers, excepting notaries public, boards of arbitration, court commissioners, justices of the peace, and constables, "be paid fixed and definite salaries" (city justices of the peace might be paid by salary). Section 2 provided that the Legislature would set the fees for the exempted officers, who would accept the fees as their full compensation. Other officers were required by law to pay all fees collected by them into the "proper treasury" and to be responsible under bond for them. Payment by fees collected were customary arrangements at the time for the exempted officers, but the delegates to the constitutional convention felt that other officials should be given a fixed salary and not allowed to keep any fees they collected.

An amendment to the article approved in 1982 provided that all officers be paid fixed and definite salaries and eliminated the provision for compensation by fees.

Article XXII

Miscellaneous

SECTION 1

Homestead exemption. The Legislature shall provide by statute for an exemption of a homestead, which may consist of one or more parcels of lands, together with the appurtenances and improvements thereon, from sale on execution.

This section provides for exemption of a certain amount of property (to be determined by statute) from sale on execution. In the original constitution, the amount was $1,500, but it was raised by statute periodically—despite the constitutional limitation—until 1988, when voters approved elimination of the dollar amount and authorized the Legislature to determine the amounts.

This article was given careful attention in the constitutional convention. There was clearly a sentiment favoring protection of a basic amount of property from sale on execution, which was provided in territorial law. Delegate Andrew Anderson observed that a homestead provision was "to protect the poor and weak—those who need protection. The money lender and the rich man take care of themselves."[90] There were, however, problems in determining what property and what amount of property should be exempt. The Mormon pattern of settlement was different from that in most other agricultural states. In the midwest and plains states, farmers usually settled on large farms and built their

[90] *Proceedings of the Convention*, 2: 1768–69.

homes on those farms, not in cities or towns. In Utah the usual practice was for farmers to build homes in towns on "city lots" of an acre or two; their farms were outside the community. This met Mormon president-prophet Brigham Young's desire that the settlers be close enough to protect and help each other and to foster the sense of community.

This practice created problems for constitutional convention delegates in writing a homestead exemption, because the general understanding of the term "homestead" was a home and some land to protect the dwelling and livelihood of families.[91] Some delegates suggested leaving the whole matter to the Legislature. Others wanted a law similar to the territorial homestead law with the exempted amounts expressed in dollars—an amount which could be calculated to include the home and some of the farming properties. This view won approval, and the original article mandated the Legislature to provide for each head of a family an exemption from sale on execution of a homestead valued at $1,500. It could be made up of one or more parcels of land chosen by the head of the family.

Statutes enacted since statehood have determined the amount of the exemption and what kinds of sales fall outside the homestead exemption. The current statute provides that homesteads are *not* exempt from the following obligations: liens for taxes and assessments on the property; security interests in the property (such as a loan) and judicial liens (liens obtained by a legal process) for debts created for the purchase price of such property; and judicial liens obtained on debts created by failure to provide support or maintenance for dependent children, and consensual liens obtained on debts created by mutual contract (U.C.A. 78-23-3(2).

In *P.I.E. Employees Federal Credit Union v. Bass* (1988) the Utah Supreme Court held that a mortgage sale on a second mortgage (which created a security interest) was not a sale on execution under this section. In this case, a homeowner whose property was sold by the credit union because of defaults in payment on the note sued to recover the amount of the homestead exemption, $11,000. After reviewing conflicting decisions on the types of obligation which should be exempt under the homestead provision, the Utah Supreme Court concluded that this foreclosure sale was not a "sale on execution" within the meaning of this section. The court agreed that the term "security interest" as used in the statute was meant to embrace "any consensual security interest in the property by which the owner of said property voluntarily pledges that property as security for a debt regardless of the purpose of the debt." The court reasoned that "The owner of property should not be allowed to hold that property out as security for a debt, with the credit received very possibly contingent on that

[91] Ibid., 2: 1770.

security interest, and then have the opportunity to cut off the security by claiming a homestead exemption."

Possession of a property is not the determining factor in the application of this section, the court held in *Rich Cooperative Association v. Dustin* (1963). A property owner whose property is subject to a life estate can claim a homestead exemption under this section irrespective of the question of whether the owner is in possession of the property.

SECTION 2

Property rights of married women. Real and personal estate of every female, acquired before marriage, and all property to which she may afterwards become entitled by purchase, gift, grant, inheritance or devise, shall be and remain the estate and property of such female, and shall not be liable for the debts, obligations or engagements of her husband, and may be conveyed, devised or bequeathed by her as if she were unmarried.

This provision was in the original constitution and has not been changed. It reflected territorial law at the time of statehood, which provided for the property rights of married women. It is covered in U.C.A. 30-2-1 et seq., which makes explicit a married woman's right to contract, sue, and be sued. The wages, earnings, property, rents, or other income of one spouse may not be reached by a creditor of the other spouse to satisfy a debt, obligation, or liability of the other spouse. Family expenses as provided by statute (U.C.A. 30-2-9) and medical and dental and similar necessities for a minor child may be ordered by the court to be paid by a spouse.

The Constitutional Revision Commission studied this section in 1996 and concluded that federal and state statutes make it unnecessary. An amendment repealing this section will be proposed to the Legislature.

SECTION 3

Seat of Government. The seat of state government shall be at Salt Lake City.

This provision formerly was in Article XIX, Public Lands and Buildings. That article was repealed in 1988 and this provision was approved in an amendment that year. Former section 3, which prohibited the manufacture and sale of alcoholic beverages, was repealed in 1933.

Article XXIII

Amendment and Revision

SECTION 1

Amendments: proposal, election. Any amendment or amendments to this Constitution may be proposed in either house of the Legislature, and if two-thirds of all the members elected to each of the two houses, shall vote in favor thereof, such proposed amendment or amendments shall be entered on their respective journals with the yeas and nays taken thereon; and the Legislature shall cause the same to be published in at least one newspaper in every county of the state, where a newspaper is published, for two months immediately preceding the next general election, at which time the said amendment or amendments shall be submitted to the electors of the state for their approval or rejection, and if a majority of the electors voting thereon shall approve the same, such amendment or amendments shall become part of this Constitution.

The revision or amendment of an entire article or the addition of a new article to this Constitution may be proposed as a single amendment and may be submitted to the electors as a single question or proposition. Such amendment may relate to one subject, or any number of subjects, and may modify, or repeal provisions contained in other articles of the Constitution, if such provisions are germane to the subject matter of the article being revised, amended or being proposed as a new article.

The first paragraph of this section was in the original constitution and has not been changed. It provides for proposal of amendments to the constitution by a two-thirds vote of each house of the Legislature. They may not be proposed by initiative (*White v. Welling,* 1936). Amendment proposals are to be published in local newspapers. Beginning in 1976, they have been published with an impartial analysis and arguments for and against them in a voter information pamphlet. The proposed amendments are also posted at the polling places, along with other initiatives and referenda that may be on the ballot. A majority of the voters voting on the proposition constitutes approval; a majority of the voters who cast ballots in the election is not required (*Lee v. State,* 1962). An amendment becomes effective on the date it is approved by the voters unless another effective date is specified by the Legislature (*Snow v. Keddington,* 1948).

The second paragraph of this section was added by an amendment approved by the voters in 1970. Called the Gateway Amendment, this section was drafted by the Constitutional Revision Commission to avoid possible problems with the "single subject" requirement then in Article VI, section 23 (now in section 22). This permitted the Legislature to deal in one ballot proposition with a complex subject that might require amendment of several different sections of an article, or sections in more than one article. For example, in 1996 the proposal to allow the state to guarantee the debt of school districts required changes in five sections in four different articles. Conventional wisdom dictates that a large number of ballot proposals will cause voters to vote "no" on all of them; the history of Utah's amendment process shows that voters will approve six or eight propositions on the ballot if they seem to be understandable and important to them.

As of the end of Utah's centennial year, 1996, 140 amendments had been proposed to the voters, and they had approved ninety-one of them. Of course, this figure does not measure the real number of changes since passage of the Gateway Amendment; some single proposals produced changes in several articles.

SECTION 2

Revision of the Constitution. Whenever two-thirds of the members, elected to each branch of the Legislature, shall deem it necessary to call a convention to revise or amend this Constitution, they shall recommend to the electors to vote, at the next general election, for or against a convention, and, if a majority of all the electors, voting at such election, shall vote for a convention, the Legislature, at its next session, shall provide by law for calling the same. The convention shall consist of not less than the number of members in both branches of the Legislature.

In the early 1960s some governmental officials, business executives, and academic students of government began to focus their attention on state government, and especially on its problems of effective governance. The Commission on the Reorganization of State Government (Little Hoover Commission) began to explore the weaknesses of the executive branch, and the Legislative Study Commission pointed out the lack of staff assistance for the Legislature. In 1966 voters were asked to vote on the call for a convention to revise the constitution, along with seven proposed amendments to strengthen the legislative and executive branches and permit metropolitan governments in populous counties. The convention proposal gained the most attention and soon attracted opposition from Salt Lake City's most prominent business interests, as well as conservatives who feared change and were comfortable with the existing case law. Passage of the convention proposal would have required approval by a majority of the voters who voted in the election, and it did not even come close to meeting this requirement. Only 15 percent of those who voted on the proposal (not all those who voted in the election) approved it. The other proposals were all defeated by substantial margins, but none had such a resounding defeat as the constitutional convention. Had it passed, the Legislature would have provided by statute for the number and election of delegates and for staffing and other expenses.

SECTION 3

Submission to electors. No Constitution, or amendments adopted by such convention, shall have validity until submitted to, and adopted by, a majority of the electors of the State voting at the next general election.

There has been no serious suggestion recently for another try at a complete rewriting of the constitution. Instead, the Constitutional Revision Commission has been made a permanent body (U.C.A. 63-54-1 et seq.). It continues to study the constitution and regularly make recommendations to the Legislature for changes, and its proposals have resulted in major changes in state government. The Utah electorate seems to prefer to digest a few changes at a time.

Article XXIV

Schedule

This article is included for its historical value. It was written to provide for continuity in making the transition from territory to state by providing schedules and procedures to be followed. All contracts, laws, judgments, penal sentences, and pending cases in the courts were provided for in this schedule.

SECTION 1

Actions, contracts to continue. In order that no inconvenience may arise, by reason of the change from the Territorial to a State Government, it is hereby declared that all writs, actions, prosecutions, judgments, claims and contracts, as well of individuals as of bodies corporate, both public and private, shall continue as if no change had taken place; and all process which may issue, under the authority of the Territory of Utah, previous to its admission into the Union, shall be as valid as if issued in the name of the State of Utah.

SECTION 2

Territorial laws continued. All laws of the Territory of Utah now in force, not repugnant to this Constitution, shall remain in force until they expire by their own limitations, or are altered or repealed by the Legislature. The act of the Governor and Legislative Assembly of the Territory of Utah, entitled, "An Act to punish polygamy and other kindred offenses," approved February 4th A.D. 1892, in so far as the same defines and imposes penalties for polygamy, is hereby declared to be in force in the State of Utah.

This act for punishment of polygamy was singled out for special attention in this section, which provided for continuity of all the territorial laws in force, because it was questionable whether this law, based on congressional anti-polygamy laws, would continue in effect after statehood.

SECTION 3

Prisoners to be held. Any person who, at the time of the admission of the State into the Union, may be confined under lawful commitment, or otherwise lawfully held to answer for alleged violation of any of the criminal laws of the Territory of Utah, shall continue to be so held or confined, until discharged therefrom by the proper courts of the State.

SECTION 4

Fines, penalties, and forfeitures due the Territory—Debts of the Territory. All fines, penalties, and forfeitures accruing to the Territory of Utah, or to the people of the United States in the Territory of Utah, shall inure to this State, and all debts, liabilities and obligations of said Territory shall be valid against the State, and enforced as may be provided by law.

SECTION 5

Recognizances—Judgments—Records—Fines due counties, municipalities, and school districts. All recognizances heretofore taken, or which may be taken before the change from a Territorial to a State Government, shall remain valid, and shall pass to and be prosecuted in the name of the State; and all bonds executed to the Governor of the Territory, or to any other officer or court in his or their official capacity, or to any official board for the benefit of the Territory of Utah, or the people thereof, shall pass to the Governor or other officer, court or board, and his or their successors in office, for the uses therein, respectively expressed, and may be sued on, and recovery had accordingly. Assessed taxes, and all revenue, property, real, personal or mixed, and all judgments, bonds, specialties, choses in action, claims and debts, of whatsoever description; and all records and public archives of the Territory of Utah, shall issue and vest in the State of Utah, and may be sued for and recovered, in the same manner, and to the same extent by the State of Utah, as the same could have been by the Territory of Utah; and all fines, taxes, penalties and forfeitures, due or owing to any county, municipality or school district therein, at the time the State shall be admitted into the Union, are hereby respectively assigned and transferred, and the same shall be payable to the county, municipality or school district, as the case may be, and payment thereof be enforced under the laws of the State.

SECTION 6

Criminal prosecutions begun and crimes committed before statehood. All criminal prosecutions, and penal actions, which may have arisen, or which may arise before the change from a Territorial to a State Government, and which shall then be pending, shall be prosecuted to judgment and execution in the name of the State, and in the court having jurisdiction thereof. All offenses committed against the laws of the Territory of Utah, before the change from a Territorial to a State Government, and which shall not have been prosecuted before such change, may be prosecuted in the name, and by authority of the State of Utah, with like effect as though such change had not taken place, and all penalties incurred shall remain the same, as if this Constitution had not been adopted.

SECTION 7

Transfer of causes, records. All actions, cases, proceedings and matters, pending in the Supreme and District Courts of the Territory of Utah, at the time the State shall be admitted into the Union, and all files, records and indictments relating thereto, except as otherwise provided herein, shall be appropriately transferred to the Supreme and District Courts of the State respectively; and thereafter all such actions, matters and cases, shall be proceeded with in the proper State courts. All actions, cases, proceedings and matters which shall be pending in the District Courts of the Territory of Utah, at the time of the admission of the State into the Union, whereof the United States Circuit or District Courts might have had jurisdiction had there been a State Government at the time of the commencement thereof respectively, shall be transferred to the proper United States Circuit and District Courts respectively; and all files, records, indictments and proceedings relating thereto, shall be transferred to said United States Courts: Provided, That no civil actions, other than causes and proceedings of which the said United States' Courts shall have exclusive jurisdiction, shall be transferred to either of said United States' Courts except upon motion or petition by one of the parties thereto, made under and in accordance with the act or acts of Congress of the United States, and such motion and petition not being made, all such cases shall be proceeded with in the proper State Courts.

SECTION 8

Seals of courts. Upon a change from Territorial to State Government, the seal in use by the Supreme Court of the Territory of Utah, until otherwise provided by law, shall pass to and become the Seal of the Supreme Court of the State, and the several District Courts of the State may adopt seals for their respective courts, until otherwise provided by law.

SECTION 9

Transfer of probate causes to district courts. When the State is admitted into the Union, and the District Courts in the respective districts are organized, the books, records, papers and proceedings of the probate court in each county, and all causes and matters of administration pending therein, upon the expiration of the term of office of the Probate Judge, on the second Monday in January, 1896 shall pass into the jurisdiction and possession of the District Court, which shall proceed to final judgment or decree, order or other determination in the several matters and causes, as the Territorial Probate Court might have done, if this Constitution had not been adopted. And until the expiration of the term of office of the Probate Judges, such Probate Judges shall perform the duties now imposed upon them by the laws of the Territory. The District Courts shall have appellate and revisory jurisdiction over the decisions of the Probate Courts as now provided by law, until such latter courts expire by limitation.

During Utah's territorial period, the probate courts had assumed a broader jurisdiction than is usual in such courts, because of the antagonism between the Mormon people and the judges appointed by the president of the United States. Even after the jurisdiction of these local courts was curbed by Congress, some of the old feelings persisted, and, despite some opposition, the convention framers agreed to phase them out in the new state.

SECTION 10

Officers to hold office until superseded. All officers, civil and military, now holding their offices and appointments in this Territory by authority of law, shall continue to hold and exercise their respective offices and appointments, until superseded under this Constitution: Provided, That the provisions of this section shall be subject to the provisions of the Act of Congress, providing for the admission of the State of Utah, approved by the President of the United States on July 16th, 1894.

SECTION 11

Election for adoption or rejection of Constitution and for state officers—Voters. The election for the adoption or rejection of this Constitution, and for State Officers herein provided for, shall be held on the Tuesday next after the first Monday in November, 1895, and shall be conducted according to the laws of the Territory, and the provisions of the Enabling Act; the votes cast at said election shall be canvassed, and returns made, in the same manner as was provided for in the election for delegates to the Constitutional Convention.

Provided, That all male citizens of the United States, over the age of twenty-one years, who have resided in this Territory for one year next prior to such election, are hereby authorized to vote for or against the adoption of this Constitution, and for the State Officers herein provided for. The returns of said election shall be made to the Utah Commission, who shall cause the same to be canvassed, and shall certify the result of the vote for or against the Constitution, to the President of the United States, in the manner required by the Enabling Act; and said Commission shall issue certificates of election to the persons elected to said offices severally, and shall make and file with the Secretary of the Territory, an abstract, certified to by them, of the number of votes cast for each person for each of said offices, and of the total number of votes cast in each county.

The qualifications for voters in the 1995 election to ratify the constitution and elect the first officers for the new state were the same as those in the Enabling Act (Ch. 138, 28 Stat. 107)—males over twenty-one years of age. Some delegates wanted to let women vote on the constitution, since they were entitled to vote after its adoption, but the majority refused to accept this proposal. Nevertheless, an Ogden woman, Sarah E. Anderson (who later became a state legislator), went to court to enforce her right to register and vote. She won the first round in the district court in Ogden, but the territorial supreme court rejected her claim in *Anderson v. Tyree* (1895).

SECTION 12

Officers to be elected. The State Officers to be voted for at the time of the adoption of this Constitution, shall be a Governor, Secretary of State, State Auditor, State Treasurer, Attorney-General, Superintendent of Public Instruction, members of the Senate and House of Representatives, three Supreme Judges, nine District Judges, and a Representative to Congress.

The state officers listed were elected in 1895 to terms of office lasting until 1901. State senators were elected to staggered terms, and the representative to Congress was elected for one year, until the election of 1896. The senators of the new state—by agreement one Mormon and the other non-Mormon—were elected by the Legislature at its first session in 1897.

SECTION 13

Contest for district judgeship, how determined. In case of a contest of election between candidates, at the first general election under this Constitution, for Judges of the District Courts, the evidence shall be taken in the manner prescribed by the Territorial laws, and the testimony so taken shall be certified to the Secretary of State, and said officer, together with the Governor and the Treasurer of the State, shall review the evidence, and determine who is entitled to the certificate of election.

SECTION 14

Constitution to be submitted to voters—Ballot. This Constitution shall be submitted for adoption or rejection, to a vote of the qualified electors of the proposed State, at the general election to be held on the Tuesday next after the first Monday in November, A.D. 1895. At the said election the ballot shall be in the following form:

For the Constitution. Yes. No.

As a heading to each of said ballots there shall be printed on each ballot the following Instructions to Voters:

All persons desiring to vote for the Constitution must erase the word "No."

All persons desiring to vote against the Constitution must erase the word "Yes."

Since the leading newspapers, the Mormon church, and virtually all of the prominent politicians in both parties were strongly in favor of statehood, it was not surprising that the constitution was ratified by a vote of 31,305 to 7,687.

SECTION 15

Election of officers not provided for herein. The Legislature, at its first session, shall provide for the election of all officers, whose election is not provided for elsewhere in this Constitution, and fix the time for the commencement and duration of their terms.

SECTION 16

When Constitution in force. The provisions of this Constitution shall be in force from the day on which the President of the United States shall issue his proclamation, declaring the State of Utah admitted into the Union; and the terms of all officers elected at the first election under the provisions of this Constitution, shall commence on the first Monday, next succeeding the issue of said proclamation. Their terms of office shall expire when their successors are elected and qualified under this Constitution.

Done in Convention at Salt Lake City, in the Territory of Utah, this eighth day of May, in the year of our Lord one thousand eight hundred and ninety-five, and of the Independence of the United States the one hundred and nineteenth.

Attest: JOHN HENRY SMITH, President
PARLEY P. CHRISTENSEN, Secretary

President Grover Cleveland signed the Proclamation of Statehood on 4 January 1896. Two days later, the new governor, Heber M. Wells, took the oath of office at a ceremony in the Salt Lake Mormon Tabernacle, beneath a huge American flag.

BIBLIOGRAPHICAL ESSAY

Although there is an abundance of publications on Utah history, there is a scarcity of publications dealing specifically with the constitution. The state's pioneer past and colorful territorial history seem more enticing to writers and historians. This essay will discuss bibliographic sources that illuminate these aspects of the constitution: the history of the state, the struggle for statehood as a background for the 1895 Constitutional Convention, the constitutional convention and its framers, and sources of interpretation of the document.

The current Utah State Constitution is available in libraries in the first volume of the *Utah Code Annotated,* which gives brief summaries of cases interpreting the constitution and references to some statutes that elaborate on constitutional provisions. Copies of the constitution are available for a nominal charge at the Office of Legislative Research and General Counsel at the State Capitol. The official text of the original constitution of 1895 is also found in volume 2 of the *Proceedings and Debates of the Convention,* 2 vols. (Salt Lake City: Star Printing Co., 1898), which is available in some libraries and in the Utah State Archives, and in volume 9 of *Sources and Documents of United States Constitutions,* William F. Swindler, ed., 11 vols. (Dobbs Ferry, N.Y.: Oceana Publications, 1973–79).

HISTORICAL ROOTS OF THE CONSTITUTION

Utah History

An understanding of the history of Utah and the Mormon church is necessary to understand the Utah Constitution, because it reflects the interaction of Mormons (members of the Church of Jesus Christ of Latter-day Saints) and those not of that faith within the Utah Territory, as well as the stormy relationship between Utahns and the national government between 1849 and 1895. Histories of Utah designed to cover several different time periods, along with histories of the state's twenty-nine counties, were commissioned for the centennial in 1996, although most of these books had not been published by the end of 1997. A comprehensive history, which brings together a wealth of information not previously found in one volume is *Utah: The Right Place* (Salt Lake City: Gibbs Smith, 1995) by Thomas G. Alexander. A volume of essays on political, economic, and governmental topics, *Utah's History,* Richard D. Poll et al., eds. (Provo, Utah: Brigham Young University Press, 1978), is still a valuable source for data on Utah's officials, as well as a variety of statistics and maps.

Older histories of Utah include Hubert Howe Bancroft's *History of Utah, 1540–1886* (San Francisco: The History Company, 1889). A non-Mormon but sympathetic chronicler of Utah's territorial history, Bancroft provides interesting detail on some aspects of Utah's territorial history. The essential work for understanding Utah's economic-political struggles in the territorial and early statehood years is Leonard J. Arrington's *Great Basin Kingdom: An Economic History of the Latter-day Saints, 1830–1900* (Cambridge, Mass., Harvard University Press, 1958). Leland H. Creer's *Utah and the Nation* (Seattle: University of Washington Press, 1929), and his *Founding of an Empire* (Salt Lake City: Bookcraft, 1947), are useful short works. Orson F. Whitney's four-volume *History of Utah* (Salt Lake City: George Q. Cannon and Sons, 1892–1904) brings the perspective of a participant in historical events and includes a valuable collection of biographies of prominent Utahns. The same is true of Noble Warrum's four-volume *Utah Since Statehood* (Chicago and Salt Lake City: Clark Publishing Co., 1919). Both Whitney and Warrum were delegates to the 1895 Constitutional Convention. A short but well-written survey of Utah history by social-economic historian Dean L. May, *Utah: A People's History* (Salt Lake City: University of Utah Press, 1987), is useful. A valuable reference is Alan Kent Powell, ed., *Utah History Encyclopedia* (Salt Lake City: University of Utah Press, 1994).

Government and Politics

The history of Utah government and politics has been neglected by publishers, but it has been given attention by students seeking advanced degrees at Utah universities and elsewhere. Although few have been published, these dissertations and theses on political topics illuminate the development of governmental institutions and the political history of the Territory and state. Examples include Velt G. Erickson, "The Liberal Party of Utah" (master's thesis, University of Utah, 1948); Stewart L. Grow, "A Study of the Utah Commission, 1882–1896" (Ph.D. diss., University of Utah, 1954); and Ellsworth E. Weaver, "The Evolution of Political Institutions in Utah" (Ph.D. diss., New York University, 1953); Brad E. Hainsworth, "Utah State Elections, 1916–1924" (Ph.D. diss., University of Utah, 1968); Dan E. Jones, "Utah State Politics, 1916–1924" (Ph.D. diss., University of Utah, 1968). Some authors of theses and dissertations have published articles based on their research in the *Utah Historical Quarterly* and *Beehive History,* both publications of the Utah Historical Society. For theses on more specialized aspects of Utah politics, the holdings of the University of Utah, Utah State University, and Brigham Young University are listed on-line. The Utah Historical Society library has holdings on Utah politics, as well as some primary sources (diaries, letters, etc.) in this area. The LDS (Mormon) Church Historical Department and Archives have many collections of diaries and other primary sources, but some are restricted.

The late Frank H. Jonas was a major contributor to Utah's political history. He edited *Politics in the American West* (Salt Lake City: University of Utah Press, 1969) and wrote "Utah: The Different State" as an essay for that volume. A more recent collection of readings on western politics is Clive Thomas, ed., *Politics and Public Policy in the Contemporary American West* (Albuquerque: University of New Mexico Press, 1991), which includes Utah.

The origins of government in Utah are discussed in Leland H. Creer, "The Evolution of Civil Government in Early Utah," *Utah Historical Quarterly* 16 (1958): 23–42, and in Eugene E. Campbell, "Governmental Beginnings in Utah," in Richard D. Poll et al., eds., *Utah's History* (Provo, Utah: Brigham Young University Press, 1978). The structure of current Utah government is described in *State and Local Government in Utah* (Salt Lake City: Utah Foundation, 1992), a volume that is periodically brought up to date. Regular bulletins of the Utah Foundation, a nonprofit governmental research foundation, are good guides to constitutional and other contemporary governmental issues.

Utah's territorial courts are discussed in Clifford L. Ashton, *The Federal Judiciary in Utah* (Salt Lake City: Utah Bar Foundation, 1988). The Utah Supreme Court since statehood is featured in Stephen W. Julien, "The Utah State Supreme Court and Its Justices, 1896–1976," *Utah Historical Quarterly* 14 (Summer 1976): 267–85. A special issue of the *Utah Historical Quarterly* 61 (Summer 1993) contains informative articles on Utah courts and the judiciary. Of historical interest is *History of the Bench and Bar of Utah* (Salt Lake City: Interstate Press, 1913).

There is no published history of the Utah Legislature, although accounts of specific sessions may be found in the master's and doctoral theses on Utah politics. In addition to the *Utah Code* and *Utah Code Annotated,* there are the *Laws of Utah* for every session. The *Senate Journal* and *House Journal* from 1896 to the present are available, along with some journals from the territorial period.

Utah's territorial governors are the subject of biographical essays in Thomas McMullin and David Walker, *Biographical Directory of American Territorial Governors* (Westport, Conn.: Meckler Publishing, 1984). The governors since statehood, from Heber M. Wells to Michael O. Leavitt, are profiled in an issue of *Beehive History,* No. 18 (1992), published by the Utah State Historical Society.

Mormon History

Although Mormon history and Utah history are not synonymous, Utah was dominated by that church in the early years of territorial history, and later years were marked by efforts of the increasing non-Mormon population to end that domination. The movement from hostility to accommodation between Mormons and non-Mormons finally set the stage for statehood and cooperation in writing a constitution.

There is a large body of Mormon history. A comprehensive account of the development of the church is Leonard J. Arrington and Davis Bitton's *The Mormon Experience* (New York: Alfred A. Knopf, 1979). James B. Allen and Glen M. Leonard have written a more recent version in *The Story of the Latter-day Saints,* 2d ed. (Salt Lake City: Deseret Book Company, 1992). An older but still useful "inside" source is Brigham H. Roberts, *A Comprehensive History of the Church of Jesus Christ of Latter-day Saints, Century I*, 6 vols. (Salt Lake City: Deseret News Press, 1930). Roberts, a high church official, was also a prominent delegate to the constitutional convention and an active Democratic politician. Mormon church entanglement with the courts is chronicled in Edwin Brown Firmage and Richard Collin Mangrum, *Zion in the Courts: A Legal History of the Church of Jesus Christ of Latter-day Saints, 1830–1900* (Urbana and Chicago: University of Chicago Press, 1988).

For the serious student of Mormon history, the five-volume *Encyclopedia of Mormonism* (New York: Macmillan Publishing Co., 1992) edited by Daniel H. Ludlow is an essential resource for church history, doctrines, and practices. It is considered to be a church-approved source, despite the disclaimer in the preface.

There are also significant works on Mormonism by non-Mormons. A reasoned but critical view of Utah's late-nineteenth-century political history by a non-Mormon mayor and judge, Robert N. Baskin, is captured in his *Reminiscences of Early Utah* (Salt Lake City: Robert Baskin, 1914, photo reprint by Modern Microfilms, Salt Lake City, n.d.). A non-Mormon sociologist's views of Utah and Mormon history, Thomas F. O'Dea's *The Mormons* (Chicago: University of Chicago Press, 1957) is an insightful examination of Mormon history and culture. Catholic archbishop and historian Robert J. Dwyer, in *The Gentile Comes to Utah*, 2d ed. rev. (Salt Lake City: Western Epics, 1971), describes the cultural conflicts between Mormons and non-Mormons in the territorial period.

THE STRUGGLE FOR STATEHOOD

Territorial Issues and Politics

The struggle for statehood is a major theme during the territorial period (1850–1895). Utah's struggle is placed in the national context (with a few minor errors) in Howard R. Lamar, *The Far Southwest, 1846–1912: A Territorial History* (New Haven and London: Yale University Press, 1966), and in Lamar's "Statehood for Utah: A Different Path," *Utah Historical Quarterly* 39 (Fall 1971): 307–27. Another account is S. George Ellsworth, "Utah's Struggle for Statehood," *Utah Historical Quarterly* 31 (Winter 1963): 60–69. Tense relationships between the Mormons and their appointed governors and judges made attainment of statehood more difficult during this period. This problem is explored in Everett L. Cooley, "Carpetbag Rule: Territorial Government in Utah," *Utah Historical Quarterly* 26 (April 1958): 106–29; Clifford L. Ashton, *The Federal Judiciary in Utah* (Salt Lake City: Utah Bar Foundation, 1988), which shows the federal judges on the edge of the federal battle against polygamy; Thomas G. Alexander, "The Utah Federal Courts and the Areas of Conflict, 1850–1896 (master's thesis, Utah State University, 1961); and Gustive O. Larson, *The Americanization of Utah for Statehood* (San Marino, Calif.: Henry E. Huntington Library, 1971), a somewhat defensive account of the Mormon–federal government struggle.

A meticulously detailed inside story of Mormon leaders' campaign for statehood is Edward Leo Lyman's *Political Deliverance: The Mormon Quest for Utah Statehood* (Urbana and Chicago: University of Illinois Press, 1986). The gradual mitigation of hostility and uniting of Mormons and non-Mormons to gain statehood is recalled in Jean Bickmore White, "Prelude to Statehood: Coming Together in the 1890s," *Utah Historical Quarterly* 62 (Fall 1994): 300–15. Thomas G. Alexander's view of the Utah Constitution's territorial origins is shown in "Utah's Constitution: A Reflection of the Territorial Experience," *Utah Historical Quarterly* 64 (Summer 1996): 264–81. A lavishly illustrated short history of the struggle (based on a five-part public television series on this subject) by Ken Verdoia and Richard Firmage, *Utah: The Struggle for Statehood* (Salt Lake City: University of Utah Press, 1996), presents a broad-based view of the cultural climate and political struggles that led to the constitution.

Documentary evidence of the struggles between Utah's appointed officials and the Mormons is found in the reports of the territorial governors to the Secretary of the Interior in the Executive Proceedings Record Books, Series 242, Utah State Archives. Minutes and reports of the Utah Commission (officially known as the Board of Registration and Election in the Territory of Utah) from 1882 to 1896 are in the Archives on microfilm, Series 1126.

Part of the statehood struggle was evident in the framing of six constitutions before 1895, all rejected or ignored by Congress. The history of these six constitutions (sketched briefly in Part 1 of this volume) is found in Jerome Bernstein, "A History of Constitutional Conventions of the Territory of Utah, 1849–1895" (master's thesis, Utah State University, 1961); in Martin B. Hickman, "Utah Constitutional Law" (Ph.D. diss., University of Utah, 1954); and in Jean Bickmore White, *Charter for Statehood: The Story of Utah's Constitution* (Salt Lake City: University of Utah Press, 1996). Texts of these draft constitutions are found in the United States Senate and House Miscellaneous Documents (many now on microfilm).

Volume 9 in *Sources and Documents of United States Constitutions,* William F. Swindler, ed., 11 vols. (Dobbs Ferry, N.Y.: Oceana Publications, 1973–79), contains background notes on Utah's constitutional history and texts of the draft constitutions of 1849, 1856 (mis-titled as the draft of 1860), 1872, and 1882. It also contains other important territorial documents relating to the constitution: President Benjamin Harrison's Amnesty Proclamation of 1893, the Enabling Act of 1894, and President Grover Cleveland's 1896 Proclamation of Statehood.

The first constitution sent to Congress in search of statehood was an 1849 draft of the Constitution of the State of Deseret, a document that has had more extensive treatment than the later constitutional drafts. Dale L. Morgan, in *The State of Deseret* (Logan: Utah State University Press and the Utah State Historical Society, 1987), describes this document and also the operation of the provisional government that functioned under it until its replacement by the Organic Act of 1850 that made Utah a territory. Morgan's book still is an essential source.

However, the more recent account of this constitution's origin by Peter Crawley in "The Constitution of the State of Deseret," *BYU Studies* 29 (1989): 7–22, contradicts Morgan's traditional version that a convention produced this document; evidence points to its drafting by a small group of Mormon leaders.

THE CONSTITUTIONAL CONVENTION OF 1895

Official Records

There are few documents beyond the official record of the proceedings of the constitutional convention of 1895 to create "legislative intent" of the delegates. The verbatim record, *Proceedings and Debates of the Convention,* 2 vols. (Salt Lake City: Star Printing Co., 1898), is poorly indexed by topics and by delegate names, and it is not completely inclusive. It is sometimes hard to follow a debate when the wording of the proposal under discussion is not printed. Nevertheless, these debates are frequently quoted in Utah Supreme Court briefs and opinions.

Although committees in the convention had stenographic assistance, minutes of most committee meetings are not available. Committee reports are found in the Statehood Constitutional Convention (1895) files at the State Archives (Series 3212). The committee files contain various items: letters from interest groups, petitions, drafts of articles approved by the committee, minority reports, and indications of which state constitutions were used in preparing the various articles of the constitution.

Other Works

Fortunately, the three Salt lake City newspapers, the *Deseret Evening News* (owned by the Mormon church), the *Salt Lake Tribune* (owned by non-Mormon Republicans), and the *Salt Lake Herald* (a Democratic party voice), covered each day's sessions in lengthy, sometimes gossip-mongering, detail. From these accounts, the real flavor of the convention emerges.

Utah's convention debates are seen in the context of their western setting in Gordon Morris Bakken, *Rocky Mountain Constitution Making, 1850–1912* (Westport, Conn.: Greenwood Press, 1987), which shows the similarity of problems faced by all the intermountain states and explains how the conventions addressed in different ways the common problems of water scarcity, railroads, mining, and other economic issues. Another useful account of the major convention debates is Jerome Bernstein, "A History of Constitutional Conventions of the Territory of Utah, 1849–1895" (master's thesis, Utah State University, 1961).

The Delegates to the Convention

A search for diaries, biographies, and autobiographies of convention delegates garners data on the most prominent participants but leaves much to be found about the lives of the lesser-known. Few of these sources provide much insight into the issues and personalities of the convention. An exception is the series of diaries of Edward F. Partridge, Jr., Harold B. Lee Library Special Collections,

Brigham Young University, which contain candid comments on his delegate-colleagues and the tedium of the convention sessions. The papers of delegate-historian Orson F. Whitney, including diaries (1877–1931), notebooks, and autobiography in the Historical Department of the Church of Jesus Christ of Latter-day Saints (photocopies in the University of Utah Marriott Library Special Collections) also contain some personal observations.

Published sources on convention delegates include Gary James Bergera, ed., *The Autobiography of B.H. Roberts* (Salt Lake City: Signature Books, 1990); T. Earl Pardoe, *Lorin Farr, Pioneer* (Provo, Utah: Brigham Young University Press, 1953); *The Diaries of John Henry Smith,* Jean Bickmore White, ed. (Salt Lake City: Signature Books, 1990); and reminiscences of Charles Nettleton Strevell, *As I Recall Them* (Salt Lake City: Stevens and Wallis, 1943). University of Utah theses include Kent Sheldon Larsen, "The Life of Thomas Kearns," 1964, and Edward Leo Lyman, "Heber M. Wells and the Beginnings of Utah's Statehood," 1967. Several other autobiographies of delegates are available in the L.D.S (Mormon) Church Historical Department and Archives or the Utah State Historical Society library, but some do not include entries about the 1895 convention.

A short sketch on each of the 107 delegates is included in Jean Bickmore White, *Charter for Statehood: The Story of Utah's Constitution,* based on accounts in newspapers, biographical volumes, histories of Utah institutions, and in city, county, and family histories.

A Utah historian, the late Stanley S. Ivins (whose father was a delegate), researched a variety of sources to determine the occupations and religious affiliations of the delegates, and the number of speeches each gave in the convention. Although he wrote only one article on the subject, "A Constitution for Utah," *Utah Historical Quarterly* 15 (April 1957): 95–116, he carefully saved his research notes, which are in the Stanley S. Ivins Papers at the Utah Historical Society library. There are some errors in his data, but they are minor, and his article paints a fairly accurate picture of the convention.

CONSTITUTIONAL INTERPRETATION

Since the constitution was written, it has been subject to interpretation in hundreds of court cases and implemented by legislative enactments. A good source to start a search for the contemporary meaning of the constitution is the *Utah Code Annotated* (Charlottesville, Va.: The Michie Company). It contains brief summaries of cases following each section, generally copied from the decisions of the Utah Court of Appeals or Supreme Court without background explanation. The U.C.A. gives statutory notations and occasionally refers to law review articles that provide more information. Articles in the *Utah Law Review and Journal of Contemporary Law* (University of Utah College of Law), the *Brigham Young University Law Review,* the *Brigham Young University Journal of Public Law,* the *Utah Bar Journal,* and occasionally the *Utah Historical Quarterly,* discuss the more important court decisions, and the *Utah Law Review* regularly carries notes on recent decisions.

The creation of a Constitutional Revision Commission in 1969 provided a source of studies on the constitution. Unfortunately, most of these early studies are not available. But since the Commission was made permanent in 1977 and provided with greater staff assistance, its files contain in-depth analyses of various articles of the constitution too numerous to list. These studies are in the Commission files at the Office of Legislative Research and General Counsel at the State Capitol building in Salt Lake City. Since 1976, the lieutenant governor's office has published a Voter Information Pamphlet for each general election; it includes discussions of proposed constitutional amendments and reasons for and against changes.

A valuable source for discussions of early Utah Supreme Court decisions is Martin Berkeley Hickman, "Utah Constitutional Law" (Ph.D. diss., University of Utah, 1954). Although the articles are now somewhat outdated because of constitutional change, the special *Utah Law Review* symposium issue on Utah constitutional law in 1966 (September 1966) is still an excellent resource for historical data.

Two thoughtful discussions of the Utah Supreme Court's approach to state constitutional law are Milo Steven Marsden, "The Utah Supreme Court and the Utah State Constitution," *Utah Law Review* 1986 (no. 2): 319–29, and Associate Justice Christine M. Durham, "Employing the Utah Constitution in the Utah Courts," *Utah Bar Journal* 2 (November 1989): 25–27. Both authors examine models for state constitutional analysis and offer views on current interpretations of the constitution.

■ TABLE OF CASES

A

B

C

D

E

F

G

H

I

J

K

L

M

T

U

W

Y

Z

INDEX

About the Author

JEAN BICKMORE WHITE is Emerita Professor of Political Science at Weber State University in Ogden, Utah. She is the author of *Charter for Statehood: The Story of Utah's State Constitution* and several articles and monographs on Utah's Constitution, government, and politics.

www.ingramcontent.com/pod-product-compliance
Ingram Content Group UK Ltd.
Pitfield, Milton Keynes, MK11 3LW, UK
UKHW020924170926
475595UK00031B/60

9 780199 779284